THE
POLTERGEIST

by

William G. Roll

The Scarecrow Press, Inc.
Metuchen, N.J.   1976

The Poltergeist was first published by New American Library and is reissued by Scarecrow by arrangement with The New American Library, Inc.

Library of Congress Cataloging
in Publication Data

Roll, William George, 1926-
    The poltergeist.

    Reprint of the ed. published by
New American Library, New York.
    Bibliography: p.
    Includes index.
    1. Poltergeists--Case studies.
I. Title.
BF1483.R64 1976   133.1'4   76-25880
ISBN 0-8108-0984-2

To

J. Gaither Pratt

ACKNOWLEDGMENTS

Parapsychology is becoming increasingly interdisciplinary. In fact, it is so interdisciplinary that we are sometimes hard put to identify it as a separate area of exploration. But surely, one would think, the poltergeist must fall, or levitate, into some parapsychological niche. Just when the parapsychologist believes he has cornered the poltergeist, when he feels he has observed some strange goings-on, and when he then addresses himself to the hows and whys of these goings-on, he finds himself out of parapsychology and talking to people in psychology, psychiatry, engineering, etc.

The main role, and sometimes it seems the only role, I perform in my poltergeist studies is to direct the attention of my colleagues in other fields to the phenomena and then wait for them to come up with the answers.

The significant part of the story of the poltergeist is not the accounts of flying objects, etc., as much as the interpretations of these occurrences made possible by the people in other professions who were willing to take a look at the data. Persons who helped in this way include Drs. George Klein, Irving H. Paul, and Gertrude R. Schmeidler of the Department of Psychology, City College of the City University of New York; Drs. Theodore H. Barrett and David Blumenthal, clinical psychologists, Indianapolis, Indiana; Drs. John Altrocchi and Randell T. Harper, Department of Psychology, Duke University; Drs. Carl Eisdorfer, Ben Feather, and Walter Obrist, Department of Psychiatry, Duke University; Dr. Harry T. McPherson, Division of Endocrinology, Duke University; and Drs. John L. Artley and William T. Joines, Department of Electrical Engineering, Duke University. Most of the analyses to determine whether the patterns shown by the phenomena were statistically significant were done by Dr. Donald S. Burdick of the Department of Mathematics at Duke.

Special thanks are due the colleagues who assisted in the on-the-spot investigations, particularly Dr. J. Gaither Pratt, Division of Parapsychology, University of Virginia, Charlottesville; Mr. John P. Stump, Chapel Hill, North Carolina; and

Dr. Charles Wrege, Rutgers University, New Brunswick, New Jersey. Miss Susy Smith, who told me about the Miami poltergeist, also helped in this way.

When a poltergeist lets loose in a home, sooner or later the family is likely to call the police. Several of these officers gave generously of their time to help the poltergeist victims, and were also a significant help in the parapsychological investigations. This was true especially of Detective Joseph Tozzi of the Nassau County Police Department, New York; Chief Charles D. Allen and Officers Robert Davis and James Moore of the Smithfield Police Department, North Carolina; and Officers William Killin and David J. Sackett of the Miami Police Department, Florida.

The people primarily involved in the poltergeist studies were, of course, the persons in whose homes or businesses the events erupted. Thanks are due to them for bearing with the parapsychological investigations which all too rarely gave them significant help in dealing with their strange troubles and more often were a source of additional interruption and inconvenience.

Most of the investigations have been published in the parapsychological journals, including the *Journal of the American Society for Psychical Research*, *The Journal of Parapsychology*, the *Journal* and *Proceedings of the Society for Psychical Research*, and the *Proceedings of the Parapsychological Association*.

I asked several people to read the manuscript of the book and offer suggestions for improvements. They include Mr. W. Edward Cox, Mrs. Laura A. Dale, Miss Jacqueline A. Damgaard, Mr. B. S. Lozoff, Dr. Robert L. Morris, Dr. J. Gaither Pratt, Dr. J. B. Rhine, Mrs. Muriel Roll, Dr. Gertrude R. Schmeidler, and Mr. William Service. I am grateful to them for their help. Mrs. Donna Brown, who typed the manuscript, has shown a great deal of patience, perseverance, and good humor at what turned out to be a lengthy and difficult task. In several places she too made improvements in the text. Any remaining deficiencies are, of course, the responsibility of the poltergeist.

CONTENTS

FOREWORD

by J. B. Rhine

A book on what to do with a poltergeist is definitely needed today. This one not only tells how a parapsychologist deals with a poltergeist but also (in the Appendix) what to do with a poltergeist until the parapsychologist comes.

It is likely to be much more useful, however, in helping readers to decide what to *think* about the numerous reports of alleged poltergeists appearing in recent years.

By far the most informative feature of this book is its account of what has already been done about many of these cases. It reviews in detail the scientific study of a number of these utterly fantastic outbreaks, mainly those in which Mr. Roll himself played an active part. It is fair to say that in his diligent pursuit of this particular branch of the parapsychological field of inquiry he has been the leader, at least in the United States; this book is his progress report.

Why on earth does anyone do research on poltergeists? It is easy enough for most of us to be interested in these very odd and annoying disruptions of the household, if only out of sympathy for the families that suffer them, but it is quite another matter to be willing to invest what it takes in the patient effort, limitless inconvenience, embarrassing publicity, disturbed sleep, and tireless energy that are demanded in actual investigation. This is enough reason for there not having been more books reporting such a series of personal involvements in the interminable detail of such studies.

The timing of this book owes much to the stage of development and status of parapsychology as a whole. Poltergeists have been happening for a long time (although Professor E. R. Dodds drew attention in *Proceedings of the Society for Psychical Research* [1] to the absence of reports of poltergeists in classical antiquity), but a strong development of scientific parapsychology was needed to support a systematic investigation of them. This is because the principles of this

ix

new science provide what seems to be the only plausible explanation of these peculiar behavioral abnormalities as reported.

By the same token, these researches on poltergeists (and the book) had to wait for the psychokinesis (PK) side of parapsychology to come into prominence in active research. This PK branch of parapsychology, which deals with "mind over matter," is the one to which we must turn for a possible explanation of the poltergeist. That is why I say this bold scientific sortie across this particular frontier of parapsychology (or psi research) could not have been made without the solid gains of decades of psi research in general and the PK work in particular.

Indeed, it will not be surprising if some reviewer of the book argues that this presentation of the poltergeist as a case for legitimate study would better have come after the psi researchers had turned still another corner. They have, of course, established PK on moving targets, first on dice and other visible inanimate objects, and later on invisible electrons; they then moved on with moderate success to the PK of living targets—i.e., to measurable physical effects on plants and animals.

However, they have not yet made the same firm case for the PK of static inanimate targets—the type most involved if genuine poltergeist phenomena occur, as reported in the spontaneous movement of objects without contact. It is true a few parapsychologists appear to be convinced by the reports of PK effects on static targets. Such conviction would, however, involve a lowering of the standards by which the other types of psi ability have been acceptably established; there are still a number of improvements of technique to apply in the perfecting of a clear case; the really definitive testing is yet to come.

Why not wait then for the experimental confirmation of PK action on static targets before taking these spontaneous happenings as seriously as Mr. Roll does in his treatment? Perhaps experimental control can be superimposed on these types of phenomena so that the experimental confirmation will come from the field study itself. It seems to me that a promising beginning has been made in the investigation of the disturbances in Miami, where designated target objects were used. Or perhaps at least some added insight into the PK process may be gained so that we may be better able to duplicate the phenomena in the laboratory. In any event, the man who has had the courage to pursue his independent course in identifying his professional career with these investigations must be granted the right to choose his own time and order and way of presentation. As will be seen, Roll even has his own interpretation of the psi process itself and he attempts to draw from the results of his poltergeist studies a slender degree of lawfulness that may help in eventual understanding of them. These efforts may all be allowed under "pioneer's license" during the stage of trying to decide what to think about the "parapsychopathological anomaly of the poltergeist."

The author himself, I am sure, expects us to keep his major contribution of reported observations on the one hand, and what he himself thinks about them on the other, in the separate categories to which they naturally belong. Of our indebtedness to him for the years of investment the former represent there can be little doubt. Appraisal of the latter can be left to time and individual judgment.

FOUNDATION FOR RESEARCH ON THE NATURE OF MAN
Durham, N. C.

INTRODUCTION

A year or so before I left Denmark in 1947, to go to college in California, the studio of Sven Türck, a photographer in Copenhagen, was the scene of some strange goings-on. In the evenings, in a darkened room, knocks and raps were heard and tables and chairs levitated, apparently induced by the presence of one or more mediums. Sometimes the medium himself, with or without his chair, would fly up into the air, his journey charted by a series of Türck's photographs. Most Danes comfortably dismissed the claims of "Spirit-Türck" (Aande-Türck) as publicity stunts to sell a book of pictures showing the tables, etc., in midair. A few found this explanation too simple. One of these was the Danish author Jacob Paludan, whom Türck had invited, along with other outside witnesses, to observe the phenomena.

Paludan was a neighbor of mine in the small town of Birkeröd, where I lived while attending Holte Gymnasium. He was the book reviewer for one of the main Copenhagen newspapers and was also interested in parapsychology. Through his reviews and other publications he was, and is to this day, one of the main exponents of parapsychology in Denmark. His reviews aroused my curiosity, and he responded generously by lending me books on parapsychology and spending many hours with me discussing the topic. This was when I first heard about poltergeists (a German word, roughly meaning "noisy spirits") whose antics were in many ways similar to those in Türck's studio.

The Türck phenomena were the most convincing Paludan had experienced. He was present when the objects were photographed in midair by no less than three flash cameras and when the locations of Türck and the others could be checked by luminescent bands they wore on their foreheads and arms. Though one of the mediums was known to cheat on other occasions, Paludan was not able to figure out how the objects could be made to move into the air by fraudulent means and then be photographed from three angles. Certainly, these and the other things I learned from Paludan convinced me that there was more to explore in human nature than my biology teacher at Holte had told us.

After a B.A. at the University of California, Berkeley, with majors in philosophy and psychology, followed by a year of graduate work in sociology, I went to Oxford University, England. Here I hoped to make a serious study of the findings of parapsychology under Professor Henry H. Price, a philosopher and parapsychological theoretician. Oxford had no objection to a thesis on parapsychology. More than that, the university gave me a grant so that I could rent space for a small ESP laboratory. When this gave out, the Parapsychology Foundation, a New York-based organization headed by Mrs. Eileen J. Garrett, stepped in.

There was a great deal of interest in parapsychology among the students and faculty at Oxford, and my wife, Muriel, and I spent eight busy years there. But it was harder than I had expected to get convincing results in my tests for extrasensory perception and psychokinesis, the so-called mind-over-matter effect. I never thought of going outside the laboratory to study the poltergeist and haunting cases which were occasionally reported in the newspapers. At that time I felt certain that the only way to find out about psychical phenemona was by experimentation. Then, in 1957, Dr. J. B. Rhine invited me to spend a year at the Parapsychology Laboratory of Duke University. This seemed a golden opportunity to learn more about ESP and PK so that I could return to Oxford with more productive research methods.

However, the phenomena were as elusive at Duke as they had been at Oxford. My first encounter with what seemed to be parapsychological phenomena was not in any laboratory but in a private home in Seaford, Long Island.[1] In the spring of 1958, Dr. J. Gaither Pratt, who was then assistant director of the laboratory, and I made an investigation of "the house of flying objects," as the papers dubbed it. This case, described in Chapter 2, convinced me that field investigations have a valuable function in parapsychology—not as a way to find scientific proof of psychical phenomena but as a way to gain insights about their nature, which can then be tested under controlled conditions.

In spite of the openness at Oxford regarding parapsychology, the research opportunities were better in America, so when Rhine invited me to stay on, I gladly accepted. Then, in 1960, a new parapsychological organization, the Psychical

Research Foundation (PRF), was formed in Durham to do scientific work on the question of whether there is survival of personality after death. I was asked to become project director of the PRF. It was in this capacity, until recently the only full-time research position at the PRF, that I conducted most of the investigations reported in this book.

The founder of the Psychical Research Foundation was Mr. Charles E. Ozanne. Ozanne, who was educated at Harvard and Yale, spent his professional life as a college and high school teacher. He had a strong desire to further serious, scientific work on the survival problem. During the 1920's and 30's he conducted a series of exploratory studies with the Boston medium Mrs. Soule, but over the years most of his contributions took the form of financial assistance for the research efforts of others. He made several gifts to the Parapsychology Laboratory at Duke University and, eventually, moved to Durham to be close to the work.

In 1959 the Parapsychology Laboratory at Duke sponsored a symposium on the survival question.[2] Rhine invited Price over from Oxford so that he could read a paper on mediumship and another on apparitions. In addition, there were papers by Dr. and Mrs. Rhine, Dr. Pratt, myself, and others. Both Pratt's talk and mine focused on mediumship. The poltergeist was represented in a paper by Mr. W. Edward Cox.

Most of us who participated in the symposium came away with the conviction that the survival issue was one on which more serious work could and should be done. Ozanne had been of that conviction all along, and now he, Rhine, and I got together to see if a plan of research could be implemented. Ozanne was willing to help with funds if there was someone who could do the work. Rhine asked me how I would feel about devoting full time to the survival question. I responded positively. My interest in mediumship and my belief that research in this area could throw light on the survival question had been strengthened by the survey of past work I had done for the paper I gave at the symposium. My participation with Pratt in the Seaford poltergeist study had stimulated my interest in field studies as another way to explore phenomena which might be relevant to the survival issue.

In 1960 Ozanne gave a grant to Duke (the Psychical Research Fund) to enable us to make a beginning. I became project director of the research, remaining on the staff of the Parapsychology Laboratory. Ozanne kept in close contact with the planning and progress of the work, and then, in August of that year, made it possible for it to continue by establishing the Psychical Research Foundation as an independent research organization. The links with the Parapsychology Laboratory remained. I continued to do my work there, and Pratt became President of the PRF board of directors. Price became vice-president.

Then another parapsychological organization was created. In 1962 Rhine established the Foundation for Research on the Nature of Man, to ensure the continuation of the work of his laboratory after he reached the retirement age at Duke. As Rhine was preparing to leave the university, we converted some of the rooms in our house into a temporary headquarters for the PRF. After six years, in 1969, Mrs. Garrett and the Parapsychology Foundation came to our help for the second time. Together with an anonymous donor, she provided funds so that we could refurbish and rent two small houses in Durham. We were also able to obtain research and secretarial assistance. These houses are now the center for our work on poltergeists, mediumships, studies of out-of-the-body experiences, meditation, and other areas which touch on the survival question.

It is not the purpose of the PRF to *prove* survival. Rather, it is our purpose to investigate, impartially and thoroughly, phenomena which are suggestive of survival and to conduct experiments to determine whether or not there is a continuation of consciousness after death.

The year 1957, when I came to Durham, was not only important for me personally, it was a milestone year for the development of parapsychology as a professional, scientific pursuit. In June of that year, following a workshop in parapsychology at Duke, Rhine initiated the creation of the Parapsychological Association to serve as an international meeting ground for people engaged in scientific work in this area. I was included on the founding council as a representative of European parapsychologists—on somewhat uncertain grounds since I am an American.

The Parapsychological Association holds annual conferences at which ongoing research is presented. The PA *Proceedings* (Duke Station, Durham, North Carolina 27706), which comes out once a year and is available to the public, presents summaries of the research papers, giving an overview of current work in parapsychology around the world. The full presentation of this work can be found in the parapsy-

chological quarterlies. The principal journals in the English
language are the *Journal of the American Society for Psychical Research* (5 West 73rd Street, New York, New York
10023), the *Journal of Parapsychology* (Box 6847, College
Station, Durham, North Carolina 27708), and the *Journal
of the Society for Psychical Research* (1 Adam and Eve
Mews, London W8 6UQ England). Since 1969 the PA has
been affiliated with the American Association for the Advancement of Science.

The reader who wishes to make a serious study of the poltergeist should read the detailed reports of investigations published in the parapsychological books and journals. A reading
list will be found in the back of this book. This list also has
information about general books on parapsychology and
about experimental reports on psychokinesis. For the person
who wishes to explore poltergeist or haunting phenomena
himself, some suggestions are offered in the Appendix.

In the main, this book is concerned with poltergeists. Summaries of current poltergeist and haunting investigations and
of other researches that touch on the survival issue can be
found in *THETA* (Duke Station, Durham, North Carolina
27706), a quarterly bulletin published by the Psychical Research Foundation.

1

Poltergeists and Parapsychology

Poltergeists, phantasms of the dead, ghosts, and haunted houses are words which to most of us represent a kind of prescientific science fiction. Like Frankenstein's monster and the vampire, they are kept going because we sometimes like to escape to the misty and creepy, but completely safe, land of childish imaginations.

Nevertheless, most scientists agree that we still do not know everything about the world, and that new discoveries are still to be made. At the time of this writing, an article in *Scientific American* shows a photograph of a tiny glass ball "levitated" about a centimeter in the air by a laser beam.[1] Apparently this is the first time that a light beam has been made to lift an object. It does not seem all that incredible that there should be a new force—or perhaps an old one in unexpected surroundings—which shoots ashtrays through the air and upsets pieces of furniture, as reported in poltergeist houses. Granting this possibility, many people are likely to ask, what difference would it make if someone were to demonstrate that these things actually happen? Proving the existence of poltergeist phenomena seems no more relevant to our understanding of man and to solving his personal and social problems than if an overgrown sea creature were someday to wash up on the shore of Loch Ness, or a large white-furred ape were found in the Himalayas: The poltergeist is unlikely to pass what some scientists call the "so what?" test.

When I began work in parapsychology, the only significance I saw in poltergeist reports was that, like other spontaneous and uncontrolled cases of apparent psychical or "psi" phenomena, they had stimulated interest in experimental research. It was now time, I thought, to forget about flying objects and to concentrate on laboratory psychokinesis.

Psychokinesis, usually abbreviated PK, is made up of two

1

Greek words, the word for mind or soul (*psyche*) and the word for movement (*kinesis*). This term for "movement by the mind" was used by Dr. J. B. Rhine when tests at the Parapsychology Laboratory at Duke University seemed to show that people were able to influence the fall of dice. The story about the PK tests begins in early 1934, when a young man claiming to be a professional gambler told Rhine that he could influence dice by willpower alone. Rhine asked the gambler to show what he could do and the results were sufficiently impressive to suggest that something was really happening to the dice.

By that time, ESP testing had been going on at Duke for several years, and Rhine's first book, *Extrasensory Perception*,[2] was then at the printer's. The results of the ESP experiments had convinced Rhine and others connected with this work that a person is not limited to the known physiological organism but can reach beyond it and directly obtain information about distant events. Of course, claims for ESP did not originate at Duke. Such claims go back as far as man has left written records. What the tests at Duke and other laboratories showed was that there really is something which superstition, imagination, lucky coincidence, and the like cannot easily account for.

When it seemed that ESP must be taken seriously, the parapsychologists began to consider another possibility: If a person can know without the senses, can he also affect his physical environment without direct contact?

This question did not arise only as a logical possibility. From time to time throughout history there have been reports of persons who apparently had the ability to cause objects in their vicinity to move, to make knocks and raps heard at a distance, and to cause other strange phenomena. Occasionally movements of objects, knocking sounds, throwing of stones, and so on would erupt spontaneously at some locality without anybody being present who seemed to cause the events, even psychically. These are the so-called poltergeist cases. This word, which is German, means literally "noisy or rattling (*poltern*) spirit" (*geist*). For instance, in 858, near the town of Bingen on the Rhine River in Germany, there were falls of stones and loud noises and knockings. It was thought that the events were caused by spirits, but attempts to make them leave by exorcism were fruitless. In 1184, at the home of William Not in Wales, spirits were apparently again on the rampage, throwing lumps of dirt and tearing up clothing.

The "Stone-Throwing Devil" was the name given to a series of unexplained falls of stones at Great Island in New Hampshire in 1682. The phenomenon was studied by Richard Chamberlain, who was secretary of what was then the Province of New Hampshire.[3]

Sometimes the unexplained phenomena took place close to special individuals, raising the possibility that they collaborated with demons, or cheated—or used PK. Perhaps the most remarkable of these persons was D. D. Home (1833–1886), who could apparently cause the levitation of furniture, and of himself, in full light. Interestingly enough, he began his career as a poltergeist boy: Shortly after his mother's death raps were heard and objects moved about without visible cause when he was present. He was investigated by the British physicist Sir William Crookes, the discoverer of thallium and the inventor of several instruments.[4] Crookes, who described his tests in the *Quarterly Journal of Science,* July 1871, and again in later issues, was convinced that the phenomena were genuine. Most other members of the scientific establishment of the day were not. The religious authorities were more impressed: Home was expelled from the Catholic Church as a sorcerer.

Eusapia Palladino (1854–1918) was another so-called physical medium. The phenomena, which included raps, appearance of lights and movements of objects, were studied by a great many persons both in Palladino's native Italy, in other European countries, and in the United States. Some of the studies were conducted by a committee from the Society for Psychical Research. (This organization was created in England in 1882 by a group of scholars and scientists to make scientific studies of psychical phenomena. The American Society for Psychical Research, formed a few years later, and most other centers and laboratories for parapsychology and psychical research trace their development to the English Society.)

In their report on Palladino, the British researchers said they had caught her cheating when the experimental conditions were lax but that at other times, when the conditions were strict, there were genuine phenomena.[5]

Rudi Schneider (1908–1957) and his brother Willy were also extensively studied by researchers from Great Britain and the Continent. The phenomena ranged from movements of objects to levitation of Rudi's body. Some of the investigators were convinced of the genuineness of the phenomena, while others were skeptical. In a survey of this work, Anita Gregory described some experiments in which her late husband, C. C. L. Gregory, director of the London Observatory, took part.[6] As a guard against fraud in the experiments, which were conducted in darkness, the table with the objects to be moved by PK was shielded by infrared beams. If anybody interfered with the objects—for instance, tried to reach them with some device—an alarm or a camera, and sometimes both, would be triggered. It was found that the alarm was activated several times, but not by anything visible since the photographs showed nothing. These interruptions in the infrared light took place when Schneider said he was "going into the ray" (he was in trance at these times and it was his "spirit-control," an entity calling itself "Olga," who made this statement). Sometimes these blockings of the light came before movements of the target objects on the table.

It was against such a background of claims and counterclaims that Rhine decided to take his visiting gambler seriously, and afterward to continue PK testing with other subjects.[7] The tests were mostly with dice, the task being to make a certain die face or combination of faces come up more often than was to be expected by chance coincidence. The early PK tests were generally exploratory: The purpose was to probe, not to prove. The work went on for several years, some tests having impressive odds against chance, some being at flat chance. The Duke parapsychologists found it difficult to decide whether they had something which could be fruitfully explored in the scientific laboratory.

The turning point came in 1942, not because of any new, impressive PK tests, but because of a discovery made in the old. The people who had tested for PK noticed that a certain pattern sometimes emerged in the experiments: Usually the first trials were best and then there was a falling off, a decline, as the test progressed. A similar effect had been found in the ESP tests, occasionally with an improvement toward the end of the trials, resulting in a curve shaped somewhat like a U. Such U-curves are often found in familiar kinds of psychological tests, such as learning a series of numbers or syllables: Usually the person is best in the beginning and then there is a falling off at the middle, sometimes with an upswing toward the end. Of course when a decline took place in a PK test, the experimenters were less than happy because the decline reduced the overall results. However, it occurred to them that the effect might be a genuine indicator of psi since the decline had also been found in the ESP tests.

The Duke parapsychologists therefore decided to reexamine all the experiments that had been done up to that time for this pattern. They took all the experiments which consisted of the same number of trials and analyzed them for decline. There were eighteen such tests. The investigators were in for a surprise: Not only was there a decline, but it was much more significant than the overall results of the experiments. The decrease in scoring between the first and last quarter of the totals of the eighteen experiments gave odds of about one hundred million to one. The analysis did not stop there. A PK experiment usually consists of several smaller units because of changes of targets, say from one die face to another, and because of rest periods and the like. When these smaller sections of the experiments were examined, decline patterns were found there too. It was a kind of Chinese box effect. When the subject began with a new target or there was some other kind of break in the experiment, he tended to do well at first and then decline. Rhine and the others who were involved in these experiments and analyses could find no way in which flaws in test conditions, recording errors, or other such explanations could produce this pattern. A thorough recheck of all the results by Dr. J. Gaither Pratt, who was then at the Duke Laboratory, substantiated the finding. Since the decline was neither wanted nor expected by the experimenters who did the original tests, it was difficult to suppose that motivated recording errors could have produced it or to take seriously the suggestion that the experimenters had been cheating. The finding was impressive not only because of the immense odds against chance but also because the decline pattern was similar to the one found in ESP tests and more familiar psychological tests, and therefore indicated the lawfulness of the PK process.

The discovery of the PK decline effect convinced the experimenters more than anything else that PK was something which could be explored in a laboratory situation. As a result, PK testing took a new start. Beginnings had already been made to replace the old cup-thrown dice tests by mechanical devices to prevent the possibility that the falling dice were somehow manually influenced by the person holding the cup. Much ingenuity was now spent building and improving PK machines. Mr. W. Edward Cox, who first worked with Rhine at Duke and more recently at the Foundation for Research on the Nature of Man (FRNM), was particularly creative in devising new instruments, and reported results with PK machines involving targets ranging from falling drops of water to electric circuits. Currently a great deal of interest centers around the machines built by Dr. Helmut Schmidt. Dr. Schmidt began this work while he was senior research physicist at the Plasma Physics Laboratory at Boeing, Seattle, Washington. He is now on the FRNM staff in Durham. These machines contain a radioactive material which emits electrons at random intervals. This causes one of two or more lamps to light up. The apparatus can be used in precognition tests, where the person tries to *predict* which lamp will come on next, and it can be used in PK tests, where the task is to *make* one or the other lamp light up.

The experiments with the Schmidt machines point to an interesting aspect of the PK process that had already been noticed by Rhine in connection with the dice experiments. If a person is successfully to influence a falling die by PK so that it will come up with, say, the number six face, the PK influence has to be exerted at just the right moment. It seems doubtful that a person can watch the faces of the die as it falls through the air or rolls on a table so that he can give it that little PK push at the right instant. And it is impossible to do so if the dice or other objects are out of sight, as with the Schmidt machine. Most of the subjects who are asked to make one or the other lamp turn on, as a rule have no knowledge of the inside of the machine. If they had any such knowledge, it is doubtful whether it would help them: Which of the lamps is to go on is determined by an electronic oscillator that functions something like a wheel turning at the rate of about one million times a second. This "wheel" is divided into two or more parts, depending upon the number of lamps which are used, so that the place the wheel stops causes one of the lamps to go on. This stopping place, in turn, is determined by the radioactive material which randomly fires electrons at the rate of about ten per second. In other words, if a person is to use PK on this machine, he has to know exactly when to stop the electronic wheel, and then he must be able to influence the firing of electrons so that the wheel stops at that point.

It seems hard to believe that, in addition to ESP and PK, people have the calculating abilities necessary to perform such a feat. However, the process may be as simple—or as complex—as the interaction of vision, nerves, muscles, and the calculating processes of the brain which are necessary to perform even such a simple task as replacing a cup of coffee on its saucer. Most of our everyday activities, even the most ordinary and automatic ones, require extremely rapid and intricate calculations which feed into our perception of the environment and our interaction with it. What is exciting about PK is that this activity can apparently go on outside the recognized borders of the physiological organism.

To many people, it is inconceivable that anybody can directly influence physical objects. They find it useless even to read the experimental reports. It seems a little easier to accept ESP, perhaps because analogies come to mind with television, radio waves, and other familiar "extrasensory" kinds of communication.

If we do not ask people what they believe but instead watch their behavior, the story is often different. A golfer who has just hit the ball sometimes strains with his whole body in the direction the ball must take to reach the hole. He looks as if he is trying to exert some invisible force on the ball. Similarly, in the bowling alley, the player may seem to try steering the ball, his body leaning toward the point on the head pin that will give him a strike. The same is true for other sports and games. But what our body affirms our head denies. Most of us would scoff at the idea that body English might tell the truth.

My attitude toward poltergeists began to change in 1958. In March of that year in a house in Seaford, Long Island, plates, figurines, and other household belongings seemed to be taking on a life of their own. There were also strange thumping sounds. Dr. J. Gaither Pratt, assistant director of the Duke Parapsychology Laboratory at the time, made a firsthand investigation and then asked me to join. I shall say more in the next chapter about how the family in Seaford tried to deal with their uninvited and invisible houseguest.

To understand the interest which the poltergeist arouses in most parapsychologists, something else should be said about present-day PK work. In most PK experiments, parapsychologists have not been able to cause stationary objects to move. PK can generally only be detected on randomly moving or changing physical systems. For this reason, we cannot tell *when* PK is operating. If the die lands with the target face uppermost or if the correct lamp shows on Schmidt's machine, we do not know whether PK or chance is responsible: We only know that the total results cannot reasonably be attributed to chance.

In the Seaford disturbances, stationary objects *did* move. When a porcelain figurine took off from a table and crashed against a secretary desk ten feet away, we did not have to ask if this might be due to chance. A figurine does not fly off on its own like that. Here the uncertainty enters if one cannot be sure that somebody did not throw it, or pull it with a string, or that perhaps there was an earth tremor or some other kind of ordinary physical explanation. If these possibilities can be eliminated, then perhaps we can learn something about PK by looking at the conditions surrounding poltergeist events. For here we may see PK at its strongest and thereby we may get some real insight into this force.

Another reason why poltergeist incidents are interesting to the parapsychologist is that they touch on the survival question. People often believe that these happenings are produced by discarnate entities. This is an important question which should not be lightly dismissed.

There are other kinds of household disturbances which sometimes make people talk about spirits, namely so-called hauntings. This term also carried its own theory: Haunt comes from the same root as "home" and "-ham" (as in Birmingham); in other words, haunting means "homing," and implies that a spirit has remained at or returned to its earthly habitat.

Sometimes poltergeist and haunting are used interchangeably, but generally poltergeist is reserved for disturbances which are physically violent. In poltergeist cases there are often daily movements and breakage of plates, knickknacks, furniture, and other movable household effects, whereas in the typical haunting case such incidents are more rare and more spread out in time if they occur at all. Poltergeist disturbances are also generally of fairly short duration, rarely lasting more than a couple of months, and often less. Hauntings, however, may go on for years. The typical poltergeist case has no reference to hallucinatory experiences, such as seeing ghosts and hearing footsteps. Reports of such experiences, however, are common in hauntings.

Because poltergeist occurrences erupt spontaneously and then go on for a time before they, just as inexplicably, die down, Rhine had classified them as recurrent spontaneous psi phenomena. In our discussions at the Parapsychology Laboratory about the Seaford disturbances it became natural for us to refer to them as possible instances of RSPK, that is of "recurrent spontaneous psychokinesis." This avoids the assumption that ghosts or spirits are responsible. We are still making an assumption, namely that poltergeist effects are produced by the mind or psyche of somebody, whether or not this somebody is in the flesh. This, too, is a hypothesis that has to be proved or disproved. When I use the word poltergeist, I mean "an apparent case of RSPK."

Investigations of poltergeists are generally conducted in a private house or business—that is, away from the home base of the investigator, his own research laboratory. As a rule, therefore, he cannot impose all the precautions and controls that are possible in experimental work, and he often has to labor under a great deal of uncertainty. Poltergeist studies are not for the person who craves a neat and well-controlled research design. My task, as I have seen it, has been to collect as many observations as I could, under as good conditions as possible, given the circumstances, in the hope that some regularity or pattern would emerge in the data which would point to an explanation. This could then be put to the test in future field studies and, hopefully, in controlled experimentation.

If poltergeist phenomena—and other PK effects—are real, what does this mean? We are back to the "so what?" question.

When things happen which people do not understand and which they do not have any control over, they often speak of ghosts and spirits causing the phenomena. The word "thunder" came from the belief that the Norse god Thor was striking the clouds with his hammer. If you believe in an unseen world to begin with, it is easy to think of spirits in connection with poltergeist happenings. The objects that move are often the kind that an angry person might pick up and throw—such as glasses and plates. Sometimes the objects apparently move around corners, speed up or slow down, again suggesting that a person is the agent—albeit an invisible one. If there are noises such as knocks and thumps, these sometimes sound as if somebody is knocking on a door to come in. However, when you go to answer, nobody is there, at least not anybody you can see. Since a person is visible, and a spirit, at least as a rule, is invisible, people easily suppose that some kind of spirit is responsible for the moving objects and the knocks.

There is another thing about poltergeists—they are very

sociable. Usually nothing happens when the family is away from the house. Moreover, a poltergeist seems to be attached to one particular individual and rarely performs unless he is at home—though not necessarily near the disturbed objects.

But if a poltergeist depends on the presence of somebody, perhaps this somebody *is* the poltergeist. There would then be no need to suppose that there are such things as the spirit entities people have in mind when they speak about polter-*geists*. We know from PK experiments that many persons have the ability to influence physical objects in their vicinity: Perhaps poltergeist occurrences are concentrated bursts of PK from a living person.

This would not be the first time that processes or parts of the human self have been, as psychologists say, "projected" into the environment. Emotions which are unacceptable to us, and the consequences of such emotions, are imputed to other people or even to spirits. For instance, sexual dreams used to be attributed to incubi or succubi, demons in male or female form who made amorous advances to the dreamer. People now generally accept their own sexual impulses and those of others as natural expressions of human nature. This acceptance has produced so many changes in the private lives of people, in social customs, and in art and literature that we sometimes say that a "sexual revolution" has taken place.

We are now in the throes of another kind of revolution— one which promises to change man's idea about himself and the world even more radically. This revolution is sometimes called the "consciousness revolution" because it involves changes in the way people think about themselves and the world around them. Many people seek out experiences which give them a sense of transcending their individual selves for more meaningful relations with others and with their environment. Rock festivals, communal living, experiments with drugs and meditation, are typical expressions among the young, while an easing of life-styles and social relations, together with increased ecological awareness, runs through most age groups.

There has also been a surge of interest in aspects of the occult, such as in séances and witchcraft. The emphasis is on participating and experiencing rather than on observing and evaluating. Parapsychologists sometimes draw back in alarm, feeling that the rising tide of the occult is about to swallow their hard-earned results. They can deal with the scientific critics, whose language they speak, after all, but they find themselves in a different world from the current practitioners of the occult. Here the I Ching, the Ouija board, and astrology become answers to problems rather than problems to be answered.

I believe that far from turning our backs on this interest in the occult, it deserves the serious attention of parapsychologists. Instead of dismissing these activities and beliefs as so much faddism or romanticism, we need to stop and ask ourselves if they may not be expressions of something real, and, in fact, of the very subject matter of parapsychology. For one way of looking at ESP and PK is to regard them as evidence that the human self extends into the environment in ways that have not so far been brought out by science.

If it is true that the human self reaches beyond the known organism, then this aspect of the self may have needs which, if unfulfilled, may lead to tensions and frustrations just as do our other unfulfilled needs.

Looked at this way, poltergeist phenomena may not represent odd exceptions to the laws of nature but lawful processes which have so far escaped our attention. If poltergeist phenomena say anything, I suspect that this is not about spirits, demons, or ghosts but about human personality. Let me now share some of the experiences which have led me and other parapsychologists to raise such possibilities.

2

The Seaford, Long Island, Disturbances:
My First Investigation

NOTIFICATION: Complainant reports to Lieut. E. Richardson, Desk Officer, 7th Precinct, that strange occurrences had been taking place in her home. On several occasions bottles had lost caps and fallen down and spilled contents with no apparent reason.

The report by Detective Joseph Tozzi of the disturbances which were to persecute Mr. and Mrs. James Herrmann and their two children in their home in Seaford, Long Island, for five weeks in 1958 continues:

DETAIL INTERVIEW: On Tuesday, February 11, 1958, the complainant was interviewed by the writer and Sgt. B. McConnell and she stated that on Monday, Feb. 3rd, 1958, at about 1530 [3:30 P.M.] to 1615 [4:15 P.M.] hours she was at home with her daughter Lucille, age 13 years and her son James, age 12 years. The complainant heard noises of bottles popping their caps and on checking found that a small holy water bottle on her dresser in the master bedroom had its cap unscrewed and was lying on its side with the contents all spilled. In her son's bedroom, which is right next to the master bedroom, a small ceramic doll had its legs broken and a few small pieces had broken off a plastic ship model. In the bathroom cabinet there were two bottles with the caps unscrewed and the contents spilled. In the kitchen there was a bottle of starch under the sink with the cap off and the contents spilled. In the cellar directly under the kitchen a gallon bottle of bleach was also spilled.

There were other bottle spillings on February 6 and 7 when the children were by themselves. But it was only on the 9th that the police were called in. The events which led to the Herrmanns' request for help are reported as follows in the police report.

On Sunday, Feb. 9th, 1958, at about 1015 hours [10:15 A.M.] the whole family was in the dining room of the house. Noises were heard to come from different rooms and on checking it was found that the holy water bottle on the dresser in the master bedroom had again opened and spilled, a new bottle of toilet water on another dresser in the master room had fallen, lost its screw cap and also a rubber stopper and the contents were spilled. At the same time a bottle of shampoo and a bottle of Kaopectate in the bathroom had lost their caps, fallen over and were spilling their contents. The starch in the kitchen was also opened and spilled again and a can of paint thinner in the cellar had opened, fallen and was spilling on the floor. The complainant then called the police department and Patrolman J. Hughes of the 7th Precinct responded. While Patrolman Hughes was at the complainant's home, all the family was present with him in the living room when noises were heard in the bathroom. When Patrolman Hughes went into the bathroom with the complainant's family he found the medicine and the shampoo had again spilled. The complainant further stated that at the time of occurrences there were no tremors in the house, no loud noises or disturbances of any kind that could be noticed. None of the appliances were going at these times and the complainant has no high frequency equipment at all in the house.

In March 1958, when I became involved with the Seaford poltergeist, I had been at the Duke Parapsychology Laboratory for less than a year, and I was still a newcomer to the American parapsychology—and poltergeist—scene. We first read of the case in the papers, and then Dr. Rhine contacted the Herrmanns and Detective Tozzi. What he heard convinced Rhine and the other members of the staff that the case was worth looking into. Dr. J. Gaither Pratt took off first. When he had satisfied himself that the case was still active, he asked me to join the investigation.

On March 10, Gaither and I interviewed Hughes about his visit. He said that actually only one bottle had fallen while he was in the house. When he was with all of the family in the living room, they heard a noise from the bathroom as if a bottle had fallen over. When they went in, they found a bottle on its side on the vanity table next to the sink. This was probably a Kaopectate bottle which had been involved in a previous incident.

Hughes told us he had inspected the bathroom just before. It had been cleaned up after the last disturbance, when a shampoo bottle had fallen to the floor from the table and the Kaopectate bottle had moved into the sink. Hughes was convinced that the bottle was not then lying down: "I can swear to that!" When we questioned him further, he could not definitely exclude the possibility that someone had turned the bottle over after he had seen it as they were leaving the bathroom, but that, he pointed out, would not explain the noise of a falling bottle in the empty bathroom when he was with the family in the living room.

The disturbance which had been most convincing to Mr. Herrmann took place about ten-thirty that morning and involved this same bottle. Herrmann, who generally commuted to his work in New York City, was spending this day, a Sunday, with his family. He struck us as a straightforward person and gave an unembellished account of the incidents in the house.

That morning as Jimmy was brushing his teeth at the bathroom sink and Herrmann was standing in the doorway (he told us), he suddenly saw two bottles on the vanity table next to the sink begin to move. He wrote and signed this statement:

At *about* 10:30 A.M. I was standing in the doorway of the bathroom. All of a sudden two bottles which had been placed on the top of the vanity table were seen to move. One moved straight ahead, slowly, while the second spun to the right for a 45-degree angle. The first one fell into the sink. The second one crashed to the floor. Both bottles moved at the same time.

Both bottles had become unscrewed while they were in the cabinet under the sink. They had been placed on the vanity top while the cabinet was being cleaned.

It was this event which made the family call the Nassau County Police Department for help.

Others were to see objects in motion. On Saturday, February 15, Miss Marie Murtha, a middle-aged cousin of Herrmann, was visiting. As she was seated in the living room across from Jimmy, who was on the middle of the couch with his arms folded, a porcelain figurine on an end table next to the couch began to "wiggle" and then flew two feet into the room and landed on the rug with a loud, crashing sound—but unbroken. Lucille was at the other end of the room, and no one else was there. The movement was so quick that the figurine looked like a white streak or feather. Though Miss Murtha could not explain this or the other incidents, she did not think anything supernatural was involved. She wrote some other details for us about this incident:

> James, his sister, Lucille, and myself were sitting in the living room—I was sitting in the green chair in the corner between the secretary and the window—James and Lucille were seated on the sofa—there is a table at each end of this sofa—on one table was a lighted lamp and two figurines—we were looking at the television when the picture started to flicker—I asked Lucille to adjust it—as she went to do so the picture cleared—on her way back to her seat I asked to feel the material in her slacks and remarked that they were smart, but thought she was neglecting to set her hair. Lucille then turned to look at herself in the glass of the secretary and James said, "Auntie Marie, she is always fixing her hair"—I turned my head in his direction to answer him—as I did I saw the female figurine wiggle (like that of a worm cut in pieces) —as it went in the air it looked like a small white feather —then crashed to the rug, unbroken. The children's parents were in other rooms of the house and hearing the crash came hurrying into the living room to see what happened.

A total of 67 individual disturbances were recorded in the Herrmann house. Of these, three were unexplained thumping sounds and the rest disturbances of objects. Since the family reported all the known occurrences to the police, there is a quite detailed record of the objects which moved and the circumstances surrounding them. This was a great help for the analysis of patterns in the occurrences which may point to their nature.

A prominent feature was that the same object was often repeatedly involved. If we count all incidents in which an object moved or was disturbed more than once, we discover that 40 of the 64 incidents are accounted for in this way. In these 40 incidents, only 16 objects were involved, having been disturbed from two to four times each.

In several cases, the repeated movement of an object eventually led to its destruction. For instance, the female figurine that moved while Miss Murtha watched was to be involved in three other incidents. The second and third times it again moved about two feet into the room without breaking. But the fourth time it hit a secretary standing 10 feet away, marring the wood and breaking into bits. Another four-time repeater was a globe of the world in Jimmy's room. Several objects were each involved in three incidents, including a holy water bottle, a bleach bottle, a glass bowl, and a table lamp. A male figurine from the same end table where the female had been, twice flew against the same secretary, first breaking an arm and then shattering completely. This last incident is one of a number of disturbances which took place during the evening of Thursday, February 20. There had been another event shortly before which had greatly frightened Mrs. Herrmann and had led her to take Lucille and Jimmy with her into the hallway to seek shelter. These occurrences are described as follows by Detective Tozzi in the police record:

> On the above date at about 2145 hours [9:45 P.M.] Mrs. Herrmann was on the phone in the dining room, James was right next to her and Lucille was in the bedroom. James was putting his books away and there was a bottle of ink on the south side of the table. A very loud pop was heard and the ink bottle lost its screw top and the bottle left the table in a northeasterly direction. The bottle landed in the living room and the ink spilled on the chair, floor and on the wallpaper on the north side of the front door. Mrs. Herrmann immediately hung up and called the writer, who had left the house about 10 minutes prior to this occurrence. When the writer arrived it was learned that as soon as Mrs. Herrmann called, she had taken the two children with her into the hallway to await the arrival of the writer. At about 2150 hours [9:50 P.M.] while the children were with her a loud noise was again heard in the living room. All three of them went into the room and found the. male figurine had again left the end table and had again flown through the air for about 10 feet and again hit the desk about six inches to the east of where it had hit the first time. On this occurrence the only noise heard was when the figurine hit the desk and at this time it broke into many pieces and fell to the floor. At this time the only appliance running was the oil burner and no one was again in the room.

Gaither Pratt and I questioned Mrs. Herrmann and the children separately on their movements during this period. They corroborated the information from the police report. The three of them were standing at the end of the hall near the bathroom, out of sight of the living room, when the loud crash sounded. Mrs. Herrmann was facing the two children who were standing in front of the bathroom door.

The strange goings-on seemed completely to overwhelm and mystify the family. They were Catholic, and Mrs. Herrmann put out bottles filled with holy water to ward off the poltergeist.

This was no help at all. In fact it probably made matters worse: The Herrmann poltergeist liked bottles. There were 23 "bottle poppings," more than a third of the total number of occurrences. The bottles would loose their screw caps with an explosivé sound, fall over, and spill their contents. Nothing could be found in them—whether bleach, starch, holy water, or wine—to explain this. Five of the bottles were examined by the police laboratory in Mineola. There was no foreign matter, and the police were unable to come up with an explanation.

I tried to determine if there was any favoring of kinds of objects. If we look at the types of objects disturbed but disregard repetitions with individual objects, we see that of the total of 40 objects 18 were bottles, 16 miscellaneous objects such as figurines, lamps, plates, and the like, and 6 were pieces of furniture that toppled over, namely bookcases, night tables, the boy's dresser, and a coffee table.

Gaither and I were present in the house during one of the bottle poppings. In the evening of March 10, at 8:14 P.M. when I was sitting at the dining room table and Gaither was in the living room, there was a loud, dull noise which sounded as if it came from the floor or lower wall of the kitchen-bathroom area. Jimmy was in the bathroom, Lucille was in bed, and Mrs. Herrmann was in the master bedroom coming toward the central hallway (Herrmann was away). I investigated upstairs, and Gaither went down to the cellar. Here he found a bleach bottle in a cardboard box by the washing machine which had lost its cap and had fallen over against the side of the box. The cap was on the floor in back of the box. The bottle was only partially full, and the bleach had not spilled.

The cap had fallen right side up, it was still wet inside and there was a wet spot on the floor below it.

The noise itself was not sufficiently well localized to establish definitely that it had come from the cellar rather than from the bathroom where Jimmy was at that time. It was therefore possible that he had some time earlier staged the bottle effect and then later made the sound. We knew that Jimmy had not been in the cellar for half an hour beforehand since he and I were doing a PK game with dice (no significant results) during that period.

It was therefore important for us to establish whether or not the wet spot under the bottle cap was fresh. We found that a drop of bleach would remain on the floor for only about 15 minutes.

If Jimmy had staged the event 30 minutes before he made the noise, the spot should have faded away. But it was still wet and moist 16 minutes after the event. In addition, if Jimmy had staged the event, he would have had to drop the cap to the floor or tapped it on the concrete since we found that a drop would not otherwise come off.

To try to find a normal explanation for the bottle poppings, Gaither and I tried to make some of our own. On the theory that someone in the home had surreptitiously placed a chemical in the bottles that would generate pressure, or that pressure had arisen in some other way, we bought some pieces of "dry ice," that is, carbon dioxide in its solid state, and placed these in containers with screw caps, such as those in the Herrmann household. We found that when the top was loosely screwed on, the pressure easily escaped with a low, hissing noise without affecting the cap. When we screwed the cap on as tightly as we could by hand, the pressure increased until the gas forced its way out around the threads of the cap but without perceptibly loosening it. Of course, thousands of housewives every year do pressure canning in glass jars utilizing this principle—without complaining of "bottle poppings": Pressure escapes from the tightly closed lids without causing them to unscrew. When Gaither and I tightened the cover mechanically, we succeeded in exploding a bottle of relatively thin glass, but the cap remained on the broken neck. This had never been observed in connection with the bottles that lost their caps in the Herrmann household. When we used a bleach bottle of the type which had lost its cap when we were in the house, and when we tightened the cover mechanically, the buildup of pressure inside the bottle produced neither explosion nor unscrewing of the cap. When the pressure built up enough, the gas escaped around the cap. In general, it became clear that pressure does not cause these types of caps to unscrew and come completely off. Either the gas escapes around the threads or the bottle explodes, the cap remaining in place. We found it made no difference if we oiled the threads of the glass.

It was not possible to pin the cause of the disturbances on any other known physical forces. The police first thought that the incidents might be due to high-frequency radio waves and

THE SEAFORD, LONG ISLAND, DISTURBANCES

a person with a radio transmitter living close by was inter-viewed. But he had not used his set for several years. The Long Island Lighting Company was contacted, and installed an oscillograph in the cellar. While it was in place, there were three occurrences, including the one with the bleach bottle which took place while we were present. No unusual vibrations in the floor were associated with these incidents. The same company examined the wiring, fuse panels, and ground wires in the house and found everything in order. Before we came, Tozzi had examined all objects that had been disturbed. He had turned the television and oil burner on and off to see if they were connected with the incidents, and also checked the fuse boxes, water leaders, and ground connections as well as the electrical installations in the attic and elsewhere in the house.

No effort was spared to explore for normal explanations and to take corrective action. A lady phoned Tozzi saying that similar incidents in her house had stopped when a chim-ney cap was installed to exclude downdrafts. Consequently the detective asked Herrmann to buy a turbine chimney cap and he himself helped to put it up.

The Seaford Fire Department then checked a well in front of the house to see if there had been any change in the water level that might have caused tremors. It was found to have been stable for the last five years. Old maps of the area, before it had been built up, were examined for water or streams, but none appeared. A test truck from the Radio Corporation of America came and the crew examined for radio frequency outside the house, finding nothing unusual, and the Town of Hempstead Building Department examined the house and found it to be structurally sound, showing only normal settling cracks in the basement floor.

A conference at Adelphi College with members of the science departments and visits to the house by a professor of engineering from Cooper Union, a structural engineer, a civil engineer, and an electrical engineer from the Nassau County Society of Professional Engineers were all fruitless. Mitchell Airfield was contacted for a list of planes leaving on a runway facing the Herrmann house on the possibility that these might be correlated with the times of the disturbances. They were not. The television antenna on the chimney was removed, a crack between the concrete foundation and the main base of the house was closed, plumbing was checked, and vibrations from the circulator were examined. None of this affected the incidents.

What counted most strongly against known types of impersonal physical explanations was the fact that the incidents seemed to happen only when Jimmy was home. There were a few which could have taken place while he was out of the house, but even those might have happened as he was entering or leaving. Moreover, the incidents were clustered during his waking hours. There were none when he was asleep. The thought that was uppermost in our minds when Gaither and I began our investigations was that Jimmy, perhaps abetted by his sister, produced the incidents as childish pranks. The police approached the case with the same idea. On February 12, the day after Tozzi had entered the case, he warned both children that it would be a grave matter if they were implicated in any way. Nevertheless, the phenomena continued, some of them taking place when Tozzi was close by. One time, in the basement, a figurine of a horse fell to the floor and broke right next to Tozzi when Jimmy was next to him. The detective immediately accused the boy of having thrown the horse—even saying he had seen him do so though he had not—and subjected the boy to a long and severe grilling. Jimmy denied he had anything to do with this or any of the other incidents. Another time when there had been several disturbances, Mr. Herrmann himself accused Jimmy and said that Detective Tozzi had proof he had caused many of the events and that it was now time for him to admit this without further delay. Mr. Herrmann said that Jimmy, driven to tears, only said, "Dad, I had nothing to do with any of it." When Tozzi arrived shortly afterward, he wrote in his report, "James was sitting at the dining room table crying, Lucille was in the kitchen crying, and Mr. Herrmann was trying to bring some order to the house, as the complainant [Mrs. Herrmann] was also crying and on the verge of hysteria. At this time, the complainant and the two children went to the Liguoris' home to spend the night as they were afraid to sleep in their home. . . ."

Gaither and I found Jimmy to be an intelligent and likable boy. Nevertheless, in several cases he was in a position to cause the incidents normally. And these have to be ruled out from the evidential standpoint. If we move from the simple pranks hypothesis to that of skilled magic, where some device or devices were installed by Jimmy to produce the effects, this would have to account for such incidents as the two bottles which moved in different directions while Herrmann was watching, and the figurine flying off the end table when Miss Murtha was looking at him. There are other such incidents, including the movement of the figurine, which crashed against the secretary 10 feet away while Jimmy was standing with his mother and sister in the hallway. We found it difficult to conceive of how he could have installed an undiscovered device to cause these incidents.

The fraud hypothesis would be easier to accept if it could be supposed that the other members of the family were acting as Jimmy's accomplices. We could then simply suppose that the events described by the Herrmann family, such as the simultaneous movement of the two bottles in different directions, never occurred and that the effects that the police and others had observed had been staged. This still leaves those events which took place while Hughes, Miss Murtha, and Gaither and I were present.

Other factors make the family hoax theory an unsatisfactory one. The Herrmanns would seem to have been inviting unnecessary trouble and running grave risks by asking the police and other investigators into their home and then staging the disturbances right under their noses. A member of the Seventh Precinct Force was in the house at the time of six of the events, but the police investigations and interviews failed to reveal anything suspicious. The educational background of the parents, their professions, and the position of the family in the community would not lead one to expect a joint hoax. Mrs. Herrmann was a registered nurse who had held a supervisory position in a large hospital before her marriage. Herrmann was the interlines representative of Air France in New York City and a member of the auxiliary police of Seaford. The family was Catholic and participated actively in church and school affairs. Some of the events involved religious objects, including the movement and breakage of a statue of the Virgin Mary and the spilling of the holy water bottles. Such destructions and spillings, if done intentionally, would amount to desecration, a serious religious offense.

Gaither and I each spent 10 days with the family under circumstances which we felt gave us a close acquaintance with all its members, and we were personally unable to accept the family hoax hypothesis as a reasonable one. The Herrmanns seemed greatly upset by the destruction of their belongings and were also afraid that the disturbances might injure someone. They moved to the homes of relatives and neighbors four times to avoid the incidents, staying away six nights.

After a coffee table, a new and prized possession, turned upside down and was damaged, Detective Tozzi, who came together with Sergeant Reddy, found Mrs. Herrmann "very upset over the occurrence. The complainant was crying the whole time interviewed by the writer and stated she is ready to try anything to stop the disturbance. She doesn't believe in any supernatural powers, but stated that if this is not stopped she will even be ready to try a medium spiritualist." Later that day, Tozzi called the Rectory of St. William the Abbot to request the bishop to have the rite of exorcism carried out. He was told this was not used for the kind of disturbance that occurred in the Herrmann house.

Gaither and I had to conclude that the fraud hypothesis and other ordinary explanations were not supported by the evidence and that the RSPK hypothesis had to be taken seriously for this case.

The "popping" of the bleach bottle while Gaither and I were present was the parting shot of the Seaford poltergeist. From then on, everything was quiet and soon thereafter Gaither and I left. Had we been of any real help to the Herrmanns? It was probably a coincidence that the poltergeist left while we were there, so we could not take credit for that. Also, we had not "solved" the case, at least not in any ordinary sense, since we could point to no familiar physical force as the explanation of the incidents nor to any culprit, even an invisible one. But this in itself was a relief to the Herrmanns. While the incidents had convinced them that no member of the family was producing the incidents normally, the idea of some kind of other-worldly and evil influence had become a possibility for them as shown by the use of holy water and the attempt to have the place exorcised. At the end of our stay they had come to see the matter not as one for religion but for science. When, some years later, poltergeist disturbances erupted in a home in Newark, New Jersey (Chapter 4), Mrs. Herrmann could take it upon herself to phone the family to give them courage in facing their problem. In spite of all its destruction, the poltergeist rarely does anybody serious harm and its lifespan is relatively short.

The poltergeist has a reputation of being elusive if not plain evasive. This was not true in Seaford. Things sometimes happened in full view of people and when outside visitors were present. The extent to which it is possible to observe poltergeist events under good conditions will determine whether or not science can take them seriously. Let us, therefore, look at other cases. I shall take 1958 as the dividing line between old and new poltergeists. Let us first survey the cases published before 1958. I shall restrict myself to the cases published in serious books and journals.

3

Earlier Cases
Around the World

On January 7, 1851, in the small town of Yerville, France, an unusual lawsuit was heard in the court of M. Folloppe, justice of the peace.[1] A shepherd named Thorel had summoned Father Tinel, the parish priest of a neighboring village, Cideville, for defamation of character. Tinel had allegedly called Thorel a sorcerer and accused him of causing a number of strange incidents that were plaguing two boys, Gustave and Bunel, ages 12 and 14, whom Tinel was tutoring and who were boarding at the presbytery. The incidents, which occurred between November 1850 and February 1851, included knocks and raps, the movements of the boys' desks, and slaps by invisible hands. Gustave claimed he was haunted by a ghostly figure and recognized Thorel as the ghost. It soon became clear that Thorel had no connection with the incidents but that he had encouraged the idea that he might. In any case, he lost his suit.

However, he won an interesting case for the poltergeist literature. The sworn court testimony has several reports by eyewitnesses to the events. A farmer, named Cheval, said he saw the tongs and shovel from the fireplace in the presbytery leave their place and move into the middle of the room. When they were put back, they rushed out again. "My eyes were fixed on them to see what moved them, but I saw nothing at all." Another witness, the parish priest of Saussay, Father Leroux, said that when he was visiting the presbytery of Cideville, "I saw things which I have been unable to explain to myself. I saw a hammer, moved by some invisible force, leave the spot where it lay and fall in the middle of the room without making more noise than if a hand had gently laid it down."

In all, I found 47 poltergeist cases in the serious literature before 1958. Of these, 27 are from publications in the English language and the majority are English and American cases. The first of the 27 cases occurred in 1849 and the last in 1957. Mr. George Zorab, a Dutch parapsychologist, has made a survey of poltergeist reports in other languages covering the same period.[2] His 20 cases bring the total to 47. The largest proportion of the 47 cases comes from England and the United States, with eight cases from each. There are five French poltergeists, and four each from Germany and Holland. Italy has three cases; and Austria, India, Indonesia, Ireland, and Russia each have two. Finally, there is one case each from Belgium, Czechoslovakia, Finland, Sweden, and Switzerland.

There is no denying that the poltergeist is a citizen of the world. A more important issue for our purpose concerns the likelihood of meaningful encounters with poltergeists, whatever their national origin.

People often think that poltergeist phenomena, if not obviously fraudulent, are so shifty that it is useless to try to investigate them. This is an important consideration. Before scientists can be expected to pay serious attention to poltergeists, they will want to know what the prospects are for a serious investigation. For instance, is anything likely to happen to an object when outside witnesses have the situation under observation? The Seaford case may have been an exception.

Let us see what the chances are for getting a close-up look at the poltergeist. I shall disregard the cases with which other parapsychologists and I have been involved in recent years. They will be discussed later.

In 40 of the 47 poltergeist cases, visitors not belonging to the household were present when things happened which they could not explain normally. The Cideville case is an example.

Another question is important when it comes to studying poltergeist phenomena. This has to do with the prospects of directly observing the poltergeist movements.

In the following case, some events were observed but others only took place when no one was watching the object. Thirty to 40 persons had watched as pieces of wood were moving in a carpenter's shop in the village of Swanland, Yorkshire, England, in 1849.[3] One of the carpenters said that "on one occasion a piece of wood, starting from somewhere near me, made a series of some three or four jumps, like a frog, along the bench, about nine feet in length, at which I was sitting at work; then sprang from the bench about three yards, upon a trestle, only some four inches wide; then from the trestle on to a wheel-stool (arrangement for making a wheel) and thence straight at a closet door where we kept nails, etc., where it came to rest."

Nevertheless, direct observation seemed to inhibit the events: "Sometimes one of us would look fixedly for many minutes at a bit of wood on the floor. It never moved while we looked at it. But once let our attention be relaxed and that very bit of wood would come flying at us from some distant point."

It is not always clear whether or not it inhibits the phenomena if somebody looks at the object. However, in 37 of the 47 cases, somebody was watching the movement of an object—sometimes from beginning to end.

Perhaps the characteristic of the poltergeist which is most helpful to the investigator is its preference for certain objects and areas. All but one of the 47 cases showed this feature. In Cideville it was the boys' room and desks, and in the following case, the head of the stairs and a special chair in the home of T. B. Clarke, a businessman in Oakland, California.[4] For three days in April 1874, heavy pieces of furniture moved about on their own. An investigating committee consisting of a professor from the University of California, a lawyer, and a minister cross-examined the witnesses at length and recorded their statements.

Once when Helen, Clarke's grown daughter, walked up the stairs, he said jokingly to her, referring to an object that almost hit her the night before, " 'Nellie, look out for your head,' she replied, 'Oh! it is not time for them to begin yet.' Instantly a large upholstered chair standing at the head of the stairs, went revolving and lay down across the stairway preventing her getting up."

Later that night and also the next one, this chair again turned over. Finally, after several disturbances with other objects, Clarke said that the same chair "went revolving in mid air" in the presence of three houseguests. "This chair having been the means of great annoyance to us thus far, I placed it in Mr. O.'s [a boarder] room where it would be less likely to disturb us."

A large mahogany bureau also located at the head of the

stairs, then turned over. Clarke therefore said he ". . . brought out the chair as the lesser evil, and set it at the end of the bureau in the hall, where it had previously stood. . . . Mr. S. [a visitor] who stood at the foot of the stairs, as when the bureau moved, and in a few moments saw this same upholstered chair going through its accustomed evolutions, but this time it started downstairs, end for end, and was caught by him." The person referred to, William Sherman, told the investigation committee that the "progress of the chair down the stairs was very slow" but that it had been caught by another visitor.

When an event happens repeatedly, the idea of conducting a test involving the object or event in question sometimes occurs to one of the witnesses. The chair in the Clarke house would have been an obvious candidate.

Sometimes the tests concentrate on sound effects. In the Cideville case, Father Leroux mentioned the knocks in his testimony: "I took every precaution in listening to them, even placing myself under the table to make sure that the children could do nothing, and yet I heard noises, which seemed to me . . . extraordinary. . . . I noticed that M. Tinel seemed to be somewhat exasperated at these noises and at their persistence, especially on several nights during which I slept with him, when he woke up frightened about it all."

Another witness, M. de Mirville, did some tests in which the "cause," the name the unknown entity or energy went by in court, correctly rapped the number of letters in the names of Mirville and his children and indicated his age in the same way.

Sir William Barrett, the British physicist and one of the founders of the Society for Psychical Research, made a similar test during his investigation of disturbances that had upset a widowed farmer and his five children in a cottage near Derrygonnelly, Ireland, in 1877.[5] They seemed to center around his 20-year-old daughter, Maggie. Voices were heard and objects thrown about: ". . . they were Methodists, and their class leader advised them to lay an open Bible on the bed. This they did in the name of God, putting a big stone on the top of the volume; but the stone was lifted off by an unseen hand, and the Bible placed on top of it. After that 'it,' as the farmer called the unseen cause, moved the Bible out of the room and tore 17 pages right across. Then they could not keep a light in the house, candles and lamps were mysteriously stolen, or thrown out."

When Barrett was present and while Maggie and the children were lying motionless in bed, loud knocks and raps were heard, and "Suddenly a large pebble fell in my presence on to the bed; no one had moved to dislodge it even if it had been placed for the purpose. . . .

"I mentally asked it, no word being spoken, to knock a certain number of times and it did so. To avoid any error or delusion on my part, I put my hands in the side pockets of my overcoat and asked it to knock the number of fingers I had open. It correctly did so. Then, with a different number of fingers open each time, the experiment was repeated four times in succession, and four times I obtained absolutely the correct number of raps."

The first impulse of a family whose household belongings move about on their own is often to call the police. Constable William Higgs went to the home of Joseph White in Worksop, Nottinghamshire, England, to discover the cause of a great deal of breakage in the kitchen which bothered the family in February and March 1883.[6] The destruction was worst when a feeble-minded girl, Eliza Rose, who was visiting the family, was present. But she was not always on the scene. For instance, a tumbler fell from a chest of drawers in the kitchen near Higgs when only he and White were there.

White feared that the occurrences were warnings of a death in the family. Since one of his children was ill, he asked a physician, Dr. Lloyd, to examine the child. While the doctor was out of the kitchen, the others "saw a cream jug, which Rose had just placed on the bin, fly four feet up in the air and smash on the floor. Dr. Lloyd and Mrs. White then entered, and in the presence of all these witnesses, a basin was seen to rise slowly from the bin—no person being near it except Dr. Lloyd and Higgs. It touched the ceiling, and then fell suddenly to the floor, and was smashed."

Higgs and Lloyd examined some of the objects immediately after they had moved, but found nothing to explain the matter. Can we be certain that there was not some magical device which escaped notice? I do not think so. But this is not the issue at stake. The question is, whether poltergeist occurrences occur sufficiently out in the open to give a reasonably observant witness a good chance to discover fraud or other familiar causes if there are any. When he sees an object begin to move and when he has some control over the situation and can immediately examine the object and the place where it stood, this gives the observer a good chance to make a meaningful investigation.

In 20 of the 47 cases, incidents took place at a time when someone was looking directly at the object.

The following incidents are from a house in the village of Durweston, near Blanford, England, occupied by a widow, Mrs. Best, her daughter, and two orphan girls.[7] The occurrences began in December 1894, with sounds of knockings and scrapings and, later, movements of objects. A neighbor, Mr. Newman, who had witnessed some of them, was interviewed: "On Tuesday [December 18] between 10 and 11 A.M., Mrs. Best sent for me, and told me that Annie (the elder girl, about 13 years of age) had seen a boot come out of the garden plot and strike the back door, leaving a muddy mark." Newman went into the house and witnessed several occurrences including the flight of the same boot from the place it had fallen by the door. Mrs. Best threw it out into the garden.

Newman's report continued: "I went out and put my foot on it, and said, 'I defy anything to move this boot.' Just as I stepped off, it rose up behind me and knocked my hat off: there was no one behind me. The boot and the hat fell down together."

If the movements or disturbances of objects center in a special place or are focused on certain objects, it becomes possible for the investigator to concentrate his attention on these instead of having to keep watch over a whole house and its contents. It is much easier to rule out fraud and other ordinary explanations if one's surveillance can be limited to a certain area or to a few objects.

As I mentioned before, most of the cases show focusing. Sometimes, as in the following study by Professor C. Lombroso, the Italian physician and criminologist, the investigator took advantage of this to do an experiment.[8] The disturbances occurred during November 1900 in Turin, Italy. They were focused in the cellar of an inn and ceased when a servant boy was sent away. Before that happened, Lombroso went down to the cellar: "In the center there was a rough table, on which I made them place six lighted candles . . . I saw three empty bottles, standing upright on the ground, roll as if pushed by a foot and break against the table. To guard against trickery I touched and minutely examined with a candle all the full bottles on the shelves and made sure there was no thread or wire which would explain the movements. After a few minutes two bottles, then four, and then two more bottles of the second and third shelf, fell to the floor without a shock, as if they had been carried. After their descent—one could not call it a fall—six of them broke on the moist ground . . . while two remained intact." Later, four more broke.

Lombroso included the observations of the accountant, Pierre Merini. Once Merini, when he was alone in the cellar, saw several empty and full bottles break by themselves. He then ". . . took down a bottle which had just broken, and of which only the lower half remained. I separated it from the others, placing it some distance away. After a few moments the bottle finished cracking and burst into fragments."

In September 1903, falls of stones were reported by a Dutchman living in Sumatra.[9] The occurrences seemed to be related to a servant boy. The stones came through the roof of the bedroom, landing close to the bed. He tried to catch them "while they were falling through the air towards me, but I could never catch them; *it seemed to me that they changed their direction in the air as soon as I tried to get hold of them.*" They moved unusually slowly.

When he climbed up to examine the roof, "I saw quite distinctly that they came right through the 'kadjang.' This kadjang is of such a kind that it cannot be penetrated (not even with a needle) without making a hole. Each kadjang is one simple flat leaf of about two by three feet in size. . . . It is very tough and offers a strong resistance to penetration." Yet the stones left no holes.

The stones "fell down within a certain radius of not more than three feet; they all came through the same kadjang-leaf (that is to say, all the ones I saw) and they all fell down within the same radius on the floor." Though their descent was so slow, there was a loud bang when they hit the floor. They were warm to the touch.

Mr. A. Wärndorfer, member of the English Society for Psychical Research, went to investigate flights of tools, coal, and pieces of iron in July 1906 in a smithy in a suburb of Vienna.[10] In addition to the smith, there were two teen-age apprentices, with one of whom the phenomena seemed to be connected. Among the objects that moved were pieces of coke that were kept in a box. Wärndorfer said that he several times saw these fly after people who were leaving the shop.

People were often hit. Wärndorfer himself "was hit on the back of my right hand by an iron screw with great violence, and felt a very intense pain; some blood came at once, and a swelling was raised, which lasted for several months. . . . I remember clearly that the back of my hand was turned towards the wall." There was nobody in that part of the shop.

He had brought a small copper plate for hypnotic experiments with one of the boys: "Before having been hit I had left it lying about on several places. On being hit it struck me that many of the flying objects had dropped near it, and that on its being held in my hand, my hand had been struck. I then laid it on the smithy, and in a very short time an iron piece flew with a thundering noise against the corrugated iron roof of the smithy. I gave it to one of the boys to hold, and something dropped quite near him. On this becoming known, a neighbor came in and asked to have a try. He stood opposite me, leaning against the turning lathe, with his back against the wall; nobody was behind him. . . . He was struck in the back by a handle off the lathe."

Occasionally only one or a few objects are involved as in a case in Douai, France, where the events were focused on a mechanically operated doorbell.[11] The incidents took place in June 1907 in a house occupied by a mailman, his wife, and five children. They apparently centered around a servant girl, 16 to 17 years old.

A neighbor who several times heard the bell ringing by itself said that while she was standing on her own doorstep she spoke about it, "and it tinkled at once. This happened several times. 'One might have thought that it was defying me,' " she said.

The sounds went on sporadically for two weeks or so, the peals increasing in frequency and intensity. Then "In front of the frightened family, the bell rang violently, while the cord and the bellpull moved in unison. The whole quarter assembled, and over 300 people witnessed the phenomenon. The police were called in, but could not find the cause. Indeed, at the end of three days, in front of a policeman, the bell fell off the wall in a last peal and broke on the ground."

In a few cases, the "object" on which the poltergeist focuses its attention is a person. N. J. Murphy, a reporter, and Owen Devereux, a mechanic, went to a house at Enniscorthy, Ireland, in July 1910 where strange events victimized two young carpenters sleeping in the same room.[12] Murphy stated: ". . . we made a close inspection of the apartment. The beds were pulled out from the walls and examined, the clothing being searched; the flooring was minutely inspected, and the walls and fireplace examined. Everything was found quite normal."

The young men went to bed, the visitors taking up positions on chairs opposite the fireplace and between the two beds. Rapping noises were heard. When they stopped, Randall, one of the young men, said the bedclothes were coming off his bed.

"Mr. Devereux immediately struck a match which he had ready in his hand. The bedclothes had partly left the boy's bed, having gone diagonally towards the foot . . . and . . . appeared to be . . . going back under the bed. . . . Mr. Devereux lighted the candle and a thorough search was made under the bed for strings or wires, but nothing could be found. . . . The candle was again extinguished.

"After about 10 minutes the rapping recommenced. . . . Randall's voice again broke the silence. 'They are going again,' he cried; 'the clothes are leaving me again.' I said, 'Hold them and do not let them go: you only imagine they are going. He said: 'I cannot hold them; they are going, and I am going with them; there is something pushing me from inside: I am going, I am going, I'm gone.' My companion struck a light just in time to see Randall slide from the bed, the sheet under him, and the sheets, blanket and coverlet over him. He lay on his back on the floor. The movement of his coming out of bed was gentle and regular. There did not appear to be any jerky motion."

These cases do not suggest that there is anything evasive about the poltergeist. If it is active, it performs for strangers as well as for family and friends. Sometimes it may be stage-shy and act only when the observers take their eyes from the object in question. This, however, is more than made up for by its preference for a small stage and limited props. Hereby the witnesses can concentrate their attention on a few objects and areas.

Several of the cases to which I have already referred show the repetitive behavior of the poltergeist. Sometimes the object is a door or window. In January 1911, three young telegraph operators, Messrs. Bright, Davis, and Clark, were working in a railway telegraph tower at Dale, Georgia.[13]

The trapdoor was repeatedly opened: "In spite of fastening it with stout nails and an iron bar, it would still fly open; mysterious footsteps were also heard on the stairs, but a careful search revealed no cause for the disturbances. Then followed the raising and lowering of the window sashes . . . in full view of the three occupants, no one being near the window." They also watched as "a lantern was levitated on to the desk without having been touched, and in full view of all."

Between November 1917 and December 1918, R. P. Jacques was building a bomb shelter on his estate, Enbrook Manor, in Folkstone, Kent, England.[14] It was never tested against German air attacks but it was the target of several poltergeist missiles. And it offered no protection against them since they often came from *inside* the shelter.

When Jacques inspected it one day, the builder and his assistant, a boy, were away. "There was no one present, as both Rolfe and his assistant were at dinner. I am quite positive on this point that no person was in the dugout at the same time as myself, above or below ground. I remained there some 10 to 12 minutes inspecting the work and then came away. I closed the door at the bottom of the steps, and before taking my hand from the latch a stone came violently into contact with the inside of the door, and immediately afterwards three others in quick succession."

Eight to 11 stones followed. He went back in, found the stones by the door, and again made sure that no one else was there.

The incidents seemed to be connected with the boy. Once Rolfe took a six-pound hammer out of the shelter and then returned. ". . . within a minute I heard a little thud on the earth beside me. I looked down and there was the hammer at my feet again. It seemed to hit the ground very lightly, and despite its weight made hardly any noise. I asked the boy, who was working alongside me, to take it right out, as it was becoming a nuisance. He took it out and came back and told me he had put it at the bottom of the entrance round the corner, and whilst he was telling me I just caught sight of it settling down beside me again, just as a bird would settle down. I told him to take it away further, and he came back and told me he had put it over beside the stable, but hardly had he told me when it was back at my feet again, so we left it there."

In February 1921, Mrs. Ernst Sauerbrey, of Hopfgarten, Germany, was gravely ill and in addition was plagued by inexplicable knocks and movements of objects.[15] Dr. Scharff, her physician, could offer no help except to say that she was too ill to cause the incidents normally. Mr. Sauerbrey then called the police. "In the presence of Commissioner of Police

Pfeil, from Weimar, some objects were set out in the middle of the room at a distance of two metres from my wife's bed. It was observed that these objects also moved from the place where they were standing, without anyone coming into contact with them."

Officer Pfeil amplified, referring to himself in the third person: "A police officer set a jug of water two metres away from Frau Sauerbrey. At the very moment that he turned away, the jug was already in motion. The same thing happened with a water basin."

Beginning in July 1928 and lasting for a year, a series of disturbances was associated with two brothers in Poona, India.[16] The incidents were reported by Miss H. Kohn, a German language teacher. Her sister and brother-in-law, an Indian physician, Dr. Ketkar, had adopted the younger brother (he was about nine, his brother 17). Miss Kohn mentioned that ". . . medicines, disinfectants, ink and saccharin . . . are especially singled out for destruction. On some days the specialty is the breaking of pictures, on other days it is 'spiriting away' and breaking of eggs and the stealing of money, some of which last-named is dropped again spitefully from mid-air, and some of which is never returned. . . . we . . . actually saw the money appear in the air. . . . In every case it was most obvious that the boy was not himself doing the mischief."

Miss Kohn once did a test: "At 3:30 P.M. I went out, leaving on my table a tightly closed screw-top aluminum 'safety' inkpot, containing a glass bottle of Swan ink. By this elaborate device I had hoped to surpass the cunning of the malicious 'spirits.' "

Immediately before she returned at 5 P.M., the ink bottle had scattered in her room spilling ink all over; the aluminum container, however, could not be found: "I involuntarily looked upwards, as so many objects have been seen to descend from above . . . I called out jokingly: 'I do hope the spirit will throw back the pot, it cost me one rupee eight annas!' No sooner had I finished speaking, than I saw the missing inkpot appear in mid-air, at a distance of roughly six inches from the ceiling of my room. It fell on to the bed. I rushed to examine it, and found it as tightly screwed on as when I had closed it that afternoon."

Mr. L. Christiaens, a member of the French police, reported on a poltergeist which visited a nunnery in a small village in northern France from September 30 to November

6, 1940.[17] The phenomena centered around a 19-year-old servant girl, Josiane. "Windowpanes were broken as if cut by a saw and various sacred objects such as crucifixes and images of the Virgin Mary were broken. Tables and other objects moved about in the room of the Mother Superior, which was next to the room which Josiane shared with another servant, Maria, age 51.

"One night all Josiane's clothing was torn to shreds within a few seconds. In order to hold the poltergeist in check, the Mother Superior placed a blessed scapular on Josiane's bedside table. She then went to bed, leaving the door between the two rooms open. Suddenly the bedside table charged into her room, the scapular was flung onto her bed, and the table then retired 'with dancing steps' to its original place in Josiane's room.

"In addition to the Mother Superior, a number of other persons witnessed various phenomena. The Superior of the convent of an order of missionaries saw all the chairs overturn in the church when Josiane visited him. Two skeptical ladies invited Josiane to sleep in their room one night. The poltergeist raged until 11 P.M., with heavy blows shaking the room, movement of objects, destruction of books on sacred subjects, etc. All the eyewitnesses were interrogated by Mr. L. Christiaens. . . ."

In the poltergeist cases of the past as in those of the present, the profession most often involved in the investigation is that of law enforcement. When the phenomena seem beyond the capacity of any visible troublemaker, the family may appeal to the religious authorities. In August 1949, Rev. Luther Schulze, a Lutheran minister in Washington, D. C., was called in by a family in his parish to help with some strange incidents surrounding their 13-year-old son, Roland. He brought the boy to his own house, but the phenomena continued. In particular there was persistent shaking of Roland's bed. Since the boy could not sleep, he got up and sat in a chair. Schulze noted that this was "a heavy armchair with a very low center of gravity."

Then, while the light was on and Schulze was watching, the chair moved several inches. Roland "placed his knees under his chin with his feet on the edge of the chair. The chair backed up three inches against the wall. When it could move no further in that direction it slowly tipped over . . . throwing the boy to the floor." [18]

A Dutch couple in Indonesia, Mr. and Mrs. Krom, were

visited by disturbances in November and December 1950, in their home which was occupied also by two adopted Indonesian children, a girl of 10 and a seven-year-old boy, and by two servants. Most of the phenomena were stone throwings, the stones sometimes falling in closed rooms. Some were seen to turn at sharp angles in the air to avoid obstacles. The Dutch police inspector, J. J. W. Bijl, watched some of the stones, which "more or less floated in the air."

"One day the little native girl, Soeka, told Mr. Krom that when one threw away a stick, the thing would at once be thrown back. Mr. Krom watched Soeka throw a stick over a wall into the neighboring courtyard where nobody was to be found at the time. He heard the stick drop lightly onto the concrete floor; a fraction of a second afterwards, it lay at his feet." [19]

In August and September 1952, disturbances took place in a small house in Runcorn, Cheshire, England, belonging to Sam Jones, a widower.[20] The events occurred in a room occupied by Jones' 17-year-old grandson and an 18-year-old friend. The Rev. W. H. Stevens visited the home. ". . . after a thorough investigation had been made of the room, the two boys retired to bed at 11:30 P.M. Soon after the light had been switched off and all was quiet, the dressing-table creaked loudly and then moved. It began to shake and rock. Immediately the light was switched on movement ceased. By this time several people had entered the room . . . I pushed the table back again into the corner and, on extinguishing the light, it began to creak and was promptly pushed back again about six feet. Addressing the table I said, 'If you can hear my voice, knock three times.' Immediately it began to shake vigorously: one, two, and on the third shake I shone my torch. Simultaneously, someone switched on the light. All in the room saw the rocking table with no one near it. The shaking continued for about three seconds. The two boys were lying in bed wrapped in the clothes. I went to see if the table would rock at its own accord but it was firm on the floor."

On another occasion Stevens placed some objects on the table including a jigsaw puzzle and, in front of it, two books. "The table was out of reach of Johnny Berry [the friend] who always lay on that side of the bed. Standing near in the dark with no other person in that part of the room and quite close to the table, the contents on the table began to hurl themselves across the room. Eventually, I heard the two books fly across, then the rattle of the jig-saw in the box. That was what I was waiting for and straightway I shone my torch. The jig-saw was travelling across the room rising about seven feet in the air. The two boys were well covered in the clothes in the exact position as they had been when the light was switched off." Another visitor, J. C. Davies, described the box as being "almost in suspension above the bed ... almost as if it were being carried with directional intent."

One of the parapsychologists working in Durham at the Foundation for Research on the Nature of Man is Mr. W. Edward Cox. He is best known for his psychokinesis experiments with dice, metal balls, and other falling objects, but he has also made investigations of poltergeist cases. Between June and August 1957, a family near Hartville, Missouri, complained of unexplained household disturbances.[21] Vases and other containers had been heard to fall or had been seen in flight when Betty, a nine-year-old daughter, was home. On three occasions a pail of water overturned in the presence of several relatives and friends. Occurrences were reported in two separate houses and out of doors as well. Walnuts which were stored in one of the houses moved about. Several were seen in flight and some appeared to move unusually slowly. When Cox came, he saw a 12-inch lantern, which stood securely on a chair, fall over. He also saw a wrapped cake of soap drop to the floor from a sturdy table. Both times Cox was the person closest to the object and was unable to find any normal cause for the incidents.

The impression from the 47 poltergeist cases I have examined is that the poltergeist, for all its strange ways, is a creature of habit that will pursue its accustomed routine whether or not there are strangers about.

This is not to deny the possibility that there are many poltergeists that come and go in complete privacy—and that some of them may leave when an investigator arrives. But I think there have been enough cases where the poltergeist allowed close observation for us to make it a subject for serious study.

Some of the unpublished cases are as interesting as the published ones. Here are two, in both of which visitors to the house "experimented" with the occurrences.[22]

A doctor on the staff of a sanitarium in New York, who had heard about the Seaford investigation, sent an account of a case in Sciacca, Sicily, that occurred around 1890. His grandmother, then 25, visited the poltergeist house: "She clasped her fan tightly in her hands wedged between her knees and defied the 'spirits' to take it away. In a flash the fan was torn away and smashed on her head. . . . On one occasion my grandmother saw a policeman lock his club in a bureau drawer and defy the 'spirits' to get it. The drawer flew open and the club beat him about the head. On another occasion she saw a priest come in to exorcise the house but the Bible and paraphernalia jumped from his hands and beat him about the head and body. Black smoky stones were hurled at him. Grandmother watched the stones materialize in midair; they positively did not come through windows, walls, or ceiling. She picked some, they were hot and sooty."

Ivan T. Sanderson, the zoologist, was visiting a rubber plantation in Sumatra in 1928. While he, the host, and other guests were sitting on the veranda after dinner, small stones came sailing in from the darkness beyond the veranda and rolled to a gentle stop against the back wall.

"The host told us . . . that these small stones came all the time, particularly on certain nights and usually still ones, but not necessarily dark ones. . . . As everybody was amazed and sceptical, our host then told us to mark the stones in any way we liked and throw them back anywhere into the hopelessly thick tangle of vegetation beyond or around the garden or house. To mark them he found us chalk from his desk, a file, and pencils. The ladies used their lipsticks, and we employed all kinds of designs and devices. We all threw them back hard or lightly in every conceivable direction. Almost but not quite all of the marked stones came back onto the veranda within a matter of seconds, a few some minutes later. I would say that some fifty stones at least were so marked and thrown that night. . . . I can vouch for the fact that it would be absolutely impossible for any human . . . to trace, find, and throw back marked stones in that vegetational tangle short of clearing said tangle and sifting its entire surface."

If the 47 published reports I have examined are typical, the poltergeists. of the past were ready for either casual or serious investigators and for the tests they might devise. Let us now return to the contemporary poltergeists and see. how they compare with their predecessors.

4

The Housing Project
Poltergeist in Newark

"It doesn't hit people," I said incautiously. At that instant, a small bottle which had stood on an end table by a sofa hit me squarely on the head. This was during the evening of September 15, 1961, at my third visit to Mrs. Maybelle Clark in her four-room apartment at the Felix Fuld Housing Project in Newark, New Jersey. Mrs. Clark shared the apartment with her 13-year-old grandson, Ernest Rivers, and with an invisible force, apparently determined to destroy all her breakable belongings.

To save what little was left, Ernie's uncle, William Hargwood, a draftsman, had taken the boy to stay in his home: Objects only flew in Mrs. Clark's apartment when Ernie was there. It was at my persuasion that Ernie had returned. I told Mrs. Clark that these cases are usually short-lived—this one had begun in early May—but that the only way to find out would be to bring Ernie back. The case *was* active: Ernie had only been present for a short time when ashtrays, plates, and so on again took to the air.

In May, as we shall see later, several witnesses had been present when things moved and when Ernie was nowhere near. But in September, when I came, he was always close enough to have been able to throw the objects normally. I hoped I could either catch him doing so or else observe a genuine poltergeist event. But Mrs. Clark was not eager to see the rest of her things in pieces on the floor. She was also apprehensive that somebody might get hit. I said it was important for the scientific investigation that I witness some events myself and promised that I would pay for any further breakage if she would allow Ernest to remain. I also pointed out that nobody had been hurt by the moving objects. It

39

was then that the bottle hit me, first grazing Mrs. Clark. Ernie was on the sofa next to the table where the bottle had been. I was facing in his direction but not looking at him. He could possibly have thrown it.

The events began on Ernie's birthday, May 6, and continued until the end of the month for a total of 59 incidents. In June there was one occurrence and in August, four. At that time Ernie had moved to his uncle's. The later incidents all took place when he was back for visits.

I first heard about the case from newspaper reports,[1] but only took it seriously when Dr. Charles D. Wrege, then assistant professor at the Department of Management at Rutgers University, told me about some things which had happened when he was in the apartment. I met Wrege in September at the convention of the Parapsychological Association in New York City.

The first incident in the case was the fall of a small jar from Mrs. Clark's bedroom dresser to her floor on May 6. But it was only two days later, Monday evening, May 8, that things really let loose and she became convinced that something strange was going on. That evening, while she and Ernie were having dinner in the kitchen, four punchbowl cups in the living room, which is connected by an open doorway to the kitchen, came off their hooks on the bowl and crashed to the floor, one by one. Mrs. Clark and Ernie were alone in the apartment. A little later, several bottles in the bathroom and back hallway fell to the floor and broke. One of these, a bottle of mercurochrome in the bathroom medicine cabinet, came into the living room and broke on the floor. Mrs. Clark said that the bathroom door was closed at the time. She then put the rest of the bottles on the floor in the bathroom to prevent further breakage. A neighbor, Mrs. Holland, had now arrived, and while she was with Mrs. Clark and Ernie, who were watching television in the living room, she saw a cologne bottle from the bathroom fly into the living room. It did not come in a straight line, Mrs. Holland told me, but was "turning a jig in the air." Mrs. Holland said that the door to the bathroom was closed.

During the next three days, there were 20 other incidents. Mrs. Clark was greatly frightened, and twice she and Ernie left to stay with the Hargwoods.

The Newark Housing Authority made an investigation. Irving Laskowitz, director of the Tenant Relations Division, wrote me that an examination was made of "every inch of the Clark apartment and the basement of the building. Nothing was found to physically explain the happenings." There were no incidents in the apartment adjacent to or above Mrs. Clark's.

Mrs. Clark's fear was caused not only by what she could hear and see but also by what she suspected was the unseen cause of it all. In searching for an explanation, her thoughts went to Ernie's father, a man of violent temper who had died two years before. She thought he had come back and was causing the incidents to get Ernie away from her.

The news about the "project poltergeist," as the papers dubbed it, spread around the city, also reaching Dr. Wrege. He had been interested in parapsychology for a long time and responded to the opportunity of making a firsthand acquaintance with a poltergeist. Nothing happened during his initial visit to the apartment, but the next evening, on May 13, there were nine incidents during the hour and a half he was there.

Shortly before midnight, there was a commotion caused not by the poltergeist but by a different kind of spirit. A group of drunks banged on the front door, demanding to see "the boy with the flying objects," and then tossed a stone through a window. Wrege went to the phone in the kitchen to call the police, taking Ernie with him. As he was about to pick up the phone, he saw a water glass from the counter fall to the floor. But he did not have Ernie under full observation and could not be certain that he had not thrown it. In any case, Ernie was extremely upset at that time, as much by the outside as by the inside disturbances, and Wrege put his arm around the boy to comfort him. He made his call, holding the phone with his left hand, the right arm tightly around Ernie. Wrege had just finished the conversation with the police and was still holding on to Ernie when "there was this tremendous crash in the living room. The closest lamp to us, one of two crockery lamps, had crashed to the floor. Ernie could not have done this physically because of my control over him—but since neither of us actually saw the lamp fall (it was around the corner out of sight) I suspected the use of strings and the like. I checked the remains of the lamp and the cord to see if any strings or wires were attached. There were no such objects and . . . I do not know how this event could be attributed to trickery. . . ." The lamp landed on the floor about three feet southeast of the table on which it had stood and 15 feet from where Ernie had

been in the kitchen. The boy seemed extremely frightened at
this point and asked Wrege to call his uncle to take him out
of the apartment. Wrege did so. Shortly afterward Hargwood
and also the police came.

Wrege examined the table on which the lamp had stood
for traces of explosives and other foreign matter but found
none. He considered the possibility that the fall could have
been caused from outside the apartment by an arrangement
of strings operated by some unknown accomplice. The fact
that he had found no string might be because it had been
pulled away when the lamp fell. However, such a string
would have had to be fastened at some time earlier in the
evening. Wrege said he could not conceive of having over-
looked any such device since he had examined the apartment
for concealed mechanisms. He also had to reject the possibility that Ernie might have surreptitiously placed a string
around the lamp and then passed it to someone outside after
Wrege had examined the apartment since he stayed close to
the boy while the two were in the apartment.

After the police had left and when Hargwood and Wrege
were cleaning up the broken pieces of the lamp, with the aid
of Ernie, Hargwood suddenly cried out, and a glass ashtray
fell to the floor in Mrs. Clark's room. The ashtray had been
on the end table by the sofa where the lamp had stood and
it grazed Hargwood's chin as it moved into the bedroom.
When this happened, Wrege said that "Ernest was holding
the dustpan handle with two hands as I swept the pieces into
the pan. Mr. Hargwood was to my left by the door of Mrs.
Clark's bedroom, picking up other pieces of the lamp. He
suddenly moved back and there was the sound of glass hitting
the floor of Mrs. Clark's room." This same ashtray had
moved twice earlier that evening.

Shortly afterward, when Ernie went into the kitchen to put
the lamp pieces in the trashcan, there was another incident.
Hargwood was in the living room close to the back hallway,
and Wrege was in Mrs. Clark's room picking up the ashtray
that had just moved when a pepper shaker struck Hargwood
in the back.

At this time, all were eager to leave. Then, when Ernie
had gone out the front door and Hargwood was preparing to
turn off the kitchen and living room lights, he again cried
out, and Wrege saw a salt cellar smash against the living
room wall behind the sofa. Hargwood said it had hit his
head a moment before. Again, there was no possibility that

Ernie could have caused the event. The salt cellar had moved twice during the previous days, each time hitting somebody.

Immediately after the crash of the salt cellar, when Ernie was still outside the apartment and Hargwood was again on the point of turning off the lights, Wrege now being in the apartment close to the front door, a heavy ceramic ashtray from a bookcase near the front door fell to the floor between Hargwood and Wrege. Again, Ernie was not in the room and could not have thrown the object.

The events continued intermittently; for instance, Mrs. Holland told me that once when she was about to enter the apartment with Ernie, the television set fell over as he put his key in the door. No one was in the apartment.

I first visited the Clark apartment on September 9. This was the last day of the convention of the Parapsychological Association and in the morning I had been chairman of a panel discussion on postmortem survival; it seemed fitting to end the day with a visit to a poltergeist. Nothing happened, however, and I left, asking Mrs. Clark to phone should the phenomena resume. No sooner had I come back to my hotel than I received a call from the Clark apartment that the poltergeist had returned. I hurried to Newark and found that five objects had broken or had moved various distances while I was gone.

Mrs. Clark refused to stay the night, and Mr. Hargwood brought her to his home. The family accepted my offer to stay in the apartment with Ernie. The single incident that evening was when a light bulb fell to the floor in Ernie's room when he said he was in bed and I was in Mrs. Clark's room. The next morning, shortly after 8 o'clock, when Mrs. Clark had returned and was in the kitchen and I was in the bathroom, there was a sound from the hallway and I found a brush from the hall closet on the floor. Ernie was in his room next to the hallway. He said that his door had been shut.

Later that morning, while Ernie was seated on the sofa in the living room, he remarked to his grandmother, "I saw your bag open and close." This bag lay on a chair in Ernie's room which was visible from his position on the couch. Mrs. Clark examined the bag and found that a purse with 15 dollars had disappeared. In the meantime Hargwood arrived. When he, Mrs. Clark, and I were in the living room and while Ernie was in the hallway outside Mrs. Clark's room looking for the wallet, a sound was heard from her room and we found the wallet on the floor, minus the 15 dollars. Since Mrs. Clark's room was next to the hallway, it would have been easy for the boy to toss the wallet without discovery. His grandmother then sent him downstairs with the garbage. When he came back, he brought two dollars with him, saying he had found the money by the front door.

Mrs. Clark said that recently, during Ernie's visits to the apartment, wallets belonging to her daughter (Mrs. Hargwood) and two friends had disappeared. During this period Ernie had found about 40 dollars in cash and various other objects. Mrs. Clark tended to interpret these events paranormally. However, she was not completely credulous: Ten minutes after the boy had found the two dollars, she said, "Ernie, come here a minute." And she emptied the boy's pockets, looking for the remainder of her money, but found nothing. After that, she asked him to go out again to see if more money would appear. He brought another two dollars, then three and, finally, a 10-dollar bill. This brought the total to 17 dollars. The poltergeist was returning the money with interest!

I came back on September 13 for some hours in the evening. For part of this period Ernie was present but nothing happened. My last visit was on September 15, again in the evening. That day and the night before, seven objects had moved, Mrs. Clark's wallet had again disappeared, and, Ernie said, a Vaseline jar and a bottle of liniment had fallen to the ground in front of him in the courtyard outside the apartment. In all cases, as in those that happened earlier that month, Ernie was or easily could have been at the place where the movements originated. There were no cases like those in May when Wrege or other adults said that Ernie was in one part of the apartment while something happened elsewhere.

Since the events ceased whenever I came, it seemed that the poltergeist preferred privacy and that I was an inhibiting influence. I therefore left for short periods after Ernie arrived in the evening of the 15th, hoping that this would induce the poltergeist to return. On six occasions, objects moved while I was immediately outside the apartment so I could respond to the crash. At one time an ashtray hit the control button on the television which Ernie was watching, turning it off. When the last incident took place, I did not hear anything, at least not consciously, but entered the apartment on an impulse: An ashtray stand was rolling on the floor and the boy was seated quietly on the sofa.

In the course of the evening, I seemed to be getting closer and closer to the disturbances. But as I became more hopeful of a definite observation, Mrs. Clark became increasingly more alarmed and insistent that Ernie must leave. It was at that point, as I was trying to persuade her to let the boy remain, that the bottle hit me on the head (p. 39). The bottle came from the side table by the couch, next to where Ernie sat. At the time of the incident, I was facing in his general direction but not looking directly at him. I looked up at once when the bottle hit and found Ernie sitting quietly as usual. But I could not rule out the possibility that he had thrown the object.

A little later Ernie left the apartment, returning immediately afterward with a small bottle belonging to Mrs. Clark which he said had hit him on the head. He then left again, but came back shortly afterward with Wrege, whom he had met outside. The boy said he had been hit by another bottle.

The easiest explanation of these incidents was that Ernie took objects from the apartment outside with him. The next time he was on the point of leaving, Wrege and I asked if we might search him. He agreed and we found a piece of wood under his shirt. Ernie said he had no idea of how it got there. Wrege and I speculated that this was the next object to be "found" and that his shirt front was the hiding place for the objects that followed him out of doors and perhaps for the money he said he found in various places.

The discovery of the piece of wood and the fact that nothing happened when I or others had Ernie under observation, indicated that we were faced with an ersatz poltergeist.

My contact with Wrege had impressed me that he was a skeptical and careful observer. The conclusion, which he and I shared, that the present incidents were not parapsychological did not alter my opinion that the earlier phase of the case, when Wrege was in the apartment with the boy, probably included genuine effects. In other cases, both in the United States and Europe, there have been instances where a first and apparently parapsychological phase was followed by fraudulent simulation.

If a case includes events for which apparently reliable and serious investigators were unable to find ordinary explanations, it would be, in my opinion, a mistake to reject it because it also included incidents apparently due to fraud or other familiar causes.

Far from causing me to lose interest in the "project poltergeist," the indication that Ernie might be simulating the events suggested that the psychological dynamics, which I suspected were at the root of the disturbances, still existed. Therefore, in addition to a series of psychological tests that we had arranged for Ernie to take at New York University, plans were also made to bring him to the Duke Parapsychology Laboratory, where I then had my office, for further testing.

In the meantime Ernie moved back to Mrs. Clark's apartment, an event that was followed by a flurry of disturbances: Among other objects, the kitchen cupboard, the washing machine, and the refrigerator fell over. This last item belonged to the housing project. Having been mainly a family problem, the poltergeist was now encroaching on public property. The housing project and the county authorities became involved. With the consent of Mrs. Clark and Ernie, he was brought to a temporary shelter for children. After this, the State Board of Child Welfare took the responsibility for looking after him.

The visit to Durham was arranged with the aid of Miss Marjorie Cummings, supervisor of the New Jersey Board of Child Welfare, and Mrs. Rose Lemberg, case work supervisor at the board's Essex County district office. Since the disturbances seemed to be stimulated by the presence of Mrs. Clark, she was also invited to come to Durham.

Ernie and his grandmother arived on December 16. This was the first time since November that they had been together and that same afternoon there was an incident. Ernie and Mrs. Clark were walking along a narrow hallway outside my office when a book that had been on my desk fell to the hallway floor. Ernie might easily have thrown it since nobody was watching him and he could have picked it up when he was leaving the room. Anyhow the episode seemed to indicate that the poltergeist whether pseudo or genuine was still active and, most importantly, was ready to be confronted on laboratory territory. But it was late in the day and Ernie and Mrs. Clark were eager to get to their hotel. I brought them to the Jack Tar Hotel, asking them to get in touch with me if anything should happen.

When I came home, there was a message that the incidents had resumed in the hotel. I hurried back and found Ernie sitting on the floor holding on to the television set. He and his grandmother told me that an ashtray had fallen and that a glass in the bathroom had smashed while Ernie was there. Then a table lamp, which had been placed on the floor for safety's sake, turned over, and the phone fell down. Mrs. Clark claimed she saw the phone as it landed, at the same time watching Ernie who was seated on the floor clutching the television set to prevent it from falling. It seemed possible, however, that he might have caused the fall of the phone without detection by pulling the cord.

I stayed in the hotel for a couple of hours in the hope that there might be additional incidents while I was present. At 10:20 P.M. while Ernie was in the bathroom, there was a crash. When I came in, I found the light fixture in the sink. The plastic frame covering the bulb was bent in a way that would be consistent with someone having grabbed it and pulled it from the wall. Since the disturbances were destroying hotel property without happening under conditions that allowed for observation, I proposed that Ernie return home with me while Mrs. Clark remained at the hotel. They both liked that suggestion.

As my wife, Muriel, opened the door for Ernie and me late that evening and I told her about the events in the hotel, she at once suspected that we had an invisible companion. Our house has a long hallway, on one side lined with shelves with porcelain and other breakables of the type poltergeists delight in. Muriel had a mental image of all this crashing to the floor behind Ernie as he walked down the hall. I reminded her of my abilities as a poltergeist suppressor and we were allowed entry on the condition that I share the guest-room with Ernie.

Nothing happened at the house for the week that Ernie stayed there. Nor did anything happen at the Jack Tar. Gaither Pratt went to the hotel with a screwdriver and quietly repaired the poltergeist damage.

The fact that even the Duke Parapsychology Laboratory did not discourage the phenomena gave us an opportunity for closer observation than we had been able to achieve so far. Though the episodes from September on were suggestive of trickery and though the case had become atypical, extending for such a long period of time and over such wide terrain, there was no clear proof of fraud. But the events on December 18 caused me to reject the parapsychological hypothesis for the later phase of the occurrences. The laboratory had an experimental suite with a one-way mirror between two of the rooms. Gaither cooperated as the observer in one of these while I brought Ernie and Mrs. Clark into the other, asking them to remain there while I attended to some matters. After a while, Mrs. Clark left the room for a moment, and Gaither saw Ernie take two measuring tapes from a table and quickly hide them under his shirt. Mrs. Clark then returned, left again, and at that time Ernie threw the two tapes after her. I was summoned by Mrs. Clark who said there had been another poltergeist incident. She showed no suspicion of her grandson, and Ernie, in turn, denied any knowledge of how the tapes had moved.

This confirmed my doubts about the events that had taken place since September. Until we had actually seen Ernie throw the tapes, it had been at least conceivable that the reason no events had been observed by outside witnesses since then was that they inhibited the phenomena. I now felt I could safely conclude that all or most of the latter incidents were fraudulent.

The discovery of fraud and the absence of phenomena which the boy could not have easily caused convinced me that the parapsychological aspects of the case had passed. However, it opened up a new avenue in a study I hoped to conduct with the "lie detection" method. In this, a series of questions are asked while the person is connected to a polygraph. This measures the electrical potential of the skin, blood pressure, heart rate, and breathing. If he tells a falsehood, this is likely to result in an emotional reaction which produces a change on the graph. Since we now had an incident, Ernie's throwing of the two tapes, which we definitely knew was caused fraudulently, and since he denied having done so, I planned to question Ernie while he was attached to the polygraph, hoping to demonstrate that he was lying when he said he did not know what caused the tapes to move. We could then compare this part of the polygraph record with the record produced when Ernie was questioned about the first phase of the disturbances in which Wrege and others had failed to find evidence of fraud. I decided to question Ernie about the most convincing of these, the fall of the lamp in the living room while he and Wrege were in the kitchen. If Ernie disclaimed any knowledge of how the lamp fell and if the polygraph record supported his claim but indicated that he was lying when answering the question about the two tapes, then this would give added confidence to the lamp incident. Following the interviews concerning the lamp and the tapes, I hoped to be able to throw light on the other incidents in the case and to discover exactly when the real poltergeist had bowed out.

My expectations were not fulfilled. The lie detection interviews did indeed support Ernie's claim about the lamp but, surprisingly, I could find no evidence of lying when he denied knowing how the tapes moved.

This failure did not come as a complete surprise. Just before the polygraph examination, Dr. Ben Feather of the Duke Department of Psychiatry had given the boy a hypnosis interview. It turned out that not only did Ernie deny any knowledge of the tapes when he was awake and normal but even when he was in a fairly deep hynotic trance. Feather therefore was of the opinion that the boy threw the tapes while in a state of dissociation. Since the polygraph method cannot reveal acts of which the person is not consciously aware, Feather predicted that this method would fail.

The Newark case was of special interest because of the simulation of earlier and apparently real effects. As will become clear later in this book, poltergeist occurrences seem to be connected with psychological or family tensions. If these tensions remain after the genuine incidents have ceased, it is understandable why the person should perpetuate the events by normal means—especially if he has found that the poltergeist events caused a reduction in the tensions, as by bringing about a separation in the family.

What did surprise me in the Newark case was that Ernie seemed as unconscious of the fraudulent events as he had been of the apparently genuine ones.

This finding has important consequences. First of all, it stresses the need for the investigator to be on his toes throughout the investigation. Even though he or his colleagues may be convinced that they have observed poltergeist occurrences under foolproof conditions, they cannot therefore assume that all the events reported are genuine.

The Newark case also throws doubt on the lie detection method as a useful tool for sifting genuine from spurious poltergeist effects. It may, however, have given a clue about the nature of the poltergeist. If the same tensions in a person can be expressed in either real or simulated effects, this suggests that the process in some respects is the same in the two cases. I shall come back to this possibility later.

Our purpose in bringing Ernie and his grandmother to Durham was mainly to study the psychological situation in the family. This aspect of the research will be discussed in Chapter 13. The purpose of Ernie and Mrs. Clark, on the other hand, was to get help in dealing with the destructions in the house and if possible to make them stop. The psychologists and psychiatrists who participated in the study suggested that the best course of action would be to separate Ernie and his grandmother, at least temporarily. These recommendations were passed on to the Board of Child Welfare of New Jersey.

In January Mrs. Lemberg wrote: ". . . we are pleased to report that Ernest has been placed in a group setting, in accordance with your recommendation and our own feeling about the situation. Upon his return from Durham, Ernest was placed in a temporary foster home for a period of two weeks until these plans could be worked out. Ernest adjusted very well in the foster home, the foster mother is a particularly competent person and was able to meet many of Ernest's needs during this period. Ernest had an opportunity to visit the group placement before permanent placement there and appeared to be very pleased with it.

"Ernest's relatives will be able to visit him while he is there. However, our worker made it clear to Ernest that he could decide who he would like to visit him."

5

A Biting Poltergeist
in Indianapolis

"Mysterious bat-like bites" appeared on the arms of Mrs.
Renate Beck, her mother, Mrs. Lina Gemmecke, and Linda,
Mrs. Beck's 13-year-old daughter, according to a newspaper
report on March 13, 1962. Strange movements and breakages of objects in Mrs. Beck's house in Indianapolis were also
described. According to the newspaper story it was in the
midst of these breakages that "Mrs. Beck felt the sting on her
left arm and discovered three small puncture marks resem-
bling the bite of a bat. Mrs. Gemmecke felt similar pains at
intervals and found identical marks on her left knee and left
arm." [1]

The shades of vampires were dispelled soon after my ar-
rival in the home on March 16. The family lived in a two-
story house close to town. The house, which belonged to Mrs.
Beck, also had an apartment which took up part of the first
floor. It was vacant at the time. The three bedrooms used by
the family and the kitchen were on the second floor, and
this is where the family—and the poltergeist—spent most of
their time when they were home. Until I left on the 22nd, I
occupied Linda's room, and she moved in with her mother.

I found Mrs. Beck to be an intelligent and level-headed
woman in her early thirties. She gave an unemotional account
of the events, much less dramatic than the newspaper's. In
fact, one of the main events described there, the fall of a
vase, she said was probably caused by her as she leaned
against the bookcase on which it rested. Nevertheless, she
was convinced that something unusual was going on. She
verified that "something" bit her and showed me the marks,
which were still clearly visible. There were not three but five
small punctures on the skin and they looked nothing like bat
bites (they appeared above her right wrist, not her left arm).

51

Mrs. Beck told me that on Saturday morning, March 10, she and Mrs. Gemmecke were in the kitchen when a cup, which Mrs. Gemmecke had just placed on the sink counter, flew across the room and smashed against the wall 10 feet away. Mrs. Beck had heard of incidents like this connected with the death of someone and glanced at the calendar to fix the date in her mind. When she saw it was March 10, she remembered with a start that this was her father's birthday. They had not heard from him for about 20 years but thought he was alive in Germany. He and Mrs. Gemmecke were separated in 1943.

It was about half an hour later, as the two of them were sitting at the kitchen table, that the five stings or puncture wounds appeared. That seemed to be the end of it, but then, at about four o'clock, when they were back in the kitchen, Mrs. Gemmecke suddenly screamed and clutched her left arm where five or six puncture marks appeared. After dinner, at about eight o'clock, when Mrs. Beck was in her bedroom and her mother was in the bathroom, the latter again received five or six punctures, this time on the leg. Altogether she was wounded on 14 occasions, the number of individual punctures ranging from one to eight.

I was present in the house during some of them. On the evening of the day I came, Mrs. Beck and I were discussing the disturbances in the kitchen. Mrs. Gemmecke, who was alone in her room, suddenly called out. When we rushed in, we found one puncture mark on her upper right arm. Ten minutes later, when we were back in the kitchen, she again cried out. When I came into her room, I found her clutching her arm over the sleeve. I rolled the sleeve up and saw four puncture marks, from two of which blood was flowing. Two days later, also in the evening, she received three more punctures, this time on her right breast. When I came in, I found her pressing a cross against them. She was in bed, and on the point of falling asleep, she said. I examined the bed for insects and foreign objects, looked on the floor beneath the bed, and also checked for needles and other objects in her hair. I found nothing. I could, of course, not exclude the possibility that a pin was secreted some other place and that the wounds were self-inflicted.

Mrs. Gemmecke said she thought the bites were due to a spider or some other animal. This seemed unlikely. Several times clusters of five or more punctures came at the same time. It is difficult to suppose that one or more spiders or insects could produce these marks simultaneously without ever being seen. It is even less likely that a larger animal, such as a bat or a mouse, could have made them and escaped detection. I do not think Mrs. Gemmecke took her own theory seriously. I never saw her look for insects nor heard her ask others to do so. Her use of the cross suggests a different belief.

I looked in on Linda who was in the adjacent room when her grandmother was wounded on the chest. She was sitting on the bed calmly watching television with a horseshoe clutched in her hands. As far as Linda was concerned, this was fully effective. She was never bothered by the bites or any of the other goings-on. In fact, Linda seemed to have no connection with the incidents at all. During 29 of the occurrences, she was not at home, while Mrs. Beck and Mrs. Gemmecke nearly always were.

In all cases except for the first, the victim of the "bites" was Mrs. Gemmecke. The distribution of the marks on her body as well as the number varied widely. Those I saw were within an area of two and a half inches but otherwise seemed to be randomly scattered. There was nothing to suggest the "bat bites" about which the newspapers wrote. One cluster of punctures was on her throat, another on her right breast, five on her legs or thighs, and four on her arms, both the right and the left. Usually she was alone when she received them, but four times she was with her daughter or with visitors to the house.

The simplest theory is that the marks were due to some minor skin disease and were only thought to be bites when attention was drawn to them. However, this apparently cannot account for the punctures from which the blood was flowing which were seen by me and others. The most reasonable ordinary explanation, in my opinion, is that the wounds were self-inflicted by Mrs. Gemmecke, presumably in a state of dissociation. This of course would not explain the five punctures on the wrist of Mrs. Beck unless we suppose that she also entered a dissociated state and wounded herself when she and her mother were in the kitchen the morning the events began.

Whatever the explanation, the punctures occurred within the period of time covered by the poltergeist disturbances, or rather, within the first two weeks when most (71 out of 76) of the unexplained movements were recorded. Mrs. Gemmecke told me she had never received such wounds before.

She was greatly upset and frightened, though the punctures could not be considered serious and never became infected. She suffered from diabetes and the punctures resulted in large discolorations of the skin which sometimes lasted long after the wounds themselves had disappeared.

Her most unpleasant experiences were in the early morning hours of Tuesday, March 13. There had been eight movements of objects the previous afternoon and evening, and Mrs. Beck had called the police. At about two o'clock in the morning she was downstairs with a policeman and Emil Noseda, a friend of the family. Mrs. Gemmecke was in the kitchen upstairs. Noseda told me they suddenly heard Mrs. Gemmecke scream that she was "glued" to the closet door in the kitchen. She freed herself and started down the stairs when she again screamed. They found puncture marks on her thigh from which the blood flowed. She then sat down on a couch downstairs but had been there only 15 minutes when she again screamed and said she was being choked. Noseda told me, "We heard Mrs. Gemmecke scream. She was sitting on the davenport; felt choked. Policeman saw skin pinched as if by fingers, pin marks came then." After this, Noseda took Mrs. Gemmecke home with him, and she had a rest from the strange attacks until she returned later in the day.

Poltergeists are rare creatures and, fortunately, biting poltergeists are even rarer. A case that in some respects is similar to the present one took place in Bristol, England, in 1761–1762.[2] It was investigated by a Henry Durbin. As in the Indianapolis case, two people, Molly and Dobby Giles, 13 and eight years old, were the victims. On one occasion, Durbin reports, "We saw their arms bitten about 20 times. . . . their arms were put out of bed, and . . . they could not do it themselves as we were looking at them the whole time. We examined the bites and found on them the impression of 18 or 20 teeth . . ."

Also as in the Indianapolis case, one of the victims, Dobby, was affected more often than the other. In addition to bites and movements of objects, some of which were also witnessed by Durbin, the girls sometimes were pushed or pulled by an invisible force. This is reminiscent of Mrs. Gemmecke's impression that she was "glued" to the closet. Apparent chokings were also reported in the Bristol case. Durbin said that "I saw the flesh at the side of her [Molly's] throat pushed in, whitish as if done with fingers though I saw none."

I have taken this account from a book by a British expert on the poltergeist, Dr. A. R. G. Owen. In Owen's opinion, poltergeist woundings are "real but extremely rare."

Psychiatrists and psychologists occasionally have patients whose emotional problems result in psychosomatic reactions, including skin rashes. In hypnosis experiments, it is sometimes possible to create distinct localized effects such as welts on the skin. Religious stigmata, for instance, where wounds appear on the hands and elsewhere, corresponding to Jesus' wounds, perhaps fall into the same category.

Owens discusses the possibility that poltergeist woundings are also of this type. Mainly because of the rapid way in which they appear, he suggests that they are due to an external source rather than to a process in the victim's body.

The last punctures were those that took place Sunday, March 18, on Mrs. Gemmecke's breast. The end of the punctures coincided with the beginning of new phenomena: Knocks and raps. This change took place while I was present. The first series of knocks came late in the evening of Sunday, March 18, when I was upstairs with the family and with Howard Renollet, a distributor of vitamin products used by Mrs. Beck in the small restaurant she operated in Indianapolis. Shortly afterward there was another series. I suspected some children were playing a prank by knocking on the front door or wall. I did not investigate, since I did not want to leave the family alone upstairs. Next evening there were two similar series of knocks when I was upstairs with the family. I hurried down but could find no one either in the downstairs room or outside. Tuesday was quiet, but on Wednesday, March 21, the family heard three series of knocks in the early evening. I was at the police station reading a report of the disturbances. No sooner had I returned to be with the family upstairs than three loud knocks came from downstairs. I rushed down but found no one either inside or out.

These new phenomena were both a challenge and a frustration. I did not want to leave the family to take up a station downstairs in case there might be movements upstairs that I would miss. In fact, at one time when I was investigating the downstairs knocking, an object did move upstairs. I could not be certain that some youngster was not playing cat and mouse with me, since he might be out of the way by the time I reached the front door. Fortunately, I got help.

Shortly after nine, Dr. David Blumenthal came. David is a clinical psychologist in Indianapolis with whom I had collaborated in a previous study. When I first read about these incidents in the newspapers I asked him to contact the family for a preliminary appraisal of the case. It was at his recommendation that I made this study.

David had been present only 20 minutes when again there was a series of distinct knocks. They sounded about the same as before but that time they came from upstairs. This ruled out an outside source. Now it seemed possible that somebody in the family was continuing the prank. It could not be Mrs. Beck since she was with David and me in the kitchen when the sounds came. However, Mrs. Gemmecke was in her room and Linda in the room next to it, and both were alone. Five minutes later the knocking resumed and we counted seven distinct knocks. The people were in the same places as before. We were certain that the sounds did not come from the kitchen but from the other side of the house, the rooms occupied by Mrs. Gemmecke and Linda. David and I rushed into the two bedrooms. Linda was in bed, wrapped in a blanket and reading. Mrs. Gemmecke also was in bed in her room.

We found we could reproduce the sound by knocking on the frame of a large painting that was hanging over Mrs. Gemmecke's bed. She therefore could have been suspected of having made it. In order to watch her, David remained in her room while I went back to the kitchen with Mrs. Beck. Five minutes later, there was a similar series of knocks. David was watching Mrs. Gemmecke, I was with Mrs. Beck in the kitchen, and Linda was in the bathroom. No one else was in the apartment. Since the sounds seemed to come from the painting or possibly from the wall between Mrs. Gemmecke's and Mrs. Beck's room (occupied at the time by Linda, since I was using her room), the only normal explanation seemed to be that Mrs. Gemmecke was producing the sounds by knocking against the wall underneath the covers. As far as David could see, however, she was lying quite still. To exclude the possibility that she was making the knocks in this way, David took both of her hands in his. Shortly afterward, just before ten o'clock, there was a series of knocks when I was still in the kitchen with Mrs. Beck. Linda was now in bed in her mother's room. The door was open and the lights were on. Linda's bed stood against the wall opposite the wall to Mrs. Gemmecke's room, and the area between this wall and the bed could be seen from the kitchen. The moment I heard the knocks I went into the hallway and from there had a full view of Linda lying quietly in bed. It did not seem possible that she could have left the bed, knocked on the wall, and returned without my seeing it. Mrs. Gemmecke was also in bed, her hands held by David. This time he was certain that she could not have produced the sounds. We were unable to explain them normally.

At ten o'clock, when everybody was in the same rooms as before, knocks were again heard. At 11:40 P.M. Linda was asleep in Mrs. Beck's room. David was with Mrs. Beck in Linda's room and I was with Mrs. Gemmecke in her room. I had helped her to the kitchen for some food and then to the bathroom. The knocks came just as Mrs. Gemmecke was lying down. Again, David and I could discover no way in which any of the three women might have produced the sounds normally.

The sounds were not erratic but tended to center in two areas, the downstairs room first and later Mrs. Gemmecke's room. They seemed to persecute her in much the way the puncture wounds had done before. She was extremely upset by them. To allay her anxiety, David and I told her they were made by fellow investigators who were assisting in the case and not to worry about them.

Mrs. Gemmecke had come to the States three years before from Germany. She had lived through the air raids of the war and seen her house destroyed. But she had never come across anything like this before. At one time she cried out, *"Ist Amerika verhekst? So war es nie in Deutschland!"* (Is America bewitched? It was never like this in Germany!)

But most of the events in the Beck home were neither bites nor knocks but conventional poltergeist rampage among the household furnishings. There were 76 such incidents compared to 25 series of knocks and 14 puncture incidents.

The occurrences were concentrated in the period from March 10 to 24, when there were 110 incidents all told; there were three later in the year and two the following February. All the incidents took place in Mrs. Beck's house. There were none in her restaurant nor in Mr. Noseda's home nor the hotel where the family took refuge during the periods of most turbulence. Mrs. Beck had been operating her restaurant for about a month and earlier had worked in a restaurant owned by Mr. Noseda, who now was retired. He told me that Mrs. Beck was highly capable and dependable during the 10 years she worked for him. Mrs. Beck was divorced and lived alone with Linda for several years till her mother came from Germany.

Linda's Scotch terrier, Peanuts, did not seem to be affected by the events. The only possible exception was when the dog "suddenly screamed" for no apparent reason immediately before the first incident, the flight of Mrs. Gemmecke's cup.

The home was situated on a quiet street and there were no reports of anything unusual going on, either in the empty downstairs apartment or in neighboring houses. It therefore seemed unlikely that impersonal physical forces such as tremors caused by traffic, earth movements, and the like were responsible. The events ceased when the family left the house and also when everyone was asleep. The most likely ordinary explanation was that one or more members of the family perpetrated the events as a prank.

On four occasions during my stay, Linda was either not at home when the disturbances took place or else she was in a different room. In five cases, her mother was not in the area in question. There were two incidents which none of the three members of the family seemed to be in a position to cause normally. On Sunday, March 18, I was seated in the kitchen with Mr. Renollet. At 10:35 P.M. there was a sound from the direction of Mrs. Gemmecke's room as if something struck the floor. Linda was in bed in her mother's room and Mrs. Gemmecke was in bed in her own room. I looked at Mrs. Beck who had just been in her bedroom and was in the hallway walking toward the kitchen. I rushed into Mrs. Gemmecke's room but found nothing out of place. Five minutes later, as I walked downstairs with Mr. Renollet, I found a long-handled bathbrush on the staircase outside and below Mrs. Gemmecke's room. Apparently this was what caused the noise. At the time of the sound, I was watching Mrs. Beck through the open kitchen door and had a full view of her. She was not making any unusual movements. At the same time, I had a view toward the entrance of the bedrooms of Mrs. Gemmecke and Linda. I felt certain that neither one could have thrown the brush without being heard or seen by me.

It might have been supposed that the brush had been "planted" on the step earlier and the sound made later to make it seem as if the incident took place then. But this possibility had to be ruled out because I was the last person to have been on the stairs before the sound was heard. I had been downstairs at 10:15 P.M., 20 minutes before the sound, to make a phone call. Nothing was out of place then. I was certain I could not have missed an object of this size lying directly in my path, particularly since I was on the lookout for objects out of place or for mechanisms that might cause the movements. It did not seem possible that any of the three women could have thrown or placed the brush on the stairs during the following 20 minutes without discovery since I was attentive to any unusual movements by them and had the area under observation.

I also considered the possibility that the sound was made first, presumably by Mrs. Gemmecke, who then put the brush in place. This too seemed implausible. Neither Linda nor her grandmother could have left their rooms or thrown anything to the stairs during the five minutes between the sound and the discovery of the brush without my observing this from the open kitchen door. Mrs. Beck and Mr. Renollet were in the kitchen during this period and neither of them had been on the stairs.

There was another incident I could not completely dismiss. This happened in the early morning hours of Thursday, March 22, after the knocks David and I heard. Linda was in bed, Mrs. Beck was seated at the kitchen table, and I was in Mrs. Gemmecke's room where an alarm clock had just fallen. Suddenly a small glass vase from the kitchen table flew through the open door and fell to the rug by my feet. The vase did not break; nevertheless there was a loud explosive sound. I was facing Mrs. Beck but not looking directly at her. It was possible, therefore, that she might have thrown the vase. However, this would not explain the sound, which was as loud as a pistol shot. I at once examined the vase. There was no sign of foreign substances on it or on the floor. Unusually loud sounds are often reported in connection with poltergeist incidents.

I was not the only one who had been present when incidents took place which could not be easily dismissed. One of the other visitors was Edward Lacy, Jr., photographer for the *Indianapolis Star*. He struck me as a serious and sensible person who was more interested in finding an explanation for the events and in helping Mrs. Beck than in getting material for a melodramatic newspaper account. To avoid disruptions from curiosity-seekers, he agreed to keep my visit from his paper.

Lacy told me that early Tuesday morning, on March 13,

he was sitting in the kitchen with Mrs. Beck. No one else was in the house. He had opened all the doors to improve his access to and view of possible disturbances. He noticed that a milk bottle was lying on the floor of the kitchen closet. He also left this door open. He then went out to the hall to make a phone call, all the time keeping watch on Mrs. Beck, who remained in her chair next to the door. At 2:30 P.M., when he was seated by the telephone table in the hall and looking into the kitchen where he could see Mrs. Beck behind the door, he suddenly heard her scream and saw her start up from the chair. At the same time he heard and then saw the milk bottle move into his field of vision from the closet. Mrs. Beck was about six feet from the bottle, on the other side of the kitchen doorway, and could not have reached the bottle. Since he himself opened the closet door and saw the bottle shortly before, it seemed impossible for Mrs. Beck to have tied a string to it or interfered with it in any other way. The bottle "bounced" along the floor he told me. The event was similar to the movement of a glass which Linda told me she saw on her mother's bed, it "went bump, bump . . . bouncing like it was dancing" and then rolled off.

Noseda told me about an event that took place while he was there the afternoon of the same day. He was seated by the kitchen table when the parchment kitchen lamp fastened to the wall above the table fell down. Mrs. Gemmecke was in the room, her daughter and granddaughter being elsewhere in the house. Noseda checked the nail, and found it to be firm in the wall. He then replaced the lamp. About 20 minutes later, while he was still at the table, it fell again. In both cases he was the closest person. He could not explain these incidents, particularly not the second after he himself had checked the nail. I also examined this nail and found it solid. (I first thought that the lamp might have been balanced on the nail and fallen down accidentally; however, it was impossible to achieve this—the lamp would not stay up unless the wire frame was behind the head of the nail.) Altogether this lamp fell six times.

There were also times when Mr. or Mrs. Noseda were with members of the family in one part of the home and something happened in an empty room. On the afternoon of Saturday, March 24, when he was in the bathroom and Mrs. Noseda was in the hall together with Mrs. Beck, who was seated next to the phone, and Mrs. Gemmecke was in her own room, a phonograph record flew out of Mrs. Beck's room to the hallway, landing by the feet of Mrs. Noseda. No one was in Mrs. Beck's room. A few minutes later, Mr. and Mrs. Noseda, Mrs. Beck, and Mrs. Gemmecke were all in Mrs. Beck's room, when a toothbrush moved from the empty bathroom to the hall. Shortly afterward, Mrs. Beck collapsed, apparently of nervous exhaustion. While Mrs. Noseda was watching her, an alarm clock moved from the bedside table to the door. My confidence in Noseda was increased by his description of some events that were caused normally by Mrs. Beck. The circumstances were as follows.

Following the violent knocking incidents Wednesday evening and Thursday morning, March 21 and 22 and after I had left, the disturbances apparently ceased, and the family breathed a sigh of relief. But the respite was short-lived and the poltergeist signaled its return by a series of knocks close to midnight on Friday. Next came nine movements or breakages of objects. Mrs. Gemmecke then blacked out and fell in a closet, remaining there for more than an hour. Mr. Noseda was called back and found her nude and hysterical, screaming "The devils are here." Eventually everyone went to sleep and things quieted down until Saturday afternoon. At that time the first of 22 additional movements of objects began. This was the worst day of all. Noseda telephoned a Catholic priest for help, and it was suggested that the family pray the rosary in Mrs. Beck's room. The Nosedas were Catholics, and so was Mrs. Gemmecke; Mrs. Beck, however, had left the Church. As they were praying, Mrs. Beck collapsed on the floor, apparently in a dissociated state, for as she was lying there she knocked on the floor. A priest then arrived, and while he was in the hallway and Mrs. Beck was lying on her bed, he saw her throw an ashtray. Noseda described Mrs. Beck as being "almost in a coma." Though there was nothing else to suggest that Mrs. Beck was prone to such episodes, I did not find it difficult to suppose that the intoning of the rosary to a lapsed Catholic, following what was an exhausting evening and day, could have brought on an unusual psychological state. In this connection, it is noteworthy that the only unusual experience that Mrs. Beck said she had had before the present events was a hallucinatory or visionary experience in a church where she had gone to pray. That we are not dealing with attempts at deceit is supported also by the lack of concealment. She neither hid her knocking on the floor nor her throwing of the ashtray.

If Mrs. Beck was in a poor state that day, her mother was

even worse. I mentioned her collapse in the closet. In the evening, Mrs. Beck decided it best to take her mother to the hospital. However, Mrs. Gemmecke fainted in the downstairs room before Mrs. Beck could get her into the taxi. As before, when she had had problems, Mrs. Beck called the police for assistance. When a sergeant came, Mrs. Gemmecke was still lying on the floor. He went upstairs to speak to Mrs. Beck. While he was there, Mrs. Gemmecke revived and, in a hysterical outburst, threw an ashtray and turned three pieces of furniture over. The sergeant saw this as he came down the stairs. It seemed clear to him that here was the instigator of all the disturbances, which had brought several investigations and visits by members of his department. He arrested Mrs. Gemmecke on a charge of disorderly conduct.

As far as the police and newspapers were concerned, the case of the strange "bat bites," knockings, and movements of objects had been solved and the culprit had been clearly identified as Mrs. Gemmecke.

The poor woman, elderly and diabetic, persecuted by the poltergeist woundings and knockings, now had to spend a night in jail. The next day, Sunday morning, March 25, Mrs. Gemmecke was taken to a hospital by the prison authorities for treatment and then returned to jail. Later that day Mrs. Beck secured her release on 100-dollar bail.

Her stay in jail was the last straw to Mrs. Gemmecke. With the police joining forces with the poltergeist, she felt she had no choice but to leave the country. Her decision was reinforced by the judge who took her case under advisement until April 5, with the understanding that the charges would be dropped if she had left by then. At noon, Saturday, March 31, Mrs. Gemmecke left by plane for Kassel, her home town in Germany.

I knew nothing of these developments till later. As Mrs. Beck wrote me, in spite of the sadness of the departure, it may have been for the best both for Mrs. Gemmecke and the rest of the family.

The Indianapolis poltergeist presented some unusual innovations among the standard poltergeist throwings. Just as there often is "focusing" on special objects, on kinds of objects, or on areas where objects are disturbed in a particular poltergeist case, so different poltergeists sometimes have characteristics and patterns of their own. In the Seaford case, it was bottle poppings, and in Indianapolis, knocks and wounds. I have come across only one case in which there were probably no movements of objects at all but which still had to be classified as a poltergeist or RSPK case since unexplained physical events took place repeatedly and spontaneously in the vicinity of a person. This case is described in the next chapter.

6

Strange Lights in Clayton, North Carolina

For about two hours during a July night in 1962 I was lying in a flower bed in the small town of Clayton, North Carolina, looking for some strange lights which had stirred up the whole town. I was gazing up at one of the windows of a white frame house occupied by Mrs. Pearl Howell and her two grown children, Frances and Robert (Bobby). Down the street and on the other side, in a house occupied by Major H. Parrish, Dr. Carl Eisdorfer was surveying the front and east side of the home. I was on the west side.

Inside the Howell house were the three members of the family and a police officer, Robert Davis. All the lights in the house were out, and everything was quiet. The venetian blinds were closed in Frances' room. This occupied the front and southwest corner of the house. It was the side window of Frances' room on which I was concentrating.

At 1:15 A.M. Davis left and joined Carl on the other side of the street. Five minutes later, Frances' window lit up in a series of weak but unmistakable flashes of light.

Davis and Carl had not seen anything, probably because the lights were too weak and because insect netting, which covered the window, is more opaque when the observer is at an angle to the window than when he is in front. But the Howells did see something. The house lights were switched on and, when Davis went to inquire, Mrs. Howell told him there had been eight flashes in Frances' room. This was consistent with what I saw, though I had not managed to count them. As I shall explain later, Carl had come to Clayton to help in the psychological study of the case. At that time he was associate professor of medical psychology in the Department of Psychiatry at Duke.

About an hour later there was a similar series of flashes, one of them rather stronger than the others. Again Davis had left shortly before and again Carl was observing the front of the house. The flashes came very rapidly and looked like those a neon tube sometimes gives off when it is turned on. (There were no neon lights in the room.)

Nothing much could be concluded from these sightings. Nevertheless they were important to me. Aside from the satisfaction of seeing the lights, the fact that they came from inside the house was added evidence that we were not dealing with a prowler who had shone a light into the house to frighten the family.

The lights I saw were clearly demarcated by the window frame. It did not seem possible that they could have come from outside through the other window, since Carl and Davis attested that they had seen no beams of light hit either the front or the other side of the house.

It seemed more likely to be a matter of faults in the house wiring or a prank by one of the members in the family. The fact that the flashes only came after the officer left made the latter the likelier explanation. Since they occurred in Frances' room, maybe she was the culprit. But there had been other sightings which placed difficulties in the way of such a simple explanation.

North Carolina is famous for its strange lights.[1] In the mountains, close to the ski resorts, are the "Brown Mountain Lights," unexplained points of light hovering near the mountain of that name. At the other, eastern, end of the state on the coastal plain is the "Maco Light" which is seen near a railroad and is, as tradition has it, carried by the spirit of a railroad signaling man who (literally) lost his head in a train accident and is searching for it. I have not investigated either since it seemed uncertain that they were parapsychological and that I would be able to make a meaningful study. But when I read about the lights in Clayton, which were both frequent and clearly localized, I decided to look into the matter.

Clayton is a small town in the Piedmont part of the state and close to home base: It is only about 50 miles from Durham. Clayton is part of the police district of the neighboring town of Smithfield. When I learned about the case, the police had been called in and Chief Charles D. Allen was in charge. I phoned him on Monday, June 25, and he told me that the lights had first appeared about three weeks earlier. The lights, Allen said, only came on at night and seemed to follow Frances. I reached Mrs. Howell later that day. She was convinced that a prowler was trying to scare the family by shining a strong light into their home. They had received an anonymous, threatening phone call which supported that belief. Other such calls were to follow during which the person sometimes implied that he was causing the lights. But nothing had happened for several days and it seemed that the prowler had left.

On the 27th, however, I got a call from Charles Barden. Barden was a free-lance photographer in Clayton who had taken photographs connected with the case for the newspapers. He had become interested in the phenomena and was to be a great help in the study.

Barden said he had been at the house the previous evening and seen several flashes. They seemed faster than flashbulbs, he said, having more the speed of electronic flashes. He "never saw anything like it before." Nothing had been found which could cause them. He and the police had decided that there would be no further publicity. They would welcome collaboration with parapsychologists.

That same evening I went to the Smithfield police station to get an impression of the situation. I learned that most of the lights were much stronger than the ordinary lights in the house—and that these were always turned off when the strange lights flashed. It seemed impossible to pin down the source, except that all agreed it was not the light bulbs and lamps in the house. Later that night I went to the Howell home and met the family.

The family had been in the house for six months. They liked it and also liked their neighbors. Mrs. Howell had reared her two children single-handedly since her husband died, 19 years before. She and Frances were both waitresses, working in the same restaurant.

Frances was a taciturn, rather heavyset 19-year-old girl. She told me that the lights began two or three weeks ago and that Bobby had seen them first. Bobby, the more communicative of the two, was 22 years old and working as a car mechanic. His room was at the east end of the house facing the porch and opposite to Frances'.

One evening between eleven and eleven-thirty o'clock, Bobby told me, he was in bed when he saw a "light flash, real bright." He thought it was lightning and went to the door to look at the weather, but it was clear and he went back to bed. "Then the light came again; my sister jumped up and hollered. She thought somebody had a light in her room." The family called the police and they came and checked the house and neighborhood. They found nothing. On the matter of the source of the lights, Bobby made an interesting remark when he told me about some of the more recent incidents: "It don't make a bit of difference whether the [venetian] blinds are pulled or closed." Obviously, this would only be true if the source were *inside* the house but this was an assumption that the family was unable to accept. And indeed how could that be? Barden and the police had examined the house and found nothing that could create the bursts of light that were seen. It seemed unlikely that electronic flashlight equipment could be concealed somewhere. The home, a white frame building, was of simple construction and sparsely furnished.

Chief Allen told me that he had sought the advice of electrical engineers at the University of North Carolina in Raleigh and was told that flash equipment with a remote control was the most likely explanation. He had searched for this and any other clues, but found nothing. There seemed to be no place to hide the type of equipment needed for such lights. There was also no smell or smoke associated with the phenomena, and no residues of chemicals or burned areas were ever found. This and the fact that the lights often followed each other in close succession, with only a fraction of a second between each, made it difficult to suppose that Frances was igniting some chemical that would produce them.

Frances' room was not the only place where the lights shone. Bobby told me that once when he was sitting on the living room couch opposite the bathroom door, he saw three or four great bright flashes in the bathroom when Frances went toward the bathroom door. The bathroom window, I noticed, had a heavy cloth curtain, apparently upholstery material, which attenuated the light considerably. Again, it seemed difficult to suppose that such bright lights could penetrate from outside.

When I arrived on the evening of June 27, the house was filled with relatives and I did not expect anything to happen. Earlier that day the family said there had been no less than five anonymous phone calls.

About 10:30 P.M. Frances and Mrs. Howell left for an errand in Frances' car. About half an hour later, I received

a telephone call from the police: Frances had come to the
police station saying that the light had "hit" her car. This
happened when she and Mrs. Howell were pulling out, about
75 feet from the back of the house. It had happened once
before.

By 11 P.M. they had returned, and I was discussing the
incidents with Mrs. Howell in the kitchen when Frances and
Bobby exclaimed that they saw a flash as Frances went into
the bathroom. I went into the sitting room to watch for
further events. Nothing happened, and I suspected that I was
inhibiting the incidents. I therefore went outside, taking up
a station by the bathroom window, having first told Frances
to go to the bathroom to see if this would stimulate the
events. Again nothing happened.

At 11:20 P.M., as I was returning through the kitchen
door from the outside, I saw three clear, but not blinding,
flashes of light as Frances was on the point of leaving the
small hallway outside the bathroom. Though I could not be
certain that Frances was not playing a trick, since I did not
have her in view, or that the lights did not come from outside, at least I knew that they were still occurring.

There were no further incidents and I left some time after
1 A.M. But shortly after, the lights came on again and the
family called the police.

The officer who responded to the call that evening was
Robert Davis, an alert young man who seemed determined to
get to the bottom of this strange problem. He told me later
that as he entered through the kitchen door he saw the light
flash in the front of the house. He then took up a station
on the couch directly facing the bathroom. Because of the
lights in her own room, Frances had moved to the living
room couch outside her room.

Probably because of the many sleepless hours and her
anxiety, she became sick and went to the bathroom. Davis
reported that "just as soon as she opened the door, it flashed
on her twice real quick." Frances had not turned the lights
on, he said. He went outside to search the area, but found
no one. Later on, when Frances again needed to go to the
bathroom, he shone his flashlight as she entered. Apparently
this kept the other lights away.

The phenomena were at their strongest from 3:45 to 4:15
A.M. During this period, Davis was with Mrs. Howell and
Frances, who were both on the couch in the living room,
Bobby Howell being asleep in his room. And all this time,

Davis said, the front bedroom, where the lights were flashing, was empty. They eventually stopped and Davis left about a quarter to five in the morning.

The next evening, I was told to go to the police station for important news. Waiting there were Allen, Barden, and Davis. It was a very happy police chief who told me that earlier in the day an electrician had examined the house wiring and had found and repaired a short in the main wire leading to the house. Allen was certain they had the problem licked. I was doubtful: If the incidents were due to an electric short, why should they happen in such close proximity to Frances?

The news had also spread to their anonymous harasser. He phoned in the afternoon and said "that light won't be on tonight, but I'll be around." So the family did not even have a brief respite.

In any case, the Howells had little confidence in the electrical repairs. Mrs. Howell pointed out that if the trouble were in the wires, the lights should have flashed two evenings during the weekend when the family was away, yet the neighbors, who continued to watch the house, reported nothing unusual.

There were no lights on the evening of June 28. Apparently the faulty wiring—or the prowler—was the explanation.

The next evening, June 29, I phoned the family to hear if there had been any developments. There had been no lights, but earlier in the day the caller had left another message: "Lights will be on tonight—better not have police." And, at 1 A.M., Barden phoned me to say that the lights had started again. That night two policemen were involved. While one was on the street and the other in the house, they saw three flashes in Frances' room. There was no prowler in evidence.

On the 30th another short was found, this time in the switch controlling the ceiling light in Frances' room. When the door to the room was slammed, the light sometimes came on. The wiring and the wall switch were changed. Nevertheless, that night the flashes continued.

The evening of Tuesday, July 3, was particularly lively. The light "flashed all night," according to Davis and James Moore, the other officer who was working on the case. Moore, also a younger man, struck me as responsible and concerned about the family.

At 11:20 P.M., while Davis was making a phone call from the house, he saw a flash in Frances' room at the same time that he saw the girl in the doorway to the room, which was otherwise empty. I did not ask Davis to whom he was talking. However, the mayor of Clayton, R. L. Cooper, who by this time was also participating in the investigation, told me independently a few days later that it was he to whom Davis was speaking and that Cooper was in radio contact with three men outside the house. Cooper immediately put them on the alert for a prowler or anything else suspicious. They saw nothing except for the light which flashed in Frances' room.

Charles Gordon was the owner of the Howell house. He was in the house construction business and felt he knew the house. He told me he had been in the building business for 25 years and now had his own firm.

The same evening, the night of July 3, he was watching the house from the Webb home across the street when "I saw the front part of the house lit up." Gordon said the light must have come from the inside since he saw no beam or other indications of an external source. He then went over to the Howell house, but the lights seemed to have died down. Remembering that the phenomena sometimes started up again when Frances went to the bathroom, he asked her to do that. She went up to the sink to turn on the water, leaving the door open. Gordon reported: "When she turned the spigot, it shined." He was standing in the doorway looking at her. Frances had "one hand on the spigot, one by her side." The flash was not as bright as those that had been reported earlier, and it did not blind him. To see if this effect could be produced by others, he sent his wife to the bathroom and then went himself, but there were no more lights.

In the early morning of July 4, at 5:40 A.M., when Moore was in the living room and Frances was in her room, the light flashed. The door was open, Moore told me, and he could see both of Frances' hands. She had a glass in her left hand and her right was in her lap. Mrs. Howell was on the couch next to Frances' door and Bobby was asleep on the other couch. No one else was in the house. The flash was reddish, as it sometimes was said to be at dawn.

Although the prowler theory could not explain the lights, the police were still looking for someone they could identify as the Howells' tormentor. At 1:30 A.M. the same morning, Davis saw a man in the neighborhood who behaved suspiciously and fled when Davis approached. Davis had the block surrounded but the man had disappeared. Davis therefore concluded that he must have lived in one of the homes. Whether or not this was the phone harasser, later that morning Moore received a call at the station from an unknown person who "just laughed." A few days later, when I was in the house in the early morning, the phone rang and I answered it. The party said nothing and hung up. These two incidents seemed to support the Howells' claims about the anonymous phone calls.

Nevertheless, evidence was building up that the lights were not due to any known source, either outside or inside the house. At the same time, it was clear that Frances had some focal role in the disturbances, very much like the people around whom poltergeist disturbances take place.

While there was some progress in the poltergeist investigation, the same could not be said for the police investigation. Chief Allen was losing patience. And on July 5 he took Davis and Moore off the case. They told me that Allen had complained that the two of them "were just up there, holding the girl's hand." Instead he put an older officer, Otto Creech, on the case, hoping he would resist such temptations. The two younger men naturally felt bitter. I commiserated with them, but at the same time I understood Allen's frustration. Here were the light flashes for all in the house and neighborhood to see. Davis and Moore had spent whole nights inside and outside the house. They had thoroughly searched the house and had also repeatedly combed the neighborhood without finding any explanation and without significantly inhibiting the lights.

Officer Creech fared no better than his younger colleagues. He told me on July 6 that during the previous night he had been in the house and seen the lights flash twice, but found no clues.

Another visitor that evening was James W. Boyette, an electrician from Smithfield. Mrs. Howell had asked him to help in the investigation. He told me that he was sitting in a chair in the living room, opposite the door to Frances' room at 1 o'clock in the morning when a strong flash came on. Frances was in the room and the door was open. He estimated the strength of the light to be about 200 watts. It "seemed to start up to a brilliance and then die down . . . had a yellow glow." If the light had come from the outside, he thought it would have to be at least 500 watts to penetrate the venetian blinds. About two and a half hours later it came on again, this time more white than yellow, but of about the same strength. Both times, he told me, he rushed into the room with Creech and searched it. After this they searched outside the house, both times to no avail.

Boyette was certain that the light fixtures in the room could not have produced such a strong light.

Mr. Strickland, a lineman in Clayton who had helped re-wire the outside of the house when the short had been found, was also in the house and witnessed the second of the two flashes. He described it to me independently as "a bright light, like a 150-watt bulb. Bright yellowish." Frances was in bed, he said, and the venetian blinds were closed. Whatever the explanation, "it's not in the wiring of this house."

Davis and Moore were now speaking about a 17-year-old neighborhood boy as somehow being connected with the incidents. But the only evidence was that he was a "book-worm" and that he had never been seen during any of the disturbances. The two officers were trying their hardest to prove their competence.

With Officer Creech succeeding no better than the two others, Chief Allen stepped in himself and made a thorough search of Frances' room. At the end of the investigation, I received a small envelope containing the only foreign objects found in the room: A dusty, squashed pink birthday candle and what looked like part of a child's tooth and some loose filling.

At Allen's request, the house wiring was thoroughly checked and all the wiring in Frances' room disconnected. The police were not the only ones who were worried. Charles Gordon said that Cooper was talking about condemning his house.

I continued to come to Clayton, in all spending 10 nights in the house and in various observation posts outside. Allen had now come to the conclusion that the phenomena were outside the scope of conventional police methods and that the explanation must be in some unusual energy source. He therefore gave me a free hand in directing the investigations by his officers—except that he asked me to stay in the house with Frances and to post Creech outside!

Sometimes we tried an experiment: While I was observing inside and Creech was outside the bathroom window, I asked Frances to go to the bathroom, hoping to stimulate the lights in this way. Another evening I covered the windows of the bathroom and Frances' room with opaque sheets of cardboard so that, if the lights came on, both the family and I would know for sure whether or not the source was inside the house. Creech was again stationed outside. I also removed the main light fuse from the fuse box so that I could be certain that the lights were not caused by someone flicking on a lamp or using the house current in some other way. But the lights stayed away. It seemed as if they avoided situations that would reveal their origin.

Since I seemed to put a hex on the lights, I kept away at different times, hoping that Creech and the others would be able to observe the light under good conditions.

On July 10 several flashes in the Howell house as well as in Parrish's were reported to the police by Mrs. Howell (Parrish had no phone). Davis and Moore responded. Allen had come to realize that the failure to locate a culprit had nothing to do with the efficiency of his two young officers.

Moore told me that at ten minutes to eleven that night, as he was approaching the house from the back and while he was 10 feet from the kitchen window, "all of a sudden, the kitchen lit up." The light "flashed right in my face through the window [over the kitchen sink]." He was walking between the car shed and the house, to check the bathroom window. When the light shone, he was looking at the top of the trees where people at various times had reported lights. "When I looked down, it was fading . . . it comes on quick and goes out in a fading motion." It was a pinkish light, he said, which lit up the whole window. By a fortunate coincidence, the house was empty at the time: All three members of the family were out on the street talking to Davis about the previous disturbances.

For several hours that night, Davis took up a position on the Webb porch to watch the Howell home. During this time, Boyette was in the house with the family. At 3:15 A.M. Davis told me that he saw a light come through the front door of the Howell house. When he went over, Boyette said the flash came from the bathroom while Frances was there. Boyette was on the living room couch and only the family and he were in the house. Boyette told me independently that he was seated on the couch in front of the bathroom door and that the light flashed once as Frances was opening the door to leave. The door was open about a foot when the light came on and Frances was immediately behind it. The light was not as bright as previously; he estimated it to be about 60 watts. It seemed to come from the window. Davis had observed nobody suspicious outside. There had been several other flashes that night, mostly in Mrs. Howell's room where Frances had moved, hoping to escape the lights.

By this time everybody in the neighborhood was looking for strange lights. A great many were reported. It seems likely, however, that most, perhaps all, of these sightings were of ordinary lights which were usually unnoticed but which gained a new meaning in the context of the Howell lights. This was probably true for some of the lights there as well. For instance, on one occasion when I was present, a visitor struck a match in the bathroom and Bobby thought it was one of the lights.

At another time Parrish told Cooper about some lights he had seen in his house. Cooper simulated the effect with his flashlight, demonstrating that this was the kind of light Parrish had seen. Since the police and other searchers usually carry flashlights, this probably increased the sightings.

Conceivably, some of the outside sightings were nevertheless connected with *the* lights. Bobby told me that once, when he was standing outside the front of the house, "what looked like a bug went around the window. When it came back to where it started, it went to the center of the window and then a big flash appeared. The flash looked like it was on the inside of the house." It came on in Frances' room. Bobby observed, "when you stand in the inside, it looks as if it's on the outside; when you go outside, it looks as if it's inside."

Parrish told me that once, when he was standing in his bedroom window looking across the street to the Howell home, he saw "a bug—a little red light—crawl around the window. When it hit the middle piece, it flashed out." His 12-year-old son had watched the light too: It was "littler than a penny; it went all around."

The home of Mr. and Mrs. Clarence Webb was almost directly opposite the Howells'. Mr. Webb told me that he had seen a "little light" several times on the outside of the Howell house. The first time, he saw it on the bottom of Frances' window. "The little light would blink five times as a rule." Mrs. Webb said she had seen "a little thing like a cigarette light go around the window, and [it] was on door too—sometimes it gets a little bigger." She had seen this "a lot of times." Once, 14-year-old Andy Webb told me he saw a "dim" flash on the west side of the Howell house. He woke up his mother, and, five minutes later, Mrs. Webb told me she saw "a light about the size of a plate on the

Howell porch. When the light left, the [Frances'] room lit up."

It was impossible to determine whether or not these were lights from fireflies, flashlights, or some such source which were noticed only because they were followed by one of the genuine light phenomena.

The sightings which created the greatest stir in the neighborhood came on the evening of July 10. That night the Parrish family feared that the prowler had shifted his target: At a quarter past ten, Mrs. Parrish was awakened by two light flashes in the bedroom. Since this house was opposite the Howells', it seemed likely that the lights came from there. In any case, five or 10 minutes later, as Mr. and Mrs. Parrish watched, the lights flashed in the Howell house, and Mrs. Howell called the police. The belief that the lights had spread to another house increased the tension and anxiety in the neighborhood. Parrish, Bobby Howell, and Clarence Webb fetched their guns to deal decisively with the prowler. At 11:30 P.M. Davis was called to the neighborhood to quiet down the incipient but aimless posse.

The next day Cooper said he would condemn the house unless the case was solved. The house would then have to be vacated and possibly torn down. It was clear to me that from now on I had better spend every night in Clayton.

On July 11, I stayed in the house until shortly after 1 A.M. when I said I was returning to Durham. However, I stationed myself outside, hoping that my absence would allow the phenomena to resume. Nothing happened for as long as I was there—until 4 A.M.—nor was anything reported afterward. This situation was repeated the next night with the same results.

I suspected that I inhibited the lights, so on the evening of the 13th, I stayed away from the Howells' altogether and spent the night watching from the Parrish home. That day, Davis told me, while the family was out, he had searched the Howell house very carefully for any clues to the phenomena. He found nothing suspicious.

Since Davis did not seem to put as great a damper on the phenomena as I apparently did, I asked him to stay in the Howell house while I observed the front of the house from the Parrish house. At 11:35 P.M., while Davis was sitting on the living room couch opposite the bathroom, and while Frances was in the bathroom, Davis reported two brief flashes there. The door was open and Davis observed Frances with her right hand on the water spigot and a glass in her left hand as the light came on. She had gone to take some pills. Mrs. Howell and Bobby were asleep in their rooms. I saw no beams of light hit the house from the outside or anything else from my location that would explain the light. After this, I asked Davis to have Frances go to the bathroom to see if the lights would recur while I took a position immediately outside the bathroom window. However, they did not come on again.

The increasing number of observations by Davis and others and the absence of evidence of trickery and other normal explanations made me feel that the PK hypothesis had to be taken seriously as a possible explanation. If the lights in the Howell house were instances of PK, the source was apparently Frances. The next step was to try to discover if there was anything about her that would help explain these bursts of energy. I therefore wanted to give her and the other members of the family psychological and psychiatric tests. Following these I hoped to be able to provide some recommendations to them on how to deal with the phenomena.

I asked Drs. John Altrocchi and Carl Eisdorfer to join the investigation. To acquaint them with the situation, I asked them to come along on some of my evening excursions. John was then assistant professor of psychology at Duke.

On July 14, shortly before 11 P.M., Carl and I arrived at the Parrish house. The Parrish family continued to be co-operative and helpful, wishing to assist as best they could. At eleven-thirty the Howell house was dark. About an hour later, we saw Davis enter the home. As we learned afterward, there had been five flashes in Frances' room plus one in the kitchen, and Mrs. Howell had called the police.

When Carl and I spoke to Davis afterward, he said that as he was entering, there was another flash in Frances' room. Her door was open and he looked in immediately. Apparently she was asleep in her bed. Mrs. Howell was seated on the living room couch by the door and Bobby was sitting on his haunches by the door to his sister's room, looking in. Davis noticed that Bobby cast a shadow across the living room floor. A light coming through the west window of the room might have caused the shadow to fall this way and Davis speculated that this is where the light source was. To test this hypothesis I took up an observation post outside the west window. It was then that I observed the lights come on *inside* the room as described in the beginning of this chapter.

The next evening, July 15, John Altrocchi and his wife, Stella, came along. I spent about an hour and a half in the flower bed while they were observing more comfortably from the Parrish home and while Davis was with the Howells. There were no lights that night.

The Clayton lights were close to extinction. The last came 20 minutes after the Altrocchis and I had left at 2:45 A.M. and was observed by Jimmy Moore who had called in after some earlier incidents. It was only a faint light which flashed in Frances' room while she was there and Moore was in the kitchen.

The Clayton lights were turned out not by any prowler, visible or invisible, but by a Mr. Johnson, owner of the restaurant where Mrs. Howell and Frances worked. For a long time, he had suffered two extremely sleepy waitresses coming to work every morning. He had suggested they find another house. But, aside from the lights, they liked this one. Also, Mrs. Howell believed that sooner or later their tormentor would be caught and brought to justice. When Mr. Johnson finally fired both of them, this convinced Mrs. Howell that they had to move. Another house was found and on July 16 they moved. The move was successful: The lights did not follow the family to the new house—nor were any reported in the old. And Mrs. Howell got her job back. (Frances, however, had to change to another restaurant.)

When the family moved, it was not possible to tell whether or not the phenomena would start up in the new location or perhaps be replaced by some other unexpired phenomena, which sometimes happens in poltergeist cases. However, I felt I had enough of a picture of the case to offer some interpretation and guidance to the family and the town officials.

I therefore suggested that the parties mainly involved in the case get together for a meeting to review the case and decide on further studies. On July 18, this was called in the office of Mayor Cooper. Also present were the Howells, Chief Allen, Officer Davis, Charles Barden, Dr. Altrocchi, and Dr. Portia Hamilton. Portia is a psychotherapist and a member of the Advisory Committee of the Psychical Research Foundation.

It was generally agreed, first of all, that the lights could not be dismissed in terms of ordinary faults in the wiring or electric current in the house; secondly, that they could not be explained as trickery perpetrated by one or more members of the family; and thirdly, though the Howells still stuck to the prowler theory, it was clear to the rest of us that the flashes were not produced, in any ordinary manner, by somebody outside the house. No one, except the Howells, believed that the anonymous caller was responsible for the events. His first call came more than two weeks after the onset of the phenomena and after the troubles of the Howells were common knowledge in Clayton. Apparently this was somebody who was cashing in on the mystery. It is not uncommon for families who have gained fame or notoriety to be the victims of crank phone calls.

In view of the fact that the incidents were so closely connected with Frances, we were left then with the hypothesis that she was the energy source. But trying to explain this to the Howells was not easy. I pointed out that we all produce electricity in our bodies, including the brain, but that this generally can be measured only at short distances from the person. However, I said that there had been cases where people produce physical energy many feet away from them and that it was with the possibility in mind that the lights in the Howell home were examples of this phenomenon that we had made the investigation.

In the hope of learning more about these energies, I suggested that the family take some medical tests at Duke. At that time, no one knew whether or not the lights would start up again, so it seemed that such studies might be of value also to the Howells.

But this suggestion made no sense to them. It was not difficult to see their point of view. Referring to the analogy I had drawn with the electricity which is produced by the human body, Frances came in with, "Well, electricity in your body don't make telephone calls." Mrs. Howell remarked, "I just don't believe one person's got enough electricity in their body to make no light like that." They also pointed out, again quite correctly, that strange lights had been reported in the Parrish home.

The others tried to encourage the family as best they could to respond to my suggestion. Mayor Cooper in particular was emphatic. He pointed out that the town had gone to great expense to help the family, and that they, in turn, should do their bit to help clear up the problem. Unfortunately, it turned out that the Howells, particularly Frances, had great trepidations about any kind of examination or testing.

At the end, however, the family agreed to take an exploratory psychological test in their new home. After three more

visits to Clayton, two with Carl and one with John and
Portia, Carl administered this on August 9. I shall later say
something (Chapter 13) about the psychological factors that
may be connected with poltergeist disturbances.

In the meantime, some new disturbances started up at the
new home: At the end of July and the beginning of August,
on two occasions, someone or something tore a window
screen from a window and at one time somebody seemed
to be shaking a screen door. During the first of these incidents, Mrs. Howell and Frances said they saw a hand move
across the screen. The second time, Moore was called and
found the screen partially torn off. Were these incidents new
expressions of the unknown energy that earlier produced the
lights, or was a real prowler responsible? Since there were no
other phenomena, the latter hypothesis seems the more
plausible. Then these incidents, too, stopped and the Howells
finally had peace.

7

Recent European Poltergeists

An all-day bus ride from Reykjavik, where my plane had landed, followed by a 50-mile drive in a hired car along a two-track road on the north coast of Iceland brought me to Saurar, the home of an old sheep farmer, Gudmundur Einarsson, and his family. Saurar is one of the old Icelandic farms, rare nowadays. It dates from the time when the building material was driftwood and grass turf. When we came late in the day on May 23, 1964, and I was told we had arrived at the farm, the only suggestion of human habitation was a possible chimney stack coming out of a grassy mound in the middle of a field. We were on the north side of the house and this explained the absence of windows and doors. From its southern exposure, the structure almost looked like a small conventional home.

But Saurar was not conventional even for old Icelandic homesteads. There had been strange goings-on which made people in the neighborhood talk about visitations by drowned fishermen.

I was in Europe that year to give the presidential address to the convention of the Paràpsychological Association at Oxford University, and I used the occasion to visit people and places of parapsychological interest.[1] Saurar entered my itinerary when I saw an article about the disturbances in the *New York Times,* as I was about to leave the States.[2] It said that the Reverend Sveinn Vikingur, a retired Lutheran minister and president of the Icelandic Society for Psychical Research, had been to the farm. I contacted Vikingur before I left and arranged to meet him the next day when my plane stopped in Reykjavik on the way to England.

Vikingur told me that the incidents had begun on March 18. He had been at the house on the 21st, with other members of the Society for Psychical Research, and had stayed for three hours. Nothing happened then, but earlier in the day, when the family was having lunch, they said that the kitchen table had moved. The visitors were shown pieces of broken crockery and a kitchen cupboard which had fallen over several times and had now been fastened to the wall.

The incidents continued during April, and Vikingur thought they might still be going on. But there was no way of finding out short of visiting the farm. To protect themselves from reporters and curiosity-seekers, the family either did not answer the phone or claimed all was quiet though the disturbances might still be going on.

I was naturally eager to make the trip. Here was an opportunity to study a case in a social and cultural setting different from any I had come across before. It would be interesting to see whether the incidents conformed to patterns familiar from other cases. Vikingur agreed to come along to introduce me to the family and help as a translator.

When we came to Saurar, we were met by Einarsson and his wife, Margrét Benediktsdóttir. (In Iceland women keep their maiden name when they marry, thus the different last names for Einarsson and his wife. This seems to be an Icelandic first for women's lib, but is not. One's last name in Iceland stems from the *father's* first name—with the suffix "-dóttir," for daughter, or "-son.") The home was also occupied by two grown children, a daughter Sigurdborg and a son Benedikt. While we were there, another grown son, Björkvin, who lived in a village close by, was visiting.

The family remembered the first incident clearly: On Wednesday, March 18, at 1:40 A.M., the old couple was awakened by a sudden noise. An oval table standing between their beds had moved about three feet into the room. It weighed about 60 pounds and measured three by four feet. They thought it was an earthquake. Strangely enough, nothing else had been disturbed, but there had been an earthquake the year before when cups, bottles, and other objects fell to the floor and the walls developed some cracks.

The next day after lunch, the men went to work. Mrs. Benediktsdóttir said she and Sigurdborg went outside to enjoy the nice weather. "Then we suddenly heard a noise from within and rushed back into the kitchen. Then we saw that everything we had left on the kitchen table—cups, dishes, knives—lay on the floor and almost every piece broken." The incidents continued throughout the day, the kitchen table and the oval table in the main room (which served as the parents' bedroom and sitting room) being particularly active. To satisfy the craving of the oval table for a central position, they placed it in the middle of the room and put a chair where the table had been, in front of the window. When they were out of the house and it was again empty, they heard "a terrible noise," and found the chair broken on the floor at the other side of the table.

Obviously, the earthquake theory had to be given up. Not only were there no reports of seismic disturbances in the area (and the other homes remained quiet), but there was an element of selection of objects which could not be explained by the earthquake theory. And neither the wooden floor in the sitting room nor the earthen floor in the kitchen showed cracks or anything else that pointed to a normal physical cause.

Though hospitable, the family was reticent in discussing the events. People in these isolated farmsteads do not easily open up to strangers—and particularly not about things that might bring other uninvited guests. By and by, however, we were able to piece the story together. Björkvin in particular became frank and open as we became better acquainted. He still professed a belief in the earthquake theory (by then two geologists had been at the farm, one with a seismograph, and had dismissed this possibility). At the same time, Björkvin wanted us to have all the relevant facts, even if these went against his beliefs. He recalled that the night the oval table first moved, Sigurdborg woke up not feeling well. She went into her parents' room and saw what she thought was an old man who walked up to the table and then suddenly vanished. She woke up her mother and told her about the experience.

We did not speak to Benedikt, the younger son. He was mentally retarded, as a result of a childhood illness. He spent most of his time away from the farm, looking after the sheep. Sigurdborg said Benedikt had some clarivoyant abilities and once "saw" a shipwreck before it happened. Björkvin said his brother warned a friend who was a fisherman that he would drown and told him to take a job on land. The friend only laughed. Later Benedikt warned him again and a few weeks afterward he drowned. But since Benedikt was away when many of the incidents took place, it is unlikely that he had any connection with them.

On Thursday the 19th the oval table moved twice. The next day after lunch, when Sigurdborg was alone in the kitchen, the men being out and her mother in the living room answering the phone, she suddenly saw the kitchen cupboard begin to move. She grabbed her radio which was on top of it just before the cupboard crashed to the floor. Sigurdborg was by now thoroughly upset and went to Reykjavik the next morning to stay with her sister. She had only been gone about an hour when the cupboard fell again. The kitchen was empty, Mrs. Benediktsdóttir and Björkvin being in the adjacent room. They heard the noise and, when they came in, found the cupboard on the floor.

The phenomena continued, the most active period beginning a few days after Vikingur's first visit and lasting until April 3. Pictures fell off the walls, the dishes on the third shelf of the cupboard fell to the floor, and in the scullery dishes on the second shelf fell, all others remaining in place. The kitchen table moved "many, many times." The oval table continued as another focus for the events. Thursday before Easter it moved twice, the last time falling and breaking. They tried to tie it down, but the two parts of the top came off and moved into the room. After Sigurdborg had left for Reykjavik, a tray hanging on the wall moved across the room and landed on her bed. This tray fell at least five times and a clock and barometer moved three times. The gas cooker and the butter maker also moved.

Sometimes objects were actually seen in movement. Sigurdborg saw both the kitchen cupboard and the table move, and Björkvin said he often had seen objects in motion.

A reporter and a neighboring farmer had been present during some of the events but had not seen anything themselves. Could the case be a fraud perpetrated by the family? They seemed truthful and sincere people who, if anything, played down the events. When we made a second trip, on the 28th, we stayed at the local parsonage as guests of the Reverend Peter Ingjaldsson. He spoke well of the family and thought it highly unlikely that they would be involved in trickery.

Another daughter, Arnfridur Gudmundsdóttir, who was married and lived in Reykjavik, visited her parents on March 20 after learning about the events. She told Vikingur that when she was seated in the sitting room talking to a neighbor they heard a noise "as if a strong wind was sweeping over the room and almost shaking the house." It lasted a few seconds and nothing else happened, but the incident was very sudden and frightened her. The next morning she returned to Reykjavik bringing Sigurdborg along. Björkvin had previously told us that sometimes a sound like a strong wind blowing over the house came at the time of the incidents. There were no special feelings of cold or heat associated with the phenomena.

I noticed that the family had two dogs and asked if they reacted to the phenomena. We were told that the older of the two, which was "very intelligent," would not come into the house during the active week before Easter, even when called. The other dog did not seem aware of anything and even remained asleep in the kitchen when the table was "dancing."

On April 3 Mrs. Benediktsdóttir was taken to the hospital with a minor complaint. The incidents abruptly ceased. She came back on the 11th and still things were quiet, but on the 15th when Sigurdborg returned from Reykjavik, there was a brief resurgence: The kitchen table moved twice, and some pictures fell. This seemed to suggest that Mrs. Benediktsdóttir or perhaps mother and daughter together had some connection with the events. Sometimes poltergeist occurrences seem to arise if there is tension or conflict. As with many families where the parents are approaching retirement and the children are ready to leave, there undoubtedly was some tension in the house. Mrs. Benediktsdóttir wanted to give up the farm—the winters up there are extremely long and hard—but her husband wished to remain. Sigurdborg was engaged to get married and planned to live in Reykjavik with her husband, but she was needed at home to help her parents. She had consented to stay until that spring but was now to be married in a few weeks.

When we visited the home the second time, we learned that the farmer had given in to his wife and was planning to sell the animals and move away in the autumn. With the poltergeist gone, this removed the main problems in the life of the family.

In England, places of poltergeists and hauntings have been favored territory for a long time for a small but distinguished group of explorers. In addition to active investigators such as Sir William Barrett, there have been important ghost theoreticians such as Professor H. H. Price and G. N. M. Tyrrell.[3] A newcomer to the ranks of explorers is Dr. A. R. G. Owen. And the most recent British poltergeist is the Sauchie case, investigated by Owen during a vacation from Cambridge University where he was teaching mathematics and genetics.

When I came to England in the summer of 1964, I hoped I would learn more about the Sauchie case. The opportunity came when Owen asked me to lunch at Trinity College. It seemed as natural to discuss poltergeist disturbances at the high table in the dining hall of this distinguished Cambridge college as to discuss the disturbances caused by the increasing flow of traffic through town.

Owen told me that his involvement with the Sauchie poltergeist had stimulated him to write a book, which he had just about finished at that time. This later came out under the title *Can We Explain the Poltergeist?* and is an excellent survey of European cases.[4] The case of greatest interest is the Sauchie poltergeist because Owen visited the place and closely questioned the witnesses.

The activities took place between November 22 and December 2, 1960, in a house in the Scottish village of Sauchie. They were focused around Virginia Campbell, an 11-year-old, shy and somewhat withdrawn child, the youngest of an elderly couple who used to work an isolated farm in Ireland. At the time of the incidents, Virginia was staying with her brother and his wife in Sauchie while her mother was working in a neighboring town. Her father had remained in Ireland to sell the farm. Virginia was enrolled in the local primary school. The family physician, Dr. W. H. Nisbet, had found her in good health. When the disturbances began, he noted that she was going through a time of rapid pubescence and physical development. Apparently she was also going through a time of emotional turmoil. Sometimes she would enter a dissociated state when she would speak about her life in Ireland and lose much of her ordinary reticence.

The incidents began on November 22 with "thunking" noises close to Virginia. They ceased when she went to sleep. This continued on the next day. There was also some movement of furniture. The minister of Sauchie, the Reverend T. W. Lund, was called in. The knocking continued when he was present and under circumstances when he was certain that no one was producing them. He then saw a large linen chest raise itself slightly from the floor and move 18 inches into the room and then return. The next day, Thursday, November 24, when Virginia was in bed, he saw her pillow rotate 60 degrees while her head was on it. He did not think she caused the event normally.

Nisbet was also present that day and saw a peculiar rippling or puckering motion pass over the surface of the pillow. In the evening of the following day, as he kept watch while Virginia was going to sleep, he heard spells of knocking even when the girl was lying quietly on the bed without bedclothes. From time to time, the linen chest, which was standing by itself, moved distances of about a foot. Once he saw the lid open and shut several times in succession. The pillow continued to move, rotating as much as 90 degrees. Nisbet's colleague, Dr. William Logan, was also present during some of the events and saw the rotation and rippling of the pillow.

The incidents fell off sharply in the beginning of December, with only minor happenings in January and February. In March they ceased altogether.

Poltergeists usually restrict themselves to some area, such as a person's home. Not so the Sauchie poltergeist. Not only did the incidents follow Virginia when she went to stay with relatives in a neighboring town, they also went with her to school.

Miss Margaret Stewart, Virginia's teacher, said that she seemed a normal little girl when she joined her class in mid-October 1960. At first, Virginia was very shy and Miss Stewart found it difficult to establish any real rapport. She thought this was because Virginia came from isolated rural surroundings and because of language differences which made it difficult for her to communicate with her classmates.

Virginia had been absent from school for two and a half days when she came for the afternoon session on Friday, November 25. Virginia's sister-in-law, Mrs. Campbell, had explained the reason for her absence to the headmaster and he in turn told Miss Stewart that the child had a poltergeist. The teacher was not familiar with this word and thought that her pupil was suffering from an "obscure but mild ailment." The afternoon Virginia returned to school, Miss Stewart was glancing over the class during a period of silent reading, when she saw the lid of Virginia's desk moving slowly up and down. There were at least three such motions; each time the lid turned on its hinge from the normal rest position slightly below the horizontal to an inclination of about 45 or 50 degrees above the horizontal. The teacher naturally first thought that Virginia was opening the desk to look for something. She then saw that the girl had both of her hands, palms down, on the top of the lid as if trying to keep it down. She also had her feet on the ground, so she was not lifting the lid with her knees. Miss Stewart did not know what was moving the desk. She stared silently at Virginia, and Virginia stared silently back. None of the other pupils seemed to have noticed the incident.

About a quarter of an hour afterward, a desk behind Virginia, unoccupied at the time, slowly rose about an inch and then settled down slightly out of line in relation to the row of desks. This time, Miss Stewart rushed over to the desk, expecting to find strings or other mechanisms that would explain the event. She found nothing. Since none of the children seemed to have noticed anything, she thought it was best to cover up the situation as far as the class was concerned. Feeling that she should say something to Virginia to explain why she had come, she asked, "Are you feeling better, Virginia?" The girl replied, "There's nothing wrong with me." Immediately afterward Miss Stewart went to the headmaster and told him of the events in the classroom. The headmaster, in turn, described the events in the Campbell home and Miss Stewart learned that a poltergeist is not an ailment, at least not in the ordinary sense of the word.

On Monday, November 28, Virginia was back at school. During one of the morning periods, she had difficulties with an assignment and went up to Miss Stewart's desk to have it explained. While the girl was standing to the left of the desk with her hands clasped behind her back, and while the teacher was writing and explaining, she suddenly saw the blackboard pointer, which was lying on the desk, start to vibrate and move until it reached the edge of the desk when it fell to the floor. At the same time, Miss Stewart felt a vibrating movement in the desk and this began to rotate in a counterclockwise direction. She looked at Virginia who still had her hands clasped behind her. The girl began to cry and said, "Please, Miss, I'm not trying it." Miss Stewart said, "It's all right, help me straighten the desk up."

There were a few other incidents in school. The children had become aware of the situation, but they and the teachers did their best to minimize matters and protect Virginia from the reporters and curiosity-seekers who soon began hounding her.

Finally, the events ceased. Writing on March 20, 1961, when all was quiet, Miss Stewart told Owen that Virginia was much more out-going than before and that the tension seemed to have left her.[5]

If any country can be designated as the homeland of the poltergeist, this has to be Germany. It is natural that the center of poltergeist explorations should be in the same country. The place is the *Institut für Grenzgebiete der Psychologie und Psychohygiene,* a formidable name which, for all practical purposes, translates as parapsychology. It is located at Freiburg University, West Germany, and is headed by Dr. Hans Bender, professor of psychology. The Institut is devoted to research in parapsychology in general, but the poltergeist has always been particularly close to Bender's heart. When I visited in the summer of 1964 there had been three particularly interesting cases I had not heard of before since they had not appeared in the parapsychological journals.

In 1948, in the mountain village of Vachendorf in Bavaria, a family of refugees from Bohemia, a couple and their 14-year-old daughter, were temporarily lodged in a room in an old mansion. On one occasion, the two beds in the room were bombarded by stones, tools, and other objects. After the mother had returned the tools to the box, she closed it and then sat down on it, only to see the tools mysteriously appear one by one in different parts of the room. Another time, she saw linen belonging in the attic appear in the air and fall to the floor. Once her husband was sitting in front of a closed glass cupboard when a wooden shoe came out of it and hit him on the head.

When the daughter left Vachendorf for her holidays, the phenomena in the farm ceased but were reported to have resumed in her new location.

Three years later, in 1951, a Catholic priest from the village of Neusatz in Baden asked the Freiburg Institut to investigate strange phenomena in a farmhouse occupied by a mother and her 30-year-old mentally retarded son. Linen was cut up, clothes torn, and the living room curtains disappeared several times without a trace. In the stable, the tails of the cows were braided. The Freiburg team connected the curtains to a device that would trigger a film camera if activated. This was a great success as far as the family was concerned since the camera apparently kept the poltergeist away. But it was a disappointment to the poltergeist explorers.

Dr. Bender has been particularly interested in the reports of objects coming through walls and other obstructions without leaving any opening.[6] Such penetrations of matter by matter probably are the greatest challenge by the poltergeist to the theories of physics. Apparently such penetrations took place in the following case.

In 1952 the Department of Public Health in the town of Neudorf in Baden had asked Bender's help in dealing with an unusual situation that had developed in the home of the mayor. On one occasion, the day before Bender came, the mayor, his grown son, and daughter-in-law had watched in amazement as a collection of nails appeared about eight inches below the ceiling of a bedroom and then fell to the floor. The mayor's 13-year-old son, Bernard, was lying on the bed next to his mother. The nails belonged in a locked cupboard in the kitchen, but there was no accounting how they came into the upstairs bedroom. The mayor had also seen a clothes pin climb up a door to the top and then fly off at a right angle. Others said they saw objects move out of a wall at great speed. When they were picked up, they felt warm.

The incidents were focused around Bernard and only happened when he was present. When he went away on vacation, they ceased for good. To try to get an understanding of the case, the Freiburg team gave the boy psychological tests. They found evidence of psychological tensions of the type connected with puberty as well as signs of frustration and aggression. Bender suspected that these tensions were connected with the phenomena.

It was 1968, and four years after my previous visit, before I was back in Europe. Again the occasion was the annual convention of the Parapsychological Association, but this time it was to be held at Freiburg University. I was looking forward to this meeting because I knew that there had been three new German poltergeist cases and that we were going to hear about them from Bender and his co-investigators.

The first erupted in June 1965, when Bremen newspapers told about a poltergeist on the rampage in what must be its favored element: A china store. Glasses, vases, and porcelain objects jumped from their shelves and dashed themselves to pieces on the floor. Police officers were called in but were unable to explain the incidents. However, when a 15-year-old apprentice, Heiner, was sent home, the turmoil stopped. A person who knew something about parapsychology and suspected poltergeist activities had advised dismissing the boy. Bender was brought into the case two days afterward. The discussion with witnesses and reconstruction of the events convinced him that here was a genuine case.

Heiner was an unfortunate and unhappy boy. He was born out of wedlock and had been brought up by his grandmother. She could no longer take care of him so he was sent to Bremen to his mother who was now married and had another child. She showed little interest in Heiner, and he was forced to take the apprenticeship in the china shop. Here one of his jobs was to collect empty bottles, and he was known for continuously breaking them. As a result of these incidents, he was given a lengthy examination in a psychological laboratory, an occasion which proved highly traumatic to the boy. It was after this that the paranormal breakages began.

Following his discharge, Heiner was referred to a psychiatric clinic, and the events there "flabbergasted the psychiatrists and psychologists," according to Bender. With his help, arrangements were made to bring the boy to Freiburg, where he began work as an apprentice with an electrician.

In March 1966, Heiner was helping install wires in the basement of a new school. Part of the job consisted of drilling holes in the concrete walls for plastic plugs and screws. The foreman observed that no sooner had the screws been fastened than they would come out. One of them was seen to follow Heiner as he walked through a passageway. Bender and his colleagues were now called in. They placed two hooks in the concrete wall and fastened each with two screws. After they had assured themselves that the screws were tight, they asked Heiner to stand in front of the wall at a distance of about two feet from the hooks. While they were observing the wall and Heiner, the screws again became loose. This appears to be the first time a parapsychologist has successfully induced a poltergeist movement.[7]

Next month, additional phenomena occurred, including the breakage of neon lights in the presence of the boy. But then, as the genuine phenomena began to wane, Bender found that the boy sometimes produced the events by trickery. About that time, Bender had to discontinue his observations since the parents regarded the incidents as a work of the Devil and Bender as his accomplice! Before this, however, the German parapsychologists had completed most of their studies, including PK and ESP tests. The PK tests, in which Heiner tried to influence dice falls and a pair of scales, were unsuccessful, but the boy gave highly significant ESP scores, both in telepathy and clairvoyance tests.

Some time ago an institute for public opinion research, in collaboration with the Freiburg Institut, sampled the attitudes of Germans toward poltergeist phenomena and haunted houses.[8] Seventy-two percent of the population attributed the reports to superstition, while 18 percent were convinced that such cases may be genuine (10 percent had no opinion). In 1969 a fresh poll taken in Bavaria showed that the proportion of believers had risen by 10 percent. This apparently was the result of the Rosenheim poltergeist and the investigation by Bender and his team. At the end of November 1967, a law office in the Bavarian town of Rosenheim was the scene of occurrences which the lawyer, Mr. Adam, and his secretarial staff were unable to explain.

Neon tubes in the ceiling were unscrewed, light bulbs exploded, and fuses were blown without apparent cause. Telephone calls that were never made were registered and caused a sharp rise in the bill. To prevent anyone from surreptitiously using the phones, only one was left in operation. Nevertheless, hundreds of calls were recorded by the telephone exchange when the staff claimed no one had used the phone. The number for calling to learn the time, 0119, was recorded particularly often.

Because of the apparent electrical nature of the disturbances, the Rosenheim Maintenance Department was called in to make an investigation.[9] P. Brunner, assistant director of the maintenance department, himself told the convention participants about his findings. He had come to the office expecting to uncover a normal explanation. But when a voltage amplifier was installed, he found deflections of up to 50 amps though the fuses, which should have blown from such strong currents, remained intact. The technicians could find no cause for this but put in an emergency power unit to make certain of an even electric flow. Nevertheless the phenomena as well as the deflections continued.

It was at this point, at the beginning of December, that Bender joined the investigation. The Freiburg group noticed that the unusual occurrences took place only during office hours and then they noticed that things only happened when a 19-year-old female employee, Annemarie, was present. When she walked through the hall, light bulbs exploded, the ceiling lamps swung, and other things happened. Bender's team then put up a video recording unit and were able to photograph the swinging of the lamps. As fas as I know, this is a historical first. No other scientists have so far succeeded in filming a poltergeist incident.

New phenomena arose including the rotation of pictures on the walls. The pictures would turn 360 degrees around the hooks and fall off. Also drawers opened by themselves, and finally a heavy storage shelf, weighing about 400 pounds, moved from its position against the wall.

The telephone effects were particularly interesting. A counter was installed with the aid of the phone company and it was found that the time number was often dialed four or five times a minute. Sometimes this number was called as many as 40 to 50 times in succession when no one in the office was using the phone.

Dr. Bender then asked Dr. F. Karger, a physicist on the staff of the *Max-Planck Institut für Plasmaphysik*, and Dr. G. Zicha of the Technical University in Munich, to help in the investigation.[10] In Karger's report to the Convention, he said that on December 8, 1967, he and Zicha set up a line recorder with a voltage magnifier in the passageway of the office to record the main line's voltage. During a period in the afternoon lasting an hour and a quarter, the recorder registered about 15 strong deflections at irregular intervals. During some of these, the investigators heard loud bangs similar to those produced by discharging spark gaps. They tape-recorded the sounds. The physicists then installed instruments to record the electrical potential and the magnetic field near the recorder and also the sound amplitude in the office, in the hope that these might point to the nature of the disturbances.

They failed to find any of the effects they were looking for. In particular, they had to reject the possibilities that variation in the main's voltage, demodulated high-frequency voltage, electrostatic charging, and external static magnetic fields were responsible. In addition, they had to rule out ultrasonic and infrasonic effects, including strong vibrations. They checked the amplification system for loose contacts and the recorder for mechanical defects which might produce the deflections. All such possibilities were ruled out, including trickery. The electrical equipment was all functioning properly and there was no possibility for any known physical cause to have produced the effects. An unknown kind of mechanical or kinetic influence was apparently interfering with the equipment.

A mechanical rather than an electrical cause was also consistent with the light bulbs which burst, though the light had not been switched on and the filaments were still intact. Also the automatic fuses tripped, although the current was steady. A mechanical cause was also consistent with the other incidents, such as the movements of the pictures and lamps. One of these, the rotation of a picture on the wall by more than 90 degrees, was caught on a video recorder.

Summarizing the result of the investigations by the two physicists, Dr. Karger concluded that "the phenomena seem to be the result of non-periodic, short-duration forces," rather than ordinary electrodynamic effects. In addition to the simple movements of objects, Karger pointed out that the movements of the recorder pen and the telephone incidents "seem to be performed by intelligently controlled forces."

If one shared the belief of Miss Stewart, Virginia Campbell's teacher, that poltergeist is an "obscure ailment," one might almost think that it is also contagious. The most recent outbreak investigated by the Freiburg team occurred in Nicklheim, which is only 10 miles from Rosenheim.[11] Beginning in November 1968, and lasting for four months, a laborer, his wife, and 13-year-old daughter, Brigitte, were victimized by knocks on windows and doors, flying objects, and, strangest of all, stones thrown into closed rooms. On one occasion when a priest was in the kitchen, blessing the house, a stone fell from the ceiling, though all doors and windows were closed. When he picked it up, it felt warm to the touch.

Mr. Adam, the lawyer whose office in Rosenheim had been the scene of the earlier disturbances, had become interested in poltergeist phenomena and went to see the Nicklheim family. They told him that objects which disappeared from the house would later be seen falling to the ground outside. To test this, Adam placed bottles with perfume and pills on the kitchen table and then told everybody to go outside. He closed the windows and doors and joined the others. Shortly afterward, a perfume bottle appeared in the air and then a bottle with pills. This was seen when it was at the level of the roof, moving to the ground in a zigzag manner.

One of the objects apparently "tele-apported" was Bender's

own coat. It had been hung in a closet next to the kitchen. When he was with the family in that room, the wife went to the front door to let in the cat. She came rushing back into the kitchen exclaiming that Bender's coat was lying on the snow outside, next to the staircase. It was cold, and the outer door had been closed the whole time. The only normal explanation seemed to be that the wife had taken the coat out when she went to let the cat in. Bender timed the period required to take the coat from the closet, place it on the ground, and return to the kitchen. He found it would have been impossible for the wife to have done this in the eight and a half seconds she was out of the room (the timing was obtained from Bender's tape recorder which had been on all the time).

The Freiburg team now installed a container in which they placed objects that had been disturbed previously, including a figurine of one of the Beatles. Connected with these were photoelectric switches that would trigger two still cameras and one film camera. At the front of the box there was a photoelectric "light curtain" connected to a light switch. If any of the objects left the box and if anybody tried to interfere with the objects, a red light would go on.

One time, when the Freiburg team was outside with the family, they noticed that the lights connected with the camera went on. They found that the Beatle figurine had fallen over. The protective photoelectric light curtain had not been triggered. When the photographs and film were developed, they showed nothing suspicious and gave no clue as to how this event took place. On three other occasions the light curtain activated the red light, but there was no indication why this happened.

As in other poltergeist cases which seemed to include genuine effects, when these began to wane, the focal person— in this case Brigitte—was discovered to cheat. Bender found the girl's fingerprints on a dish which she claimed the poltergeist had thrown out the window.

With the possible exception of the Newark poltergeist (Chapter 4), those with which I have been acquainted have not thrown objects through walls or closed doors. In addition to Bender's cases, there are earlier ones in which this has been reported. We must therefore be open to the possibility that this is a real effect. Bender suggests that we may have to postulate the existence of "higher space." [12] This would allow "four-fold freedom of movement" and account for the apparent penetration of matter by matter. He notes that an Austrian physicist, Ernst Mach, advanced this possibility in the beginning of the century as an abstract mathematical concept, and that Mach also said that the appearance and disappearance of objects would be empirical evidence for such a higher dimensionality of space.

In two of Bender's cases, the central person was caught in trickery. The same was true for some of the incidents in the Newark and Indianapolis cases (Chapters 4 and 5). Are these not grounds for rejecting *all* the phenomena reported for these cases? And then it is a short step to dismiss the poltergeist in general.

In the early history of parapsychology, when an investigator discovered that a medium, psychic, or poltergeist person cheated or tried to cheat, that usually was the end of research with this person. There was good reason for this since the conditions of testing or observation were frequently primitive and enabled the subject to cheat.

The research worker today recognizes that he, and not the person he is investigating, is responsible for the conditions of obstruction. He also recognizes that psychic phenomena, particularly the more striking ones, in part result from special psychological conditions. As Bender suggested, and as we shall see later from the American cases, psychological tensions in the poltergeist person are important for the phenomena. If the ability to produce the phenomena disappears, but the psychological tensions remain, then we may expect those to cause the person to resort to ordinary destructive activities. Far from ignoring cases which include normal throwing incidents, we should see that they receive special study. It may help us understand the psychological process which results in genuine phenomena if we know that this can also result in ordinary destructive behavior. And vice versa, it is important to know that destructive impulses in a person can not only find an outlet in ordinary acts of aggression but also in RSPK activities.

Cox draws a distinction between "imitative" and "total" fraud. In cases of imitative fraud, a person—often the apparent RSPK agent—copies some of the genuine phenomena by trickery. Cases of total fraud, however, are entirely made up of tricks and deception.[13] Many supposed cases of haunting and poltergeist activities are easily explained in terms of "total" trickery and other familiar physical causes. Fortunately, obvious cases of fraud can often be identified without a personal investigation. Before making this investment of time, I usually satisfy myself, by talking to the family and to outside witnesses, that at least some of the events cannot easily be explained away. Nevertheless, the poltergeist investigator inevitably gets into cases which are fruitless from the point of view of teaching him anything about psychic phenomena. However, they can be instructive: If he learns how artificial poltergeists and ghosts are put together, it may be easier for him to recognize the real ones. I shall discuss some examples of the former in the next chapter.

8

Ersatz Poltergeists

"A large misty face" and "loud, plodding footsteps, tappings and knockings, far-off voices and flying objects" chased a family of five from their home in Detroit, according to a newspaper report I received in October 1965 from John Buta, who had heard of our interest in ghostly happenings.[1] At my request, Mr. Buta visited the family. On the basis of his interviews with witnesses and an experience of his own, which I shall later describe, I decided to make an investigation.

When I came on October 6, 1965, I was met by a very fearful Mrs. Mary S. and her four children. Just the night before, they told me, their dog and a neighbor's dog had been playing in the living room. Suddenly the dogs stopped playing and went up to the entrance of the dining room where they began snapping and biting as if they were fighting something. Then, according to Gail, the 14-year-old daughter, a cocktail shaker, which was standing on a metal bookcase in the corner, "rose up . . . as if it was thrown at the dogs." Mrs. S. told me she was reading the Bible at the time. She felt a cold breeze and noticed that the dogs reacted in a peculiar way. Then the shaker fell. The 12-year-old son, Gregory, a seventh-grader to whom I spoke separately from Gail and his mother, gave substantially the same account, saying that when one of the dogs "started sniffing, chasing after something, the thing picked the blue vase [the cocktail shaker] and threw it at the dogs."

The other dog belonged to a friend of the family, Annie, a woman in her twenties. Shortly after the shaker fell, she announced that she saw something. Mrs. S. recalled: "I heard Annie say, 'Look! Look!' I said, 'Which way is he coming?' So I had my Bible open and I started toward the back of the dining room and put the Bible on the table. All went into the bedroom and shut the door, all hollering and all piled into the bed." Gail told me that she heard footsteps in the hall as she was lying with the others in the bed. She saw a misty shape form at the door and then the figure of a man appeared. "I saw him from the waist to the neck; he had on a tie, a white shirt and a dark suit."

Gregory told me he ran with the others into the bedroom, but didn't see any mist or shape: "Haven't ever seen anything; don't want to either." Mrs. S. said that she once saw 12 people or "things" in her house. However, she did not see the man in the bedroom that Gail reported. Mrs. S. "just felt it." One thing was certain and that is that the family was genuinely scared. Gail refused to go into the back kitchen and bedroom alone even while I was in the home.

Before I went to Detroit, John Buta told me over the phone that he, too, had seen something. On the Friday before I came, he was sitting in the living room when somebody said that they saw a man and woman on the hallway wall. Then John himself saw a misty shape about three feet off the floor and six by eight inches in size. It seemed to be two inches or so away from the wall and to have a kind of egg shape. He said he felt no particular fear and went up to the wall. When he moved his hand back and forth across the area, he noticed that the hairs stood up as if affected by static electricity. I mentioned this to Dr. John Artley, professor of electrical engineering at Duke. He said such a reaction might indicate an electrostatic field. An electrostatic voltmeter might register this and he lent me one to take along. It could measure from 600 to 3,000 volts. Neither of us expected that such a primitive piece of equipment would be much use on the trip, but there was no way of knowing without trying.

I arrived in the evening at eight o'clock and nothing happened for nearly three hours. Then, to stimulate the events, if there were any genuine ones, I suggested we duplicate the situation of the previous evening, including the reading of the Bible. Three minutes later, Annie said, "It's in here." Shortly afterward another visitor, a 19-year-old girl, Louisa, said she saw two figures against the wall in the dining room. I saw nothing myself but asked her to sketch the figures. She drew a picture of a man and a woman in what looked like old-fashioned clothing, the woman wearing a long dress with her hair piled on top of her head. The man wore tails.

Mrs. S. also saw a ghostly couple in this area. But these entities did not stay on the wall, for a little later she announced that they were moving about in the apartment.

Though this remark put everybody on their toes, ready to flee, nothing further happened and we went to bed—I in the bedroom where Gail had seen the apparition.

On my second day in the house, Mrs. S. told me she saw the figure of a tall man she often saw on the dining room wall. I asked her to outline where on the wall she saw the figure. Though I could neither see nor feel anything unusual there, I tried to take measurements with the voltmeter, placing the two leads both horizontally and vertically over the area. Nothing registered.

As Mrs. S. was describing the figure, Gail exclaimed that now she also saw it—and for the first time. But when her mother indicated the outline of its head, Gail said that this was not the right place. Apparently, mother and daughter were seeing different ghosts. Mrs. S. also said that she had never seen the couple in the old-fashioned clothes the visitor had drawn the evening before. The woman Mrs. S. had seen looked quite different and was kneeling in front of the man.

The place where the ghosts were generally seen was the west wall of the dining room. This continued into the hallway which led to the bedroom, the bathroom, and the kitchen. This wall, which was visible through an open doorway from the living room, was quite uneven, resulting in four or five different shades. I suspected that the shadows falling across the uneven wall stimulated the imagination of those present and that what they saw were projections of their own minds. This would explain why different people saw different ghosts. The shadows were like large versions of the Rorschach inkblots which psychologists sometimes use. In the Rorschach inkblots, as perhaps on the ghost wall, people can see different images, according to their emotional dispositions. It was consistent with this theory that when the lights in the hallway were out so that the wall could not be seen, no figures were reported.

After the apparitions had dissolved in this way, there was little else of interest: I had been doubtful about the physical incidents from my first hour in the house. When I came, the cocktail shaker was back in place on the bookcase. I checked the case, which was of light metal construction, but no sooner had I touched it than the shaker tumbled down. The bookcase was extremely unstable and it was easy to suppose that one of the dogs had bumped into it and that the cocktail shaker had come down as a result. I asked Gail if she had actually seen the cocktail shaker as it rose into the air.

She admitted she had only seen it after it had left the shelf.
Mrs. S. also only saw it as it was falling.

They reported a few other physical disturbances. For instance, once the light in the living room would not come on.
The family went outside the house and then the light came
on by itself. However, Gail's boy friend told me that this had
happened once before and that they found that a man who
occupied the upstairs apartment had been in the basement
attending to the fuses. The boy suspected that this might be
the explanation for the light events. Also the other physical
incidents could be attributed to normal causes or over-
wrought imaginations.

Mrs. S. probably supplied the first acts in the ghostly
drama and then other members of the family and visitors
contributed the rest—to which she in turn responded. For
instance, she did not herself see the apparition reported by
Annie and then by Gail after the cocktail shaker incident
but only felt it and then fled to the bedroom with the rest.

When Mrs. S. first mentioned her experiences to her
daughter, Gail said she told her mother to "stop it. I don't
believe all this." Then a visitor as well as Mrs. S. said that
"the thing" was after Gail. It was then that Gail saw the
shadows on the wall, heard the footsteps, and had other experiences. Eventually, she became the one in the family who
was most affected. In fact, she thought that one of the figures
went with her to school. Several times she saw it in her home
and outside as well.

Perhaps these imaginary spirits at one stage were reinforced by other kinds. Mrs. S. told me that "whiskey makes
it worse. When whiskey has been around, it really cuts up."

On my second evening, October 7, I left for two hours.
When I came back, Mrs. S. said that "the people" were no
longer on the walls but were walking around. She and the
others also said that there had been a sound of somebody
laughing four or five times.

About 15 minutes afterward, Gail screamed that she saw
a man by the window in the dining room. A visitor said he
saw a skeleton on the dining room wall.

As the time for my departure approached, Mrs. S. became more and more fearful. She said, "I feel I have no
heart, lungs, or organs, just completely filled with fear." She
had been thinking of moving but was convinced that this
would not solve the problem, that the "things" would follow
as they already had followed members of the family out of

doors. She was becoming hysterical, and I thought the best I could do was give her hypnotic suggestions for calm and confidence. These seemed to work, and she entered a peaceful sleep.

I then went to sleep myself but woke up at 5:30 A.M. to the sound of a penetrating scream. One of the visitors had felt (not seen) the "thing." All present had also heard footsteps in the hallway and were amazed that I had not: "Don't you hear good?" I had heard footsteps and other sounds, but they seemed to come from the upstairs apartment. Family and visitors were hysterical and it was only with difficulty that I was able to create some calm. Before I left, I advised Mrs. S. not to have people in the apartment who were so "sensitive." She agreed that if it had not been for the scream, she would not have become so frightened. I kept in touch with the family. During the following days things became more quiet.

A ghost that evaporated even more quickly had been bothering Mr. and Mrs. H. who occupied a farm with their six children near Washington, D.C. At one time Mrs. H. felt that something was pressing down on her as she was lying in bed, preventing her from moving and talking. Later her 19-year-old daughter had a similar experience. They mentioned these experiences to the 16-year-old son, and the same night he had a "seizure" during which he lost consciousness and felt as though he were being invaded by a spirit entity.

The next evening, which was April 1, 1968, the parents, the three oldest children, and a visitor gathered around the dining room table in the hope of establishing some form of communication with the entity. But this did not help matters at all. On the contrary, it brought on two seizures for the son and one for the daughter, the latter becoming so violent that she had to be held down. The three adults felt that they were on the verge of losing consciousness and the family became so terrified that they left the house.

The next day Mr. H. phoned Dr. J. B. Rhine at the Institute for Parapsychology [2] in Durham, asking for help and advice. Dr. Rhine suggested that Mr. W. Edward Cox, a member of the Institute, and I explore the situation. We left the same day. Ed and I spent the first few hours with the family in the recreation room, where they had seen "motions." These resembled the distortions seen above a heated surface such as a road on a hot day. The family associated the distortions with the ghostly visitor. I noticed that the floor consisted of large black and white tiles. If one looked at these for some time, illusions of movement were created. This tendency to interpret normal events paranormally is very common in homes visited by poltergeists and ghosts, whether these are imagined or have some basis in fact. The misplacing of objects and normal sounds such as creaks and cracks all become attributed to the uninvited guest.

After several uneventful hours, we suggested that the family reconstruct the events of the previous night which had led up to the "seizures." Everybody arranged themselves around the table. A 15-year-old son, who had never experienced anything unusual in the house except lack of food and sleep in the recent days because of the upheaval, suddenly clutched his stomach and cried out in an attack of cramps. His sister and brother were startled, apparently interpreting this as a spirit seizure, and now exclaimed that they were feeling the heat and pressure which indicated the presence of a spirit and which came before a "seizure." Probably they and others around the table would have become fully entranced if I had not stopped the proceedings by pointing out that the younger boy only had a stomachache and that this was the sole basis on which the others were concocting a ghostly presence. The boy agreed that there was nothing the matter with him that a good meal could not fix. The remainder of the evening was spent discussing the disturbances in relation to recent family tensions.

The family had been determined not to sleep another night in the house, but at the end of the discussion they were content to go to bed in their rooms, which shortly before they had even refused to enter alone. Later correspondence verified that the ghosts had been permanently laid.

There have been many other cases where the ghost or poltergeist evaporated. Fortunately, it is usually possible to determine beforehand if a case deserves a personal study. As a rule, I make an investigation only if the phenomena have been corroborated by outside visitors or investigators. In a few cases, it is not possible to reach a judgment. The following is an example. In September 1962, I attempted to make an investigation of disturbances in a small house in Portsmouth, Virginia, occupied by a couple and their great-great-grandson. The newspapers had played the case for all it was worth. When I came, the street where the unfortunate family lived had been roped off by the police to keep curiosity-seekers at bay. I was told that the poltergeist had attracted greater crowds than a recent talk by President Kennedy. The family had moved away as much to escape the crowds as to escape the phenomena. However, while I was there, they consented to come back several times for periods of observation. During some of these, there were a few occurrences which the boy or others might have caused normally. Finally, the crowds actually broke into the house, threw furniture out of the windows, and caused severe damage. The family then left for good, and the study had to be terminated.[3]

9

The Miami Poltergeist

On Saturday morning, January 14, 1967, the clerk in the Miami police district that includes Tropication Arts, a wholesale business for Florida novelty items, received an unusual complaint from the manager and part-owner of the business, Alvin Laubheim.[1]

Patrolman William Killin was dispatched, but first he called the complaint room to learn the nature of the problem. Killin later told me that the complaint clerk had said, " 'I don't know how you're going to believe me.' He said, 'You're going to think I'm drunk. You're going to think that the complainant is a kook' . . . And so he explained to me that this person who was calling said that he had a ghost in his place of business . . . going around breaking ashtrays and he said they were just coming up off the floor and breaking. And I told him—I said, 'This guy has got to be a nut.' "

When the officer arrived at the firm about 10 minutes later, he found two people there, Laubheim and Julio, a 19-year-old Cuban refugee who worked as a shipping clerk for the firm. The three of them went into the large room at the back of the building where the merchandise was stored and where most of the disturbances had taken place. The items were placed on shelves along the east side of the room and on three tiers in the center of the room. Behind these tiers were two tables where the merchandise was wrapped for shipping and behind these were some other tables. At the far northeast corner was a large entrance facing a back alley. In the front, south part of the room were two desks, one of which was used by the assistant shipping clerk, Miss Iris Roldan, who was not present that morning. Close to her desk was the entrance to the warehouse which led to the front offices and the room where the merchandise was painted.

The three men walked to the back of the building near the large entrance. While Laubheim and Julio remained there,

Killin crossed the room to the northwest corner, taking a look down the aisles between the tiers. When he had come back to the others, he turned around and then, "I saw this glass fall to the floor and break." It belonged on the shelf behind him and landed in the fourth aisle, in the west end of the room. This was a zombie glass, a highball glass painted with palm trees and flamingoes (53rd event, see Figure 1). "So, at that time, I walked around there and there's a few other things that fell, but I didn't, you know, actually see them fall. And I told Mr. Laubheim that I was going to get a sergeant up there because—well, like I told the sergeant whenever he came up there—I says if I had handed him the report without him being there and seeing it, he would have me up at the Institute or something." Two other patrolmen and the sergeant came shortly after twelve noon. By then there had been four other incidents. When Killin was standing at the desks in the front and south end of the warehouse, looking toward the area where the zombie glass had fallen and where so many of the other incidents had taken place, he saw two boxes which stood on the floor below the south end of the third tier turn over and fall into Aisle 3 (54th and 55th events). "I was standing down by the desk and Julio and Mr. Laubheim . . . were in the general vicinity of the desk, too. And we were all looking over there and they just toppled down."

There were two further incidents and then Sergeant William McLaughlin and Patrolmen David J. Sackett and Ronald Morse arrived. Howard Brooks, a friend of Laubheim, also came. Brooks was a professional magician who was working at an ice show in Fort Lauderdale. Laubheim had asked him to help, in the hope that his special skills might point to a solution. I shall write more about him later. Together with Brooks came one of the performers at the ice show, Miss Brenda Gibson.

At twenty minutes past twelve in the afternoon, the four police officers were in the front area of the room, and Julio, Laubheim, Brooks, and Miss Gibson were on the other side of the three tiers, when a box with address books fell into Aisle 2 (58th event within cluster C on diagram). When this happened, Killin said, ". . . between Ronnie and Dave and I . . . we saw everybody . . . that was in the room . . . each one of them was standing where one of us saw them." Killin said that Morse had noticed the box beforehand and that it was six to eight inches from the edge of the shelf. They

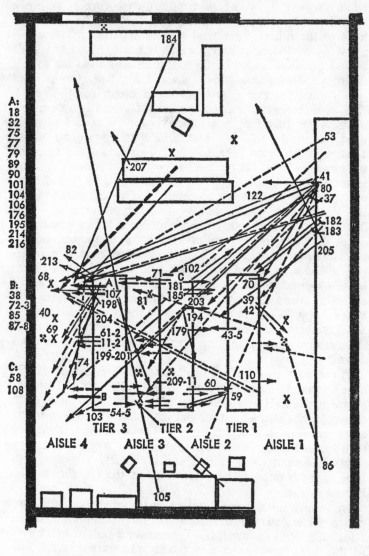

A:
18
32
75
77
79
89
90
101
104
106
176
195
214
216

B:
38
72-3
85
87-8

C:
58
108

Scale in feet

N

tested the shelves to see if vibrations or movements might cause the objects to fall: "We shook every one of them except at the extreme east [the wall tier] and nothing fell." I interviewed Sackett about this event independently and he verified Killin's satements and said that nobody was near the box.

The strange events probably began in the middle of December 1966, when there had been an unusual amount of breakage in the warehouse. Laubheim attributed it to carelessness by the two shipping clerks. The other shipping clerk was Curt Hagemeyer, an older man. The beer mugs, amber-colored glasses with a wooden handle fastened by two metal rings, were particularly vulnerable. They stood on the north end of Tier 3, the shelves closest to the west wall, and would fall into Aisle 4. On Thursday, January 12, Laubheim told me, "I set the glasses up myself and I showed it to the boy and I said, 'Now, if you put them in this position, they are not going to break or fall off the shelf.' And as I turned around and walked to the end of the counter, one of them came down right behind me" (18th event within cluster A on diagram). He had put them, handles down, on the back of the shelf to prevent them from rolling or sliding off. The glass was at least eight inches from the edge of the shelf and none of the employees was closer than 15 feet when it fell.

But this was only the beginning. "From then on, every-

Figure 1. Floor plan of the warehouse area of Tropication Arts in which most of the disturbances occurred. The numbers are only given for disturbed objects which are mentioned in the text and whose locations were reported. The arrows indicate the approximate direction and distance of motions, when they were known, of objects displaced from their original position. Arrows drawn with a solid line refer to movements when it seemed impossible, according to others present, that Julio could have caused them; arrows drawn with a broken line refer to occurrences when Julio or the places where the disturbances took place were not supervised or when it was uncertain where the objects had come from or where they had landed; and the crosses indicate the places to which objects moved whose origin was not known. The heavy lines show movements of three or more objects, as indicated by the letters and numbers. The entrance to the office area and the front of the establishment is in the southeast corner of the room. The back entrance is in the northeast corner.

thing started to happen—boxes came down—a box of about a hundred back scratchers turned over and fell with a terrific clatter over on the other side of the room and then we realized that there was something definitely wrong around here.

"And for three days we picked things up off the floor as fast as they would fall down. It was going on all day—quite violently—but not hurting anything, but things would fall to the floor. We tried to keep it quiet because we knew it would hurt our business, because we are right in the middle of a season—the beginning of a season—and it would draw a bunch of curiosity-seekers and the like, so we tried to keep it quiet for about four days. Then finally, delivery men saw those things happening and people coming in and out would see it happen and word got out and there were more and more people coming in. And somebody suggested that with the glasses being thrown around and with the girls crying in the front from fright, we had better notify the police; so I did."

The other owner, Glen Lewis, was not present as frequently as his colleague and had not observed anything unusual until Friday the 13th when he spent a few hours in the afternoon helping out in the warehouse. He told me, "I was skeptical when they told me about it over the phone, but when I was here and saw things being dropped off shelves right after I had placed them securely, then I knew something was mysterious about the whole thing. Different ashtrays, tumblers, jiggers—dropped, broke [39th, 41st, and 42nd events]. Some of the burnt leather packages fell off the shelves mysteriously [40th event]. I would put them back and they would continue to fall off the shelves" (43rd–45th events).

On Monday, January 23, there were 52 incidents, nearly a quarter of the 224 that were recorded. Laubheim told me, "Monday everything was going down and one thing was happening right after another from the time we opened up in the morning. Now there was a box of zombie glasses which is a tall glass—kind of a shell glass, and the girls paint flamingoes and palm trees on these things and they put them underneath the counter at the extreme right side of the warehouse. My partner went over and said well, in case one of these come out he wants to cover . . . it up . . . by inserting one side of the cardboard into the other so it can't be opened easily [and] . . . so no individual glass can come out the way they had been and breaking. Well, the next thing we knew, there was a terrific crash on the other side of the room and the whole box was lying upside down with all the glasses broken [122nd event]. I was standing at the other end of the counters of the shelves looking in the direction they should have come by; however, I saw nothing pass through those shelves —or pass by those shelves. However, they did—they had to cross my line of vision to break where they did." The box, which weighed about 15 pounds, had moved 24 feet, from the north end of the wall tier to Aisle 4.

Thomas Garcia was probably the first reporter to arrive on the scene. He told me that on Wednesday, the 11th, at twelve noon when he was with Laubheim and Julio at the front of the warehouse, two boxes with plastic fans fell off Tier 2 behind him. He was sure nobody was in that area. Two hours later, when he was at the north end of Tier 3, facing southeast, two beer mugs fell into Aisle 4 from the middle of Tier 3 (11th and 12th events). No one was in that aisle, he said.

William Drucker, the insurance agent for Tropication Arts, arrived on a business call on January 13. He was informed about the phenomena and shown the debris from some of the occurrences in Aisle 4. He later told me, "I went about checking the shelves to see how much they vibrate and I checked most of the shelves and I couldn't see anything but a strong tremor would knock it down because the shelves were rather substantial." He had spent about an hour and 15 minutes and was on his way out the south entrance when he heard a "thud." He turned around at once and asked those present where they had been. Miss Roldan was sitting at the front desk packing, and Mrs. Ruth May was seated behind her. Mrs. May was one of the three artists at Tropication Arts who decorated the novelty items with palm trees, flamingoes, and other Florida scenes. Julio said he was in Aisle 1 with his go-cart, packing merchandise; both ladies verified his position. Drucker told them to remain where they were and examined the room. He found two boxes, tied together, at the north end of Aisle 4, 15 to 18 inches from Tier 3 (32nd event within cluster A on diagram). He checked the tier for strings, loose shelves, and bad or tilted legs but found nothing wrong. He did not think that floor tremors could have caused the occurrence since there were no new cracks, nor could he think of any other physical explanation. Since the boxes were at least 17 feet from Julio and since Drucker had checked the shelves beforehand, he did not think Julio could have caused this event.

It was Miss Susy Smith, writer of popular parapsychological books and a personal friend, who told me about this case and suggested that I should make an investigation. Susy was giving a radio interview on the evening of January 12 about her book, *Prominent American Ghosts,* which she was then completing.[2] The station had an open line so that listeners could phone in questions or comments. One of these was Miss Beatrice Rambisz, another of the artists at Tropication Arts. The third artist was Miss Patricia Wolfe. Miss Rambisz told Susy about the strange breakages—thereby adding a chapter to her book.

Susy responded at once and arrived at the warehouse the next day. Several things took place when she was present which persuaded her that a systematic study should be made. She tried to phone me that evening, but without success. I had been in California and was returning by car across the country. When she finally reached me on January 18, I was in Shreveport, Louisiana. I took a plane to Miami the next day.

Susy had kept a record both of the incidents which took place when she was present and also of the experiences of others in the warehouse. This was of great help in getting a full picture of the disturbances. For instance, on January 13 at 1:50 P.M. Susy was sitting next to the shipping desk at the north end of Tier 1 when she heard something fall in Aisle 4. A box with rubber daggers from the southern part of Tier 3 had moved into the aisle, spilling its contents (38th event). Julio, Hagemeyer, and Lewis were in the warehouse, all in sight of her.

Sinclair Buntin was a pilot at Eastern Airlines who was visiting the warehouse at Susy's invitation. He told me that he and his wife came to the warehouse at about one o'clock, Tuesday afternoon, January 17. They had just arrived when an ashtray fell to the floor in Aisle 4 (68th event). After this, Buntin spent about 15 minutes checking the shelves and making sure that everything was put back from the edges. Around one-twenty, when he was at the front of the room, a box of combs fell into Aisle 4 (69th event). He told me that no one was near that area. About five minutes later another box fell into Aisle 1 (70th event). Again there was nobody in the vicinity and "no contraptions, or strings, or wires or anything that could cause it to move." Susy independently reported that she, Mr. and Mrs. Buntin, and Julio were in

the front and that no one else was present. The box con-
tained plastic calendars and had been on the north end of
Tier 1.

At 1:42 P.M. on the same day a shot glass came off the
north end of Tier 2 and fell into Aisle 3 without breaking
(71st event). Again Buntin was certain no one was near.

Next time, he actually saw an object in motion. This happened only three minutes after the previous event when a
box fell off Tier 3 into Aisle 4 (72nd event in cluster B on
diagram). He was in the front within 15 feet of the box and
could see it between the shelves. No one was in either Aisle
2 or 3. The box "fell at an angle which it could not have
been at if it had just been pushed off . . . about a 30-degree
angle out away from the shelf." He replaced the items in the
box and put this on the shelf about one foot in. A few minutes later it fell again while he was seven feet away (73rd
event). Again, no one was near.

Sometimes glasses and bottles which hit the cement floor
did not break, though they might have been expected to. As
a rule, however, it was difficult to determine whether this
aspect of an occurrence was itself paranormal since the likelihood of breakage depended on which part of the object hit
the floor, on the angle of impact, and so on. Shortly before
two o'clock, on the same day Laubheim came with a newspaper reporter. Laubheim showed him where the beer mugs
had been when the events started, demonstrating their position by placing one on its side with the handle down on the
top shelf of the north part of Tier 3. About five minutes later
there was a loud noise and the beer mug was found in the
south part of Aisle 4, unbroken (74th event). Susy said she
was within four feet of this end of Tier 3 and observed that
no one was near. The mug could not have rolled off the shelf:
"It would have had to fly through the air to reach this position. The shelf was examined as usual." Laubheim then replaced the mug, and Buntin made sure that it was securely
placed: "I picked that one up—propped it up and braced
it," by placing the handle down with the glass part against
a box. A few minutes later it fell again in Aisle 4 immediately below where it had stood and this time it broke (75th
event within cluster A on the diagram). Buntin was again
certain that no one was near.

At about 4:05 P.M., on the same day when Mr. and Mrs.
Buntin and Susy were still present, a Coke bottle, which had
been placed on the top shelf of Tier 3 "to tempt whatever

it might be," as Buntin said, fell to the floor and broke (77th event within cluster A on the diagram). Again, Buntin told me that no one was in the area. Susy said she and a photographer had unsuccessfully tried to make this bottle come off the shelf by shaking the tier.

Several times observers had seen objects start to move. Seeing the first stages of the movements of objects, when no one was near enough to push them and when there was no other explanation, was often highly convincing to those present that some unknown force was at play.

Miss Roldan told Susy that one day when she was talking to Julio, " . . . I saw a big cardboard carton start to move by itself. It fell down. I ran, screaming and crying."

Hagemeyer told me that on January 13 at 1:15 P.M. he was working at the shipping desk when he happened to glance up and saw a shot glass fall to the floor, near the north end of Tier 2, without breaking (37th event). "The glass came out and down—nobody in the aisle—nobody at all—not a soul." It belonged on the wall tier, approximately 15 feet from where it landed. Also, sometime that afternoon he was working with Lewis behind the shipping desk when he happened to look up and saw three small boxes move off Tier 1 and fall to the floor in Aisle 2 (43rd–45th events). "There was nobody in that aisle or the aisle on either side of it . . . there might have been somebody up by the [front] desk, but nobody [close]."

Mrs. May told Susy and me that Monday, the 16th, when she was returning from lunch through the north entrance, she saw something unusual, even for this case. A plastic tray took off from the bottom shelf of the south end of Tier 1, flew to the second shelf of the south end of Tier 2, and then flew back, landing in a large carton in Aisle 2 under the south end of Tier 1 (59th event). At about the same time, a quantity of metal key chains and a rubber alligator which had been in a box on Tier 2, spilled into the same carton where the tray had landed, the box remaining on the shelf (60th event). Julio was at the shipping desk and Lewis at the north end of the wall tier. No one was near.

Howard Brooks, the magician, first came in on Saturday, January 14. He was not in a position to observe anything of significance and, ". . . I discounted the whole thing. As a matter of fact I made a practical joke of it by showing them how—while I was standing talking to someone—I took an article from behind my back and threw it and they all jumped and said, 'there it goes again,' . . . so I wasn't convinced . . . last week. So then Monday morning I came in here and this policeman [Mr. Sackett], who was off-duty at the time, brought his wife in—he was at the other end of the aisle [south end of Aisle 3]—I was at this end and there was nobody in between and two of those cartons—about eight by 10 inches and three inches thick and weighing a couple of pounds apiece, dropped to the floor [61st, 62nd events]. I was able to see them drop through the two-by-four support—the police officer was at the other end—nobody within the area at all." Brooks was standing behind the shipping desk and saw the boxes through the shelves of Tier 3, where they had been standing. He could find no way in which this event might have been staged: "I can't buy this spook theory at this point, but something did move those, and I couldn't figure out what."

I interviewed Sackett independently and also spoke to Mrs. Sackett. Both had seen the boxes fall. The boxes had been on top of each other on the shelf and they came out as a pair: ". . . maybe a three-inch difference in their horizontal outlook . . . maybe three inches removed from the other one," Sackett said, "but they were on top of each other." And so they remained when they landed on the floor. Sackett was certain that no one had been close enough to push or throw the boxes. He examined the area where they had been, looking for evidence of trickery, but found none.

Brooks said that he returned about 1 P.M. on the 19th. Two television crewmen and Mrs. Joyce M. George, Laubheim's sister, were also present. Nothing happened for two hours, and one of the crewmen left. While Brooks was talking to the other one in the front area, Julio came by, carrying a stack of four boxes, when they heard a crash. Brooks grabbed Julio so that the cameraman could get to the area first to investigate. A beer mug had broken in Aisle 4 (101st event within cluster A). No one was near. The mug was the one that Brooks and the television crewman had placed on Tier 3. Mrs. George told Susy independently about this event. She said she was looking directly at the mug when it moved. It "sort of scooted off" the shelf, moving straight out into the air, then dropping straight down.

Once two people, watching from opposite directions, saw an object move. They described this independently. Mrs. George told Susy that she saw an Orange Crush bottle leave the top shelf of Tier 2 (102nd event). It "went way out in the air, then down with a bang on its neck. Then it bounced on its side three times." Mrs. May, who was seated at the front desk at the time, had told Susy and me about this earlier. It took place on Thursday, January 19, at around 3 P.M. shortly before I came. At the first sound—she thought this was when the bottle bounced against the shelf—she looked around and saw it land in Aisle 2. It bounced three times on its side, at least a foot high each time, moving north about three feet. Julio was at the shipping desk and Mrs. George near Aisle 2.

An important kind of observation had been initiated before I arrived: The placing of "decoy" objects in places that had been involved in earlier events in the hope that these prepared objects would be disturbed. In recognizing and seizing the opportunity to entice the effects to continue under such semicontrolled conditions, the local observers were demonstrating a truly scientific attitude toward the events and were setting an example for the subsequent parapsychological investigation.

On Wednesday, January 18, when Susy, Sackett, and Brooks were present, they placed a Coke bottle on the north part of Tier 3. Five minutes later, at 11:40 A.M., when she and Brooks were in the northwest part of the warehouse and Julio was in the north end of Aisle 2, the bottle crashed in Aisle 4 (79th event within cluster A). Susy was not certain where the other people in the warehouse were at the time, but it happened that a friend of Mrs. May, Charlotte Sheffield, was standing outside the back gate looking at Tier 3 when the incident took place. She said that no one was near.

After the Coke bottle had broken, Sackett placed a beer mug, clean of fingerprints, as a decoy where the bottle had been, and roped off Tier 3. He requested that no one go back of the rope. Susy reported: "Then everyone went out for lunch except Julio and me. Someone had brought me food and I was eating at the desk. Julio was standing beside me at the south end of the room and no one else was in the room at twelve noon. I said to him, 'This would be a good time for something to happen.' At almost that instant the sound of a shot glass landing on the cement floor was heard [80th event]. I have heard this enough almost to identify the sound by now. We found it inside the roped area between Tiers 2 and 3, about midway down Aisle 3. It was not broken. We walked back and I sat down, as we discussed the fact that the shot glasses were kept along the east wall at the back. Neither of us recalls seeing one on the shelf in that area that day" [i.e., on Tiers 2 or 3]. Though it was not possible for Julio to have thrown the glass, Susy could not be certain that someone else might not have done so, from the outside through the iron grill of the back entrance.

For the next two events, the back door was closed. Within two minutes of the previous event, Susy said, ". . . there was a loud crash of glass. At the end of Aisle 3, outside the rope, a beer mug was broken [81st event]. We did not recall seeing one of those in that area either. I went under the rope and ascertained that Sackett's decoy beer mug was still in its place on Tier 3. The back doors were now closed. No one was looking in. Julio and I were alone. I walked back to the desk and almost immediately the identical sound was repeated. This time it was the decoy mug breaking at the end of Tier 3 into Aisle 4 [82nd event]. No one was in the room except Julio and me and we were together all of this time, near the desk." (The pieces of the mug were never examined for fingerprints. When Sackett returned later that day the rope had come down and people had been in the area.)

Shortly afterward, Brooks and Miss Gibson came. He, too, did an experiment. He told me that he put out two objects on Tier 3. "There were two beer mugs that we placed as a test because it is not beyond the possibility that somebody could toss something in here and if something crashes here like a Coca-Cola bottle, how do you know where it came from? . . . but when you set it here and it crashes and there is nothing on the shelf, then we have to assume that it is the same one." At about one o'clock, one of the mugs crashed in Aisle 4 (85th event within cluster B). He and Miss Gibson were by the front desk. He was certain that the only people near Aisle 4 were television crews trying to televise the incidents (none of the objects moved when they were filmed). At about 2:20 P.M. the other beer mug fell into Aisle 4 but without breaking (90th event within cluster A). Brooks and Miss Gibson were again in the front area and none of the employees or owners were near the fall.

Between the two beer mug incidents, there were four other occurrences. At 1:23 P.M. when Brooks and Miss Gibson were in the front area, as before, he saw a plastic glass in the air (86th event). However, Brooks said he could not rule out the possibility that the glass was thrown from behind him. (It fell into the middle of Aisle 1, presumably from the south end of the wall tier.)

Seven minutes later, while he and Miss Gibson were again by the front desk, a box of rubber daggers fell into Aisle 4 (87th event within cluster B). He saw one of the daggers bounce on the floor. At about two o'clock another beer mug fell into Aisle 4 while they were in the same position (88th event). They had put out another object, a Coke bottle which they had placed against the back of the shelf in Tier 3. About 2:15 P.M., while they were still in front, it fell into Aisle 4 (89th event within cluster A). For these three last events Brooks was certain that the only people in the vicinity were the television crews.

10

Experimenting with
the Miami Poltergeist

At 3:24 P.M. I was pleasantly startled by the sound of breaking glass. I found a Coke bottle, which had been on Tier 3,
on the floor (103rd event). This event, which happened
shortly after I arrived at Tropication Arts on Thursday, January 19, showed that the case was still active. However, Julio
was close to Tier 3 and could easily have thrown the bottle
without my having seen it. About half an hour later, another
Coke bottle fell, this time without breaking (104th event
within cluster A). I was out of the room, in the front part of
the building. When I returned, I was told that Julio had been
at the north end of the room with two friends. They said that
they had been with him and that he was moving a box and
talking to them when the bottle fell.

When I came back the next morning, Friday, January 20,
a television reporter, Jerome Eden, said he had been telecast-
ing from the warehouse the night before and was alone in the
room when a Pepsi bottle moved clear across the room, crashing 36 feet away in the northwest corner (105th event). No
one else was present except a colleague of his who was rest-
ing in Laubheim's office.

Unfortunately, when I was there that morning, nothing
happened. In some of my other investigations, the phenomena seemed to decrease or stop when I arrived. It is natural
to suspect that this was because somebody was causing the
incidents by trickery and that he was afraid to continue when
he thought he was being watched. However, the police and
others, who had investigated the occurrences in the warehouse before I came, did not jinx the poltergeist. The two
police officers, David Sackett and William Killin, and the
magician, Howard Brooks, struck me as people who were

117

likely to uncover fraud if there were any, yet they had found none.

To discover if the case was still active and worthy of a serious investigation, I decided that my best course of action would be to leave the warehouse to see if this would stimulate the disturbances. Fortunately, Brooks was also present that day. I told him about my plan, and asked him to keep a careful watch in case anything should happen after I had gone.

I had only been away 10 minutes when a beer mug from the second shelf of Tier 3 fell into Aisle 4 (106th event within cluster A). When I came back, Brooks told me that at the time of the breakage, he was at the front desk at the end of Tier 2 close to one of the owners, Glen Lewis, who was at the end of Tier 1. Julio was with Albert Laubheim, the other owner, in the middle of Aisle 1, across the room from where the mug fell. Brooks noted that he himself was the person closest to the area. "There was no one near enough to do anything like to push it, pull a thread, or shove it with a wire [or] tilt the shelf." Laubheim verified that he was with Julio when this incident happened. He was asking the shipping clerk if he would be willing to work the next morning, Saturday. He said, "Let's come in tomorrow; it will be nice and quiet." It was then that the beer mug crashed.

My policy seemed to pay off, and I decided to repeat the procedure, but only to leave for the front of the building. Next time, Susy Smith was also present and she and Brooks remained as observers. At 1:40 P.M., a carton with imitation leather goods fell off the north end of Tier 3 into Aisle 4 (107th event). Julio was just on the other side of the tier. Susy, Iris Roldan, Brooks, and two friends of his were by the front desk. I rushed in and heard Susy say, "Julio, you did it!" In fact, she told me that she had not seen anything suspicious but that Julio was close enough to have pushed the box. Julio staunchly denied this, became angry and upset, and left the room saying he wanted to quit.

It had been clear for quite a while that Julio was the center of the disturbances. Many of those present therefore suspected him of throwing the boxes, ashtrays, and so forth, or of using some kind of magical devices. He was aware of these suspicions and resented them. The direct accusation brought this to a head, and it took some effort by Susy and me to placate him.

Nothing further happened until closing time. At five o'clock, when I was in the outer office with Laubheim and

Curt Hagemeyer, and when only Susy, Iris, and Julio were in the warehouse, all by the front desk, a carton with address books fell into the north end of Aisle 2 from Tier 2 (108th event within cluster C). This time there was no doubt in Susy's mind that neither Julio nor, for that matter, either of the two others could have caused the event normally: All three were with her at the front desk.

Laubheim succeeded in persuading Julio to come to work Saturday morning, January 21. This was the last day I could spend in the warehouse, at least for the present, since I had to be back in Durham on Monday the 23rd for a meeting of the Board of Directors of the Psychical Research Foundation. This was therefore a crucial morning for me because it would hardly be worth my while to return to Miami if the events only happened when I was away from the warehouse.

It seemed that I might be slowly homing in on the poltergeist since the two last incidents took place while I was in the building. I therefore decided to remain in the warehouse that day for as long as Julio was there, in the hope that something would happen when I was present and I could once and for all determine whether the case deserved further attention from parapsychologists.

Whenever something happened in the warehouse, it was the natural impulse for everyone to rush to the place where the ashtray, bottle, or whatever it was had crashed. As a result, it was often difficult to determine where people had been at the crucial time when the event took place. I therefore asked those present to "freeze" in their positions the moment something happened, if indeed something else was to happen. So as not to make Julio feel that he was under constant observation by me, I busied myself taking measurements of the warehouse at the same time that my attention was directed toward him and his activities.

At 11:10 A.M. we heard a crash. Julio was next to Susy at the front desk and Laubheim was in the northwest end of the room. Everybody "froze." At the time, I was measuring south of Tier 3, facing in the direction of Julio but without looking at him. The moment I heard the sound, I looked up and saw him at the end of Aisle 2. He had his writing board in one hand and a pencil in the other. Susy was on the phone next to him. The sound came from the east area of the warehouse and when we went to look, we found a carton with plastic combs that belonged on the south end of Tier 1 on the floor in Aisle 1 (110th event). Julio was about five feet from where the box had been. I examined the box and the area for strings and other foreign objects, but found nothing suspicious. It seemed impossible that Julio could either have pushed the box off the shelf or pulled a string without my seeing this. Only the four of us were in the warehouse. The fall of the box while I was in the room convinced me that a more thorough investigation was called for. I decided to come back to Miami, assuming that the case would remain active.

My regret at leaving the Miami poltergeist, even for a short while, was compensated by the opportunity to discuss it at the PRF Board meeting. I was particularly eager to share my experiences with Gaither Pratt, who is president of the Board, in the hope that he would join the study. As I had expected, this took no great effort. Gaither was as excited as I about the prospect of investigating a poltergeist at the height of its career. We agreed that I should get in touch with him from Miami if the case remained active. When I phoned Susy from Durham on Tuesday evening, January 24, she told me that the poltergeist was as active as ever. I returned to Miami the next day.

This time I was determined, if I could, to move the study into the experimental stage. I felt I could do so without seriously disrupting the psychological situation which might be important for the continuation of the phenomena. The last incident on Saturday had shown that I did not completely inhibit the poltergeist and the stage for experimentation had already been set by the previous witnesses and investigators who had used "decoys" in the active areas. Such focusing on certain areas and objects is characteristic of the poltergeist. In addition to making investigations easier, this recurrent feature may indicate the existence of a lawful process.

From the point of view of a scientific investigation, it would be highly desirable if such a step toward experimental control could be taken. First of all, a target area and a target object placed in it can both be closely examined for magical devices, chemicals, loose boards, and so on. It is obviously not possible to scrutinize a whole room or house with its total contents to the same degree that a small area and a few objects can be examined. Secondly, after a target place has been prepared, the experimenter can keep it under observation much more easily than the whole area where the incidents take place. It was not my plan to prevent access to these areas by the employees or owners. This would have interfered with the normal working conditions in the warehouse and therefore with the psychological situation which might be important for the activities. Instead of roping off the target areas, I planned to reexamine them whenever anybody in the business had been near them. Thirdly, once such an object has moved, there can be no doubt where it came from since the experimenter himself placed it in the target area and can satisfy himself that the object is no longer there. Furthermore, it is possible to make sure of the exact distance the object moved, as well as other details which often remain unknown for objects that have not been examined beforehand. In fact, from the point of view of evidence for poltergeist effects, movements of target objects are often more convincing than movements of other objects that occur in full view of the investigator, since the possibility of fraudulent preparation can usually be more definitely excluded in the former case than in the latter.

To avoid inhibiting the phenomena, I decided to keep in the background and to let the experiments grow out of the use of decoy objects. This had now become an accepted and natural part of the daily procedure in the warehouse.

Nothing happened when I returned on Wednesday, January 25. This was not surprising since Julio was away with a cold. He came back to work Thursday morning. While I observed but without seeming to take a direct part in the experiment, Susy placed an alligator ashtray as a target object on the second shelf at the north end of Tier 3, one of the most active areas in the room. Right in front of it, Julio himself put a cowbell that had been involved in earlier incidents. I checked both objects to see whether there were any attachments or foreign elements that might be used to stimulate an incident. I found none. I continued to check the area periodically, and always when any of the owners or employees were near.

At about two o'clock, an argument developed between Julio and Miss Rambisz. She was the person who originally called Susy and thereby initiated the parapsychological study. During the weekend, José Diaz, who occasionally worked as a medium and was the father of Julio's girlfriend had gone to the warehouse to see if he could discover whatever was responsible for the events. He said he saw a spirit entity that looked somewhat like an alligator, and he placed various objects, such as fern leaves, in different parts of the room as offerings or "playthings" for the spirit so that it would stay away from the merchandise. Since nothing had happened either Wednesday or Thursday, the employees were beginning to suspect that this ceremony had been effective. Miss Rambisz wanted the parapsychological investigation to succeed and was telling Julio that the "voodoo things" should not have been left out since they might be preventing the disturbances. Julio asked, "Well, who is paying for the breakage?" Miss Rambisz replied, "That's Al's business." This discussion was taking place in the north area of the business. Miss Rambisz and Miss Roldan were standing in front of me to my left and Julio was standing at the end of Tier 3 facing us.

I was looking at Julio, who was just about to reply to Miss Rambisz when the alligator ashtray crashed to the floor behind him (176th event within cluster A; see also Chart 1). The cowbell remained in place, so the ashtray either must have moved over or around it. I could discover no way in which Julio or anyone else could have produced this event normally. I had Julio and the others under observation and had examined the target area myself. No one had been near it since my last examination.

The timing of this event was interesting. Julio was generally not very concerned with the destructions from the point of view of the losses they represented to the owners. He also did not particularly believe in the efficacy of Mr. Diaz's preventive magic. Rather, he regarded the suggestion by Miss Rambisz as disrespectful to his future father-in-law. In any case, he seemed quite tense and angry. Some 20 minutes after the breakage, I asked him how he felt. He replied: "I feel happy: that thing [the breakage] makes me feel happy; I don't know why."

I phoned Gaither Pratt and shared these developments with him. He at once made preparations to come and arrived the same evening. On Friday morning, January 27, we went to the warehouse together. I thought that the reason I seemed to inhibit things was because of my identification as a specialist in this area and that therefore Julio felt he was under scrutiny whenever I was near. To prevent Gaither from coming under the same cloud, I introduced him to Julio, not as another parapsychologist, but just as a friend who was curious about the occurrences in a general way.

Shortly after Gaither and I arrived, a spoon-drip tray, an oblong piece of pottery in the shape of a coffeepot, used for wet spoons fell off near the middle of Tier 2 and broke (179th event). I had gone out of the room to fetch some coffee. We asked Julio to put up another tray as a replacement without announcing that this would be a target object or seeming to supervise the test. Gaither and I carefully examined the tray, at the time and periodically afterward.

Nothing happened. It still seemed that I had a hex on the poltergeist. The way I could best contribute to the investigation, it seemed, was by leaving; therefore, for short periods during Gaither's presence in Miami, on this day and the other two he spent in the warehouse, I left the room in the hope that something would happen when he had the situation under observation.

At 3:00 P.M. five minutes after I had left, when Gaither was at his observation point in the southwest corner of the room, the spoon-drip tray crashed into Aisle 2 (181st event). Gaither's report, which he wrote independently, states that when this tray had been put up "Both investigators had examined the replacement object at the time and both of us had periodically inspected it afterward in the course of our individual 'touring' of the premises to inspect objects in different parts of the room and to insure that everything was in normal order.

"During the period preceding this event I was observing the activity in the room and recording a running description of the situation on tape from my position in the southwest corner of the room. This record continued right up to the instant when the tray fell and broke. The point on the shelf where it was standing was not visible from my observation point. I could, however, see Julio. He was working in the south part of Aisle 3 and was separated from the disturbance by the tier of double shelves. I could see both his hands. In one he held a clipboard, and the other was by his side. At the time of the incident he was walking toward my position. No one was in Aisle 2 where the tray fell and broke, and Julio was the nearest person. I was not able to conceive of any way in which the falling of the tray could have been caused to happen in a normal manner." Then, while Gaither was present and I was still away, two non-target ashtrays fell to the floor and broke (182nd and 183rd events).

To assist in the investigation, Laubheim consented to keep the business open on Saturday. Julio and Hagemeyer agreed to come to work.

Gaither and I arrived shortly before 9 A.M. and Julio at

Chart 1. Events Involving Objects Used as

EVENT NO.	OBJECT	AREA PLACED IN	AREA MOVED TO	OBJECT PLACED AND/OR EXAMINED BY	TARGET AREA SUPERVISED BY
176	Alligator Ash Tray	T3 (Tier 3)	A4 (Aisle 4)	W.G.R.	W.G.R.
177	Cowbell	T3	A4	W.G.R.	
181	Spoondrip Tray	T2	A2	J.G.P. W.G.R.	J.G.P.
185	Zombie Glass	T2	A2	J.G.P. W.G.R.	J.G.P. W.G.R.
194	Zombie Glass	T2	A2	J.G.P. W.G.R.	J.G.P.
195	Alligator Ash Tray	T3	A4	J.G.P. W.G.R.	J.G.P.
198	Tab Bottle	T3	A4	W.G.R.	W.G.R.
202	Fanta Bottle	T3	A4	W.G.R.	Glen Lewis
203	Zombie Glass	T2	A2	W.G.R.	W.G.R.
204	Beer Mug	T3	A4	W.G.R.	
205	Sailfish Ash Tray	Wall Tier	A3	W.G.R.	
206	Sailfish Ash Tray	Wall Tier	Near Shipping Desk	W.G.R.	
207	Box Beer Mugs	Shipping Desk	Floor	W.G.R.	W.G.R.
212	Tab Bottle(?)	T3	A4	W.G.R.	W. Drucker
214	Iron Beer Bottle	T3	A4	W.G.R.	W.G.R.
216	Beer Mug	T3	A4	W.G.R.	W.G.R.
219	Zombie Glass	T2	A3	W.G.R.	
220	Beer Mug	T3	A4	W.G.R.	

Targets by Parapsychological Investigators

JULIO'S DISTANCE FROM OBJECT IN FEET	OTHER EMPLOYEES OR OWNERS PRESENT	COMMENTS
4	C. Hagemeyer I. Roldan B. Rambisz	W.G.R. had Julio in direct view.
11	R. Santovania	W.G.R. had Julio in direct view but had been absent immediately before this event.
8	Al Laubheim and possibly others	J.G.P. had Julio in direct view (arms and lower torso).
5	C. Hagemeyer	J.G.P. and W.G.R. had Julio in direct view.
	C. Hagemeyer	
	C. Hagemeyer	
7	C. Hagemeyer	
14	C. Hagemeyer I. Roldan G. Lewis	No investigator present.
4	C. Hagemeyer I. Roldan	W.G.R. had Julio in direct view.
5	C. Hagemeyer	No investigator present.
17	C. Hagemeyer	W.G.R. had Julio in direct view but had been absent immediately before this event.
6	R. May I. Roldan	
5	C. Hagemeyer	W.G.R. had Julio in direct view.
13	G. Lewis	No investigator present.
8	C. Hagemeyer R. May P. Wolfe A. Laubheim	W.G.R. had Julio in direct view.
4		W.G.R. had Julio in direct view.
	C. Hagemeyer	No investigator present.
13	C. Hagemeyer	No investigator present.

about nine thirty. It seemed to us that things had been particularly active when Julio was irritated or tense. Gaither's notes, made Saturday morning, say: "I would say that the atmosphere is much more relaxed [than it was yesterday], so it is doubtful if anything should be expected to happen." But this judgment was too pessimistic. There were two striking disturbances: One when Gaither was alone with Julio and the other when he and I were both there.

Again, I left to encourage the phenomena. At 10:55 A.M. Gaither was talking with Julio south of Tier 2 when he heard a crash of breaking glass in the west side of the room (184th event). He reports:

I went immediately in the direction of the noise, entering Aisle 4 from its south end. About two-thirds of the way up the aisle I found on the floor shattered glass that appeared to be the remains of a large-sized jar. The metal cap was still screwed onto the threaded opening, and the round base of thick glass was still in one piece. . . .

I asked Julio if he knew where the jar had been before it crashed on the floor. He appeared to think a moment, then he led the way to the north end of the room and pointed to a spot on the table near the back door. There we found a circle on the table that was relatively free of dust. W.G.R. and I found later that the base of the jar fitted the circle on the table, so the jar could have been standing there previously.

This incident differs in several important respects from others that happened while I was present. It occurred when Julio and I were the only two people in the room and when we were together and engaged in conversation. I had been watching Julio during the period of approximately an hour since he had first arrived in the morning. During that time I had observed nothing unusual in his actions. The jar was a relatively large one (approximately two quarts). It would have been to invite detection if such a large and "unusual" object had been placed on the shelf among the souvenirs, where it obviously did not belong, and rigged in any way to make it fall.

Assuming that the jar moved from the back table, this was the greatest distance that any of the disturbed objects traveled while an investigator was present. The distance was approximately 22 feet. The circumstances before the event and our close inspection of the situation immediately afterward did not reveal any normal explanation of how the jar came to fall onto the floor and break when it did.

The movement of the spoon-drip tray, placed as a target

object, encouraged Gaither and me to set up experimental areas in five parts of the warehouse. One of these areas was the northeast part of Tier 2, where we placed two zombie glasses and some other objects.

At 11:03 A.M., approximately eight minutes after the breaking of the glass jar and three minutes after I had returned, Gaither and I were standing just beyond the north end of Aisle 4 when we heard the sound of glass breaking in Aisle 2 (185th event). Julio was facing us at the end of Tier 3 close to Aisle 3, four feet away, and the three of us were talking about the case. Hagemeyer was in our view at the shipping desk. He was also participating in the discussion and facing the three of us. No one else was in the room. When we went to the area of the crash, we found one of the zombie glasses shattered on the floor near the north end of the aisle.

Gaither and I had both inspected that area frequently between the time when the glass was placed on the shelf and when it broke. We never found any indication of anything unusual about the situation, and we discovered nothing immediately after the disturbance that could suggest any ordinary basis for the event.

Early Monday morning, January 30, Gaither loosely tied some of the target objects with string so that they would not reach the floor if they moved off the shelves. He thought it would be interesting to see whether objects that we had prepared in this way would become involved in the disturbances. I suspected that this kind of interference would inhibit the events. Therefore, in each area, we placed another similar unattached object. Among these objects were a pair of zombie glasses of the same kind as had broken before. During the morning Julio suggested that it would be interesting to see what happened if an unattached glass were wrapped in plastic. With our approval, he took a plastic bag and placed it over the second glass. Gaither and I carefully examined the glass and bag. The two glasses were 12 inches from the edge of the shelf.

At 2:35 P.M., after I had left the building to encourage the events and when Gaither was in the middle of Aisle 3, he heard a loud noise from Aisle 2. No one was there. Hagemeyer was on the north side of the shipping desk facing south and talking with Julio, who was on the other side of the shipping desk. Gaither found the glass wrapped in the plastic cover lying on the floor four feet from its position on the tier (194th event). Surprisingly, it had not broken. He could find no evidence of how it might have been caused to fall in a normal manner.

Two minutes afterward, while Gaither was still in Aisle 2 examining the circumstances surrounding the movement of the wrapped glass, he heard a noise from the west side of the room. The remains of an alligator ashtray lay on the floor of Aisle 4 (195th event within cluster A). This was a target object which we had placed on the shelf on Tier 3. There was no opportunity for anyone to enter or leave that area of the room without being seen, and the aisle was empty when Gaither got there. He stated, "No physical explanation of how the tray fell could be found."

Gaither left Miami on Monday afternoon, January 30. I stayed two more days, until the afternoon of February 1. Fortunately my presence had become less inhibiting. Of the total of 28 incidents that took place during these two days, in 13 I was present, and in a position to satisfy myself that no one could have caused the occurrence by simple trickery. In the 15 other cases, I was often able to interview witnesses immediately afterward. In 10 of these 15 disturbances, the people who were present said that Julio was not near enough to have been able to cause the incidents.

For instance, on Wednesday, February 1, the first incident was at 9:30 A.M. when I was in the outer office with the two owners, two employees, and Patrolman Mills.

Mills had come in response to a request to investigate a burglary that had taken place during the night. Laubheim's movie camera, some costume jewelry, and petty cash had been stolen. There were also signs of small fires on various parts of the concrete floor. Julio was suspected, but not charged.

At the time of the incident, Mills stood by the open entrance to the warehouse. He turned his head at the crash, and saw Julio at the south end of Aisle 1, facing south. Glen Lewis also immediately turned his head and saw him. Neither observed any suspicious movements. Three boxes from Tier 2 had fallen into the south part of Aisle 3 (209th–211th events). Julio was about 11 feet from the shelf where the boxes had been and no one else was in the warehouse.

The last event was at 3:27 P.M. While Susy watched Julio as he was walking toward the southeast entrance, four boxes next to the door fell across the doorway (221st–224th events:

Not part of diagram). Julio was at least nine feet away and Hagemeyer, who was at the front desk, even farther. No one else was present.

Of the 13 incidents that happened when I was present, and after Gaither had left, there were eight movements of unselected objects or target objects which I had not examined immediately beforehand. Here is one such example. On Tuesday, January 31, at 12:20 P.M., I was in Laubheim's office when there was a crash from the warehouse (204th event). I hurried back (a beer mug had fallen), and, just as I entered the warehouse, there was another loud noise. A sailfish ashtray from the target area on the wall tier area broke in the north end of Aisle 2 with a loud noise (205th event). Julio had just left Aisle 2 and was headed toward the door. Hagemeyer was behind me. When the ashtray broke, I was face-to-face with Julio, so he could not have thrown it at that time. I considered the possibility that he had removed the ashtray while I was outside and then thrown it into Aisle 2 immediately before I saw him so that the crash coincided with our meeting. However, the fragments of the ashtray on the floor were spread in a fan-like pattern with the base of the fan, the area of impact, nearest Tier 1. This suggested that the origin of the movement was in the northeast part of the room, 11 feet from the spot it hit, rather than Julio's position at the southern end of Aisle 2.

In the case of a disturbance such as this, when I had not been able to examine the object immediately before the event, I speculated that some chemical or device that would disappear from sight might be responsible. A substance with this quality which is easily available is dry ice (frozen carbon dioxide). During the morning of February 1, Susy bought a large piece of dry ice which we used to attempt simulating the events. I found an easy and effective method of causing a flat object such as an ashtray to fall off a shelf. If the ashtray is perched over the edge of the shelf, with the ice used as a counterweight to keep it in place, the ashtray will fall when the ice dissolves. On one occasion when I timed this, it took seven minutes for the ashtray to fall, more than enough time for the "magician" to leave the scene. However, some vapors were emitted in the process and a large piece of undissolved ice remained and was found on the floor with the ashtray fragments. We never found any such pieces of dry ice after the disturbances nor did we ever see ashtrays or other objects perched on the edges of the shelves by the employees. I also placed dry ice *under* the objects in the hope that the pressure of the gas would cause a movement. However, they remained in place.

My attention was focused on the target areas, but I also examined the other tiers to see that everything was pushed back from the edges and firmly in place and that there were no strings or other foreign materials. I did this periodically throughout the investigation. I never found any evidence of trickery; neither did Gaither, nor the other investigators. One of these suspected that the incidents took place because objects were perched on the edges of the shelves so they would fall down by normal tremors or when somebody brushed against the objects or tiers. He therefore balanced several objects at the edges of the shelves to see if they would fall. None of them did. When Julio came upon these objects in the course of his work, he pushed them back away from the edge.

The only incident during which I saw anything in motion belongs in the category of objects which moved from non-target areas. At 10:07 A.M. on Tuesday, January 31, I was standing north of Aisle 3 facing south when I suddenly saw three boxes fall into the south part of the aisle (199th–201st events). Julio was behind me, Mrs. May was entering the room through the southeast entrance, Miss Roldan was at her desk, and Hagemeyer close to her. I did not see where the boxes came from but was told that they belonged in the north part of Tier 3. They weighed about a pound each. I could find no way in which anyone might have caused this incident normally. Julio was standing right behind me and briefly had his hand on my shoulder. None of the three others were near the event and no one else was present.

From the scientific point of view, the most interesting disturbances were, of course, the five involving target objects which moved from areas which no one had been near since my last examination. So when I came in Tuesday morning, January 31, I reduced the target areas from five to the three which had been most active.

As before, I made a practice of examining these shelves periodically, and always when somebody in the business had walked by that area or when I had been out of the room. At 9:22 A.M., when I was measuring in the northwest area of the room, an empty Tab bottle, which had been in the target area in the northwest end of Tier 3, fell into Aisle 4, about two feet from the tier in a northwesterly direction

(198th event). I had my back to Julio at the time but was close enough to Tier 3 to know that neither he nor Hagemeyer was near the area at that time, nor had been able to enter it surreptitiously beforehand. I turned my head at the sound of the crash and saw Julio at the north end of Tier 2, seven feet from the target area. Hagemeyer was at the shipping desk.

Julio and I had been joking about the "alligator" spirit Mr. Diaz had seen in the warehouse. At 11:27 A.M. Julio brought a plastic alligator and asked if he could put that on one of the shelves. I said sure, and told him to place it anywhere he wanted to, intending to examine it afterward and hoping that it would become an effective target object. Things in which Julio had shown a special interest, such as the zombie glass in the plastic bag and the cowbell, sometimes moved afterward. Nothing ever happened to the alligator, but as Julio was sitting on his haunches at the north end of Aisle 3, placing the alligator on Tier 3, there was a crash behind him: One of the two zombie glasses—the one that was not tied to the shelf—had fallen into Aisle 2 from the target area on the northeast end of Tier 2 (203rd event). When this happened, I was watching Julio five feet away. He had no contact with Tier 2 and both his hands were occupied: In the right he held the alligator, in the left his clipboard. From my position, four feet north of Aisle 3 and Tier 2, I also had this tier in view and was certain that no one was there. The only others in the room were Hagemeyer, who was at the southwest corner, and Miss Roldan, who was seated at her desk at the southeast part of the room. Neither of them was anywhere near enough to have thrown the glass. Since I was the last person to have been at the target area, none of the three employees could have staged anything beforehand.

This disturbance has an interesting aspect. I wanted to find out if the objects moved directly off the shelves or if they could be made to rise up in the air. I had therefore placed some other objects, including some notebooks, in front of the glass. These were undisturbed, so the glass must have moved up in the air at least two inches to have cleared them.

In the course of the incidents, the stock of beer mugs was depleted. It was a welcome addition to our arsenal when a new shipment arrived that morning. I took one of the mugs and put it on Tier 3 from which so many of its predecessors had perished. In addition, I took a whole box with 10 mugs and placed this on the shipping desk, since full cartons had moved from that area on several occasions. At 2:40 P.M. Julio was between the shipping desk and Aisle 3, walking toward the other end of that aisle, where I was, when he remarked to Hagemeyer—who was by the entrance in the southeast corner of the room—that "we better fill these orders." At that moment, the box of beer mugs, which was five to six feet behind Julio, fell to the floor in a northwesterly direction, that is, away from the direction Julio was walking (207th event). The mugs spilled on the floor and three of them broke. There was no one else in the room aside from the three of us, and I could find no way in which the event could have occurred normally. Certainly, Julio had no visible contact, either with the table or the box when it fell, nor had he or Hagemeyer occasion to interfere with it in any normal way before the incident.

On February 1, my last day at Tropication Arts, five target objects moved: Namely, two soft drink bottles, two beer mugs, and a zombie glass. Two of these events happened when I was present.

At 11 A.M. Susy and I were next to the shipping desk, facing south, and Julio was sitting on his haunches at the north end of Aisle 3, facing us and in partial, but not complete view, when an Iron Beer bottle fell into Aisle 4 (213th event). No one else was in the room. Julio said he had drunk the bottle 10 minutes before and placed it on Tier 3. I examined the shelf and found a moist ring where he said he had put the bottle. It had moved about three feet in a northwesterly direction.

Following the theory that an object which has been disturbed once is likely to become a target again, we took the Iron Beer bottle, which had only lost its top, and placed it in the target area of Tier 3. At 1:23 P.M. it again fell into Aisle 4 (214th event within cluster A). Julio was in the south end of Aisle 3 and I was by the front desk facing him. When we heard the sound, I was looking directly at Julio. He had a cardboard box in one hand and a pair of scissors in the other. The event took place about eight feet behind him on the other side of the tier. There seemed to be no way in which he or anybody else could have caused the incident normally at the time, or prepared it beforehand.

After the box of beer mugs fell, I took one of those which had not been completely shattered and placed it in the Tier 3 target area, instead of the undamaged mug that was there.

Again the theory was that objects which have been disturbed once are likely to become targets again. However, nothing happened to that beer mug Tuesday afternoon or Wednesday morning.

Julio then suggested that we should replace the broken mug with a new one because "maybe he don't like old one," meaning the ghost to which he jokingly attributed the occurrences. I agreed and Julio took an undamaged mug and put it on the shelf, throwing the broken one away. I carefully checked the replacement and could discover nothing suspicious about it. At 2:09 P.M., only a little more than half an hour after it had been put out, the new mug crashed to the floor in Aisle 4 (216th event within cluster A). This beer mug had been placed behind two small cartons and between a Fanta bottle and the cowbell. Like the zombie glass, it too must have moved up into the air to have cleared the obstacles. At the time of this event, I was by the front desk, looking up Aisle 3, where Julio was walking toward me with a broom in his hand. Susy and a visiting psychologist were next to me near the front desk. No one else was present. The mug moved in a northwesterly direction, its place of origin being about four feet from Julio and the direction of movement away from him. Again, I was unable to explain the event normally.

The Miami case was the first in which we had been able to impose experimental controls on poltergeist movements, and it therefore raised the possibility of PK more strongly in our minds than any other case. Later on I shall have something to say about Julio and about the physical and psychological aspects of the case.

In one respect, however, Gaither and I were disappointed in the Miami poltergeist. Neither of us ever saw an object begin its movement. In the next and final case, which I studied with another parapsychologist, we were fortunate enough to see the full movements of several objects.

11

A Demon in Olive Hill, Kentucky

At five minutes past midnight on Monday, December 16, 1968, I was walking behind 12-year-old Roger Callihan as he entered the kitchen of his home. When he came to the sink, he turned toward me and at that moment the kitchen table, which was on his right, jumped into the air, rotated about 45 degrees, and came to rest on the backs of the chairs that stood around it, with all four legs off the floor. It happened in the twinkling of an eyelid. (Roger had been in bed and had gotten up when a glass bowl fell from a bedroom dresser.)

Earlier that evening, after Roger had gone to bed, I had enjoyed a cup of coffee with his parents at that table. It was an ordinary kitchen table, having a wooden top covered with plastic, and metal legs. Roger had not been in the kitchen after we drank our coffee. At the time of the incident, I was looking directly at Roger and was convinced that he did not push the table. I could discover no other way which he or anyone else could have caused this event normally. No one else was in the kitchen. The cups and plates, which had been left on the table, crashed to the floor.

There had been many other unexplained occurrences in the home of Tommy and Helen Callihan and their five children, 14-year-old Beverly, Roger, and two younger brothers and a sister. A teen-aged girl, Pattie, whom the Callihans had more or less adopted, helped Helen take care of the home, a four-room frame house next to Henderson Branch, a small stream in the Kentucky Cumberland Mountains. This area is known for the abundance of clay, and Tommy worked at the local brickworks. The family belonged to Jehovah's Witnesses.

Helen was obviously a conscientious mother and house-keeper, and the small home was neatly furnished and carefully looked after. But this was not where the strange events began. They started in the home of Tommy's parents, John and Ora Callihan. In fact, the phenomena plagued the elderly couple in two houses. It all began in the middle of November when rumbling sounds were heard and the glass broke in a wall picture of Jesus. For several days afterward, a large number of decorative items suffered the same fate, and the coffee table and kitchen table turned over.

Visitors offered various explanations such as "raw gas," the cleansing materials used in the housekeeping, and x-rays from the television. But no one could tell the family how to turn off the raw gas, or whatever it was. Mrs. Callihan had filled two buckets with broken glass and porcelain and four crockery lamps had been destroyed. She and her husband felt they had no other choice but to leave the house, and on November 23 they moved into a house a short distance away on Zimmerman Hill. Like the first one, this was a small frame house. It had four rooms, one occupied by Marcelene, their grown daughter. Roger often visited to help with the chores. When he stayed overnight, he slept in his grand-parents' room.

After a week or so in their new home, Mrs. Callihan one night thought she saw an apparition of a man in the bedroom. She recognized him as a previous occupant of the home they had just left, who had died there about five years before.

Mrs. Callihan asked, "Where are you going?" and the vision disappeared. The next day things again began moving, and Mrs. Callihan speculated that her ghostly visitor was responsible for the events. The man, she said, was supposed to have been able "to raise the knocking spirits." But she was not quite ready to attribute the events to this source since he had been "a good man and a good friend."

By that time, the plight of the Callihans had been public knowledge in Olive Hill and beyond. The area editor of the *Ashland Daily Independent*, George Wolfford, wrote a front-page story which appeared on November 20. A reader had cut this out and eventually sent it to the Psychical Research Foundation.

On December 10, I was able to reach Mr. Wolfford over the phone. He told me he had spoken to neighbors of the family who claimed they had seen the moving objects. When, on the following day, Wolfford called and said that things had happened as recently as four days before,[1] it seemed possible that the case was still active and that an investigation would be fruitful.

John P. Stump, a student in psychology at the University of North Carolina in Chapel Hill, who also worked as research associate at the Psychical Research Foundation, left the next day, December 12, to see how matters stood.

John was hospitably received by the family. By then the crockery and other breakable knickknacks which Mrs. Callihan had salvaged from the other house had nearly all gone. Since the move to the new home, the family and visitors reported, about 90 incidents had occurred, many of them involving coffee and side tables and even heavy pieces of furniture, such as the refrigerator and kitchen table. On some days, nothing happened at all and the old couple would think that the unexplained force had left, but then the disturbances would resume with a vengeance. For instance, there were only a couple of incidents in the first week of December. However, beginning on the afternoon of Saturday the 7th, when four family pictures in the living room turned over, and continuing until eight o'clock the next morning, there were 54 cases of flying objects, tables turning over, and cabinets or dressers falling.

During many of these incidents, Mrs. Phyllis Cranks and her husband Odis, friends of the old couple, were in the house. Mrs. Cranks had witnessed several of the occurrences. When I spoke to her, she impressed me as a reliable and sensible person. She said that at about a quarter past three on Sunday morning, December 8, as she was watching Roger coming toward her, she saw a bedside stand rise up in the air behind the boy, move over his head, and crash to the floor in front of him, after having traveled about 10 feet. Mrs. Cranks had taken the other incidents in her stride, startling and mysterious though they were—some of the pictures and knickknacks had moved 15 feet or more—but so far none of the furniture had flown through the air. "That scared me worse than anything I see," Mrs. Cranks said, "because when I see that force!"

However, everything was quiet when John arrived on the evening of December 12 and things had in fact been quiet also on the two previous days. But when he returned from his motel the next day Marcelene told him that early that morning she had seen some plastic flowers in a bowl on the table of the living room slowly move out and fall to the floor behind the table. This heralded another hectic period for the family. Fortunately, this time John was present during some of the incidents. In fact, there were more than 50 incidents Friday night and Saturday morning while John was in the house. Whatever or whoever was responsible for the antics, he or it was not inhibited by an investigator.

In some cases, John was in a position to satisfy himself that there was no contrivance by any of those present and that known physical forces were not involved. On one occasion, while Roger was standing with his grandparents next to the kitchen stove, and John was looking toward the three people and the sink area which was next to the stove, John saw two bottles and a glass jar containing canned berries, which were standing on the sink unit, move into the sink at the same time, a distance of about two feet. There was no normal way in which the three bottles could have moved on their own. At the same time that he saw this, he had a view of three people. They were standing quietly making no movement during this incident. There was no one else in the area and John could find no ordinary explanation, such as string arrangements, or other means, whereby the bottles could have been made to fall into the sink normally.

A little later the same evening, when almost everyone was in the living room, and as Mr. Callihan entered the room, looking for a place to sit, John pointed to a vacant chair. At that moment the chair flipped upside down. The closest person was Roger, seated about three feet away, also in John's view. Again, there seemed to be no way of accounting for this event normally.

That night, Mrs. Callihan again had one of her strange experiences. She and her husband had gone to bed in the large bedroom, while John was sitting in the living room with Roger. Suddenly the grandmother jumped out of bed, exclaiming that she had seen a white form move toward her. She thought it looked like a "large white Catholic nurse." She seemed to touch the shape and it felt cold. A minute after this, as she was sitting in the living room trying to calm down, a small cabinet in the kitchen suddenly slid forward and a box of candy on top of it fell off. This cabinet was repeatedly involved in the incidents. John, however, was not in a position to see this event. He was more fortunate about a quarter of an hour later. Roger was sitting on a chair in front of the television set in the living room, and John was standing a few feet away looking toward Roger, when he heard a loud crack from the television's area. Roger quickly jumped away and at about the same time a cloth doily and a large plastic bowl fell to the floor behind the set, while the plastic flowers that had been in the bowl remained on the set. Then John saw the plastic flowers slowly move off the set, also landing behind it. Here he found the three objects as they had been before, that is, the flowers in the bowl and the bowl on the doily.

At the same time that these objects moved *behind* the television, a clock that had also been on the set moved *forward*, landing on the floor in front of John, about four feet from the set. Two Chinese plaster of Paris figurines on top of the set remained in place. As before, John found no strings or other contrivances. Again it seemed impossible that Roger or anyone else in the home could have caused the event fraudulently.

Since the case was still active and the poltergeist did not hesitate to perform in front of an investigator, John telephoned me that same night and I made arrangements to go to Olive Hill. When I arrived around eleven o'clock on the evening of December 14, I found 14 people crowded into the small house. The party included John and Ora Callihan, Tommy and his family, Phyllis and Odis Cranks, and John Stump. There was one incident, while I was present. The kitchen cabinet, which had been the focus of so much attention by the poltergeist, fell over again. But I was in the living room, and John was elsewhere in the house, so neither of us saw this.

Tommy and Helen Callihan wanted to get the children home to bed early so that they could have a good night's sleep before school the next day. We had not yet heard about all the events witnessed by that part of the family, so I asked if John and I could come along in order to record these events.

We left the house on Zimmerman Hill at 7:30 P.M. and shortly after were at Henderson Branch with Tommy, Helen, and the five youngsters. The children were a vivacious but well-behaved lot. None of them seemed particularly disturbed or frightened by the unusual things they had experienced. This was not true for the parents. They were both puzzled and frightened, Helen more so than Tommy. This was not surprising since she had been convinced by fellow members of Jehovah's Witnesses that the disturbances in the home of her in-laws were caused by a demon. Tommy also thought they might be due to some evil influence, but was skeptical about the demon theory. I pointed out that incidents of this type had happened often before and that scientists who had studied them believed they were due to natural forces. I said that apparently some people function rather like batteries, giving energy to such occurrences, and that there was nothing bad or evil about this energy. I said that by understanding and studying this energy, we might learn something that could be of value to people. I thought I was gaining some headway with my explanation, and somewhere in the conversation, Roger injected "It's not a demon." But Helen was unconvinced.

The children were sent to bed and the parents, John, and I continued our discussion in the kitchen. Suddenly, at 10:30 P.M. there was a crash from the bedrooms. We rushed in and found a glass bowl from the dresser in the children's room lying on the floor. Roger said that shortly before this he saw a brush on the dresser move a few inches in the opposite direction from the one which the bowl followed. He woke up Beverly, saying that he thought something was going to fall. It was then that the bowl moved.

This incident greatly upset Helen. Until then nothing had happened in her home, and she was afraid that the demon had now changed its stamping ground. Actually, as it turned out, something strange had happened before. Tommy and Helen revealed that late Saturday night, or rather early Sunday morning, when they had returned from an eventful evening on Zimmerman Hill, they heard knocking on the door but nobody was outside. And the preceding Tuesday, three knocks came from the front entrance and also from the kitchen, and again nobody could be found.

Roger now stated, "Something will happen at one o'clock tonight." This, of course, did not add to his mother's peace of mind. But it was only an hour and 10 minutes later, when Roger and Beverly were standing in their bedroom, with Roger close to the dresser, that five objects crashed to the floor: A picture, a perfume bottle, a bottle of bath oil, a bottle of rose gel, and a powder compact. The perfume bottle broke and so did a shaving lotion bottle (which had remained on the dresser). Eight minutes after that, as Roger walked through his parents' bedroom toward the bathroom, a deodorant spray can moved across his path and, at midnight as he was arranging his clothes, ready to leave the bathroom, a large metal closet fell over on a toilet bucket. At this time the parents forgot the demon theory, at least for the time being, and told Roger to "stop it." Roger, too, was becoming upset. He said he wasn't doing anything and wanted to go to his grandmother's. Suddenly, Beverly said, she saw a small glass jar slide a couple of inches on the coffee table in the living room. Roger remarked, "The table will flip over."

All the recent events had happened suspiciously close to Roger. His statements about what was going to happen next added to our suspicion that he was giving the "demon" a helping hand. It was then that the kitchen table incident, which I described at the beginning of this chapter, took place. This convinced me that the case was still of parapsychological interest. Five minutes after the table had jumped, Roger was standing in front of me in the living room with his back to the coffee table. Suddenly this flipped upside down. Again, there seemed to be no way in which Roger could have kicked or pushed this without my seeing it. The movement was as quick as the kitchen table incident. It was a heavy and sturdy table, made by a friend of Tommy's. He said it weighed 80 pounds, and John and I estimated it to weigh at least 60. Beverly was sitting behind the table, also in my line of vision. It is possible that she could have touched it without my noticing it, but I found it difficult to suppose that she could have turned a heavy table upside down in my presence without my seeing it.

I wanted to take pictures of the disturbances, but Helen prohibited this, saying, "No, this has got to stop," apparently implying that somehow or other we were responsible for the events. This opinion hardened and, as we shall see, forced us to terminate the investigation.

The events continued. At 12:20 A.M. when Roger was in the living room close to the television, and I was in the doorway between the living room and the children's bedroom with Beverly to my left and slightly behind, the bottle of rose gel, which had been involved earlier that night, moved away from the dresser. It traveled about four feet and fell to the floor close to Roger's bed. I was facing the dresser when this took place; I saw the bottle in the air and was the person closest to it. After the previous event with this bottle, as indeed after all the occurrences, John or I checked the objects and the area in which they had moved for strings, foreign substances, or mechanisms that might have been involved in a fraudulent scheme. At the same time we watched the behavior and movements of the occupants of the house, especially, of course, Roger, for suspicious actions. We never discovered anything suggestive of trickery.

While John and I could adjust our working hours to the demon's, the Callihan children had to get up for school next morning and Mr. Callihan had to go to work. An attempt was made to go to sleep. Helen put out a rollaway bed for me in the living room and John used the couch. However, when Roger was preparing to go to sleep, the curtain next to his bed moved toward him, entangling itself around his legs. Five minutes later his pillow fell to the floor, apparently without assistance from him, as John was watching the boy from the living room. Things then quieted down and it looked as if everybody might get some sleep when we suddenly heard Tommy calling out to Roger, asking him to fetch his cigarettes. John and I by this time knew that things were more likely to happen when Roger was up and about. We were not greatly surprised when a loud crash was heard and the metal closet in the bathroom again fell over. A minute after that, as Roger was just lying down on his bed, his pillow again went to the floor. He then gave up sleeping in his own bed and moved to the floor of his parents' bedroom.

Some time in the early morning of Tuesday, December 17, the kitchen stove was found to have moved from the wall about six inches and at 8:10 o'clock the last incident took place while John and I were in the house. A bottle with bath oil in it moved from the dresser in the children's room to the floor.

When Ora Callihan phoned sometime that morning to see how things were developing, Tommy told his mother, "You got nothing to worry about now, Mommy, because whatever was up there on Zimmerman Hill is now down here on Henderson Branch."

Tommy was able to take things in his stride; he even said to his mother, "You had two months of it, and now we are going to get two months of it." But Helen was not prepared to stand idly by while her belongings were ruined. Though she listened patiently to my explanation and advice, which was to let Roger and Beverly come to Durham for a short period of time, she was convinced she was dealing with a demon. I suspected that, as in some other poltergeist cases, a contributing cause was family tension. In such cases, the phenomena cease when the members of the family who are primarily involved are separated for a time. To discover the nature of the suspected tensions, I hoped the Callihans would consent to psychological studies of the boy and other members of the family. This would aid the research and hopefully enable the family to understand the strange goings-on and perhaps cause them to stop. However, Helen and Tommy would not consider a visit to Durham, even by the whole family.

Helen had formed the opinion that, far from being helpful, John and I were actually in some way in league with the demon and had brought it from the grandparents' home to theirs. This belief was unshakable. Helen said that the phenomena had just got to stop and that she would therefore regretfully have to ask us to depart. And so at eleven o'clock Tuesday morning, December 17, we had to leave the Callihan family to the mercy of their demon.

A few days afterward we were told that the family had agreed to exorcism by the Jehovah's Witnesses: In the belief that the demon was somehow associated with Roger's new clothes, these were put in a pile in the yard and a match put to them—including what the boy was wearing at the time. Roger, we were told, protested and cried. The poltergeist ignored the ceremony and continued as before. Finally, the family gave up the fight and left for Ohio to stay with relatives. There is no report as to whether or not their uninvited guest went along with them. In any case, when they came back, things had apparently calmed down, since Roger returned to school and his father to the brickworks.

Though our study of the Olive Hill poltergeist was cut short, it was unique in one respect: It is the only case I know of where two parapsychologists saw the beginning stages of movements of several objects. It was not easy for John and me to believe that we were somehow fooled—or fooled ourselves—when we saw these objects take off, with nobody near enough to push them, and when we could find no evidence of strings or other gadgets.

If we suppose that at least some of the poltergeist events I have described in this and earlier chapters are genuine, then what, if anything, can they tell us about man and his world?

12

The Psi Field:
Toward an Explanation

In September 1968, a large number of the world's parapsychologists met in Germany, homeland of the poltergeist. The
reader will recall that Dr. Hans Bender, an authority on the
poltergeist, is the head of the *Institut für Grenzgebiete der
Psychologie und Psychohygiene.* The Institut, located on a
hill overlooking the Black Forest, is the hub of parapsychological research in Germany. On Bender's initiative, Freiburg
University invited the Parapsychological Association to hold
its eleventh annual convention at this medieval center of
learning.[1]

Bender had arranged a symposium on the topic of "Spontaneous Psychokinesis" and asked me to be chairman. It was
at this symposium, entirely devoted to poltergeist investigations, that he first presented the Rosenheim case (mentioned
in Chapter 7) to a scientific audience. The assembled parapsychologists also heard the German physicist Dr. F. Karger,
of the *Max-Planck Institut für Plasmaphysik,* describe the
instruments he installed in the Rosenheim office to discover
whether or not unusual electrical magnetic forces might be
causing the phenomena. He found none.

Bender asked Dr. John L. Artley, professor of electrical
engineering at Duke University, to give the introductory paper to the symposium. This report, authorized jointly by
John and me, concentrated on a certain feature which had
emerged in two American poltergeist cases. The story of this
discovery began long before the Freiburg convention. In fact
it began long before the scientific work in parapsychology
was initiated.

From the earliest accounts of poltergeist disturbances until
the present, witnesses have generally agreed on one point:

143

At the center of the turmoil—whether this be flights of glassware and crockery, levitations of furniture, or knocks and bangs—there is some living person. Often this is somebody at the age of puberty; in any case, the person is rarely beyond the teens. Some have speculated that poltergeists are spirit entities which for some reason attach themselves to a youngster; others have suggested that the incidents are due only to the psychical abilities of the person himself without any outside aid.

I do not know of any evidence for the existence of the poltergeist as an incorporeal entity other than the disturbances themselves, and these can be explained more simply as PK effects from a flesh-and-blood entity who is at their center. This is not to say that we should close our minds to the possibility that some cases of RSPK might be due to incorporeal entities. But there is no reason to postulate such an entity when the incidents occur around a living person. It is easier to suppose that the central person is himself the source of the PK energy.

Though this simplifies the problem of the poltergeist, it does not make it simple. Many questions remain. For instance, how can human beings produce these bursts of energy? Why is it that only some people do this and not others? Does the person intentionally cause things to break and fly? What is the nature of PK energy? I believe we are beginning to unravel some of these problems. The story of my part in the search goes back to another gathering of parapsychologists.

In 1964 the Parapsychological Association met at Oxford University, England.[2] I was president of the PA that year, and the presidential address gave me an opportunity to express some ideas about ESP and PK. The title of the paper was "The Psi Field." The word "psi"—the first letter of the Greek word for "mind" or "soul," *psyche*—is used by parapsychologists as a blanket term for ESP, PK, and similar phenomena. I used the word "field" in the same sense in which we talk about magnetic or gravitational fields. According to the psi field theory, ESP and PK phenomena can be understood in terms of psi fields which surround physical objects. Like known fields, the strength of the psi field is reduced with increased distance from the source. When there is a transformation of psi energy to other energy forms, the total energy is conserved.

While it was well known that poltergeist effects generally

took place only when the agent was somewhere in the neighborhood, no one had actually measured the distance between agent and events. If the psi field is like known fields, it should become weaker with increased distance from the agent. Consequently, there should be fewer disturbances the farther away the agent is.

The first occasion to test this theory against an actual poltergeist case came up in 1967 when I was analyzing the data from the Miami case. All the incidents in Miami, with one possible exception, took place when Julio, the 19-year-old shipping clerk, was in the building. If he was away for any reason, things returned to normal. It made no difference whether Curt, the other shipping clerk, or the girls who painted the glassware and crockery were there or not. It seemed obvious that Julio was the RSPK energy source.

As a rule Julio's exact location at the time of a disturbance was not known. Generally the police officers and the other observers were only interested in knowing whether Julio or anyone else was close enough to have caused the event normally, without bothering to determine exactly where he was at the time. Fortunately, I was present during several occurrences and so was Gaither Pratt. We recorded not only the location of Julio but also which way he was facing, what he was doing at the time, and other such details. In addition, there were a few incidents in which the police and others could recall Julio's position. In all there were 32 disturbances when Julio's distance from the event was known. I divided these into five-foot groupings according to the distances from Julio. There were 10 events when he was from one to five feet away; there were also 10 events when he was from six to 10 feet away; following this, there was a decline to eight events when he was 11 to 15 feet away and to two events in the 16-to-20-foot range: One occurred in the 21-to-25-foot range. The single remaining occurrence was when Julio was from 30 to 35 feet away.

The first question to be settled was whether or not this decline could be the result of chance coincidence. A statistical analysis showed that the odds against chance were better than one hundred to one.[3] Another possibility was that the decline arose as a kind of artifact because of the limited space in which the incidents happened. The main room in the warehouse was about 30 by 40 feet. Thus the greatest distance from which anything like this could happen would be about 48 feet, the distance from one corner of the warehouse to another. Though there were no reports of disturbances either outside on the street or in the neighboring business, a wig factory, attention was naturally focused on the novelty warehouse. It is possible that some of the attenuation effect might be due simply to our not knowing about incidents that took place outside this area. Such an explanation might be plausible for the greater distances, but is less plausible for the shorter ranges. It looked as though the decrease of events with increased distance was a real effect due to the nature of the energetic process.

In familiar energy processes, not only is there a gradual decrease of energy with distance, but different types of processes result in different kinds of attenuations. When light is dispersed from a lamp bulb, the decrease of light with distance closely follows what is known as the inverse function. More particularly, the strength of the light diminishes according to the inverse square of the distance, so that light one foot from a bulb decreases to one-ninth of that strength three feet farther away.

The situation is different if light penetrates a substance such as water. A beam of light directed into a pond of water disappears much more rapidly than if it is pointed into empty space. What happens is that light energy is converted into heat as it penetrates the water. This kind of attenuation is described by another mathematical function, called the exponential decay function. The light decays, or rather is converted to heat, at a rate that can be described as the exponent of a number.

In the same way that we can predict the rate of attenuation if we know whether or not light is traveling through empty space or through some obstructing medium, such as water, the procedure can be reversed. If, for some reason, we are prevented from measuring the light directly as it penetrates the water, we can do so indirectly by taking temperature readings at various depths. If these conform to the exponential decay function, we can infer that the water is exposed to light. The figures also tell us how strong the light is.

We do not yet possess instruments for measuring psi energies directly. But perhaps we can learn something by studying their effects, RSPK incidents. At least that was my hope when I brought the figures from the Miami case to John Artley. John had come to Duke in 1956, one year before me. I first met him at the Parapsychology Laboratory where he assisted in the building of electronic instruments for testing ESP. Later he helped to build instruments for my RSPK investigations. His main area of expertise is that of physical fields, and he is the author of the textbook, *Fields and Configurations*.[4]

John analyzed the Miami data both from the point of view of the inverse function and the exponential decay function. He found that the exponential function gave the better fit.

At this point, it is well to remind ourselves that similarities between data obtained under different circumstances do not always result from the same causes. Even data produced by the same methods and under similar circumstances are not necessarily comparable. For instance, psychologists are aware that low performances in IQ tests obtained from children in the ghetto may be artifacts due to environmental conditions and not due to any innate learning capacity, though this is what the IQ test is supposed to measure. Poltergeist incidents occur in very different situations from those in which physicists and engineers measure exponential decay, and crucial pieces of information are lacking or uncertain, such as the mass and chemical composition of a moving object, its trajectory, etc. In some cases, we knew a little about velocity and weight, and I shall say something later about the relationship of these to the attenuation curves. We cannot *conclude* anything on the basis of the similarity between the two types of curves. But we can examine these curves and other patterns in the hope that they will suggest hypotheses which then can be put to test in future investigations or experiments.

If we are dealing with an exponential decay function, then in one respect there would be method in the poltergeist madness. Poltergeist disturbances would then conform to an old and established rule: The principle of conservation of energy. It is easy to see why this is so. In poltergeist disturbances kinetic energy is produced. If the energetic process is similar to known types, then the creation of kinetic energy should result from the expenditure of some other form of energy and the number of such energy conversions should diminish with increased distance from the source. In other words, we should expect our data to follow a curve such as the exponential decay function, rather than the inverse function which describes the dispersal of energy in empty space and not its conversion to some other form of energy.

To see if this was a real effect, I needed to know if it would hold up in other cases. The first poltergeist investiga-

tion I took part in was the Seaford case, explored by Gaither
Pratt and myself, and described in Chapter 2. I went back in
my files and found the figures showing Jimmy's distances
from the events. In that case there were no incidents beyond
30 feet. The number of occurrences for six groupings was
19, 9, 12, 5, 2, and 1. Again the decrease was statistically
significant, and again John Artley's analysis showed that the
exponential function gave a better fit than the inverse function.

It was the figures from these two American poltergeists
which John and I presented at the conference in Freiburg
University. As I had anticipated, the finding created a great
deal of interest. Bender had read our paper beforehand and
was able to make a similar analysis of the Rosenheim case.
It increased my confidence in the Miami and Seaford figures
when Bender told the group that the Rosenheim poltergeist
showed a similar attenuation pattern.

I had only been back from Europe three months when the
Olive Hill case erupted. This showed the most marked attenuation effect so far. The figures for the three distance
groupings up to 16 feet were 94, 12, and 1. Again the data
followed the exponential decay function. I now looked at
two earlier cases I had not yet analyzed, the Newark and
Indianapolis poltergeists. In the Newark case, the exponential
function gave the better fit, while the figures from Indianapolis followed the inverse curve more closely. However, in
that case, it is possible that the results were obscured by dual
agency. In addition to the main agent, Mrs. Beck, her mother
may have played the role of a secondary agent. If Mrs. Gemmecke caused some of the poltergeist incidents, this could
easily obscure the attenuation pattern based on the distances
between her daughter and the events.

I mentioned before that similar results are sometimes due
to different causes. It occurred to me that the poltergeist
curve could arise as an artifact which shows nothing about
the nature of the process. For instance, if the poltergeist person spends most of his time in rooms with many movable
objects and less time in rooms with few objects, the result
might be that several objects are disturbed in his immediate
vicinity and fewer at greater distances from him. For instance, if Jimmy Herrmann spent most of his time in the dining room, which had shelves with plates and cups, and less
time in the recreation room where there were fewer such
objects, and if his RSPK powers were about the same under

both circumstances, there would be more RSPK incidents close to him simply because there were more objects to be affected by his RSPK capacities in the dining room and because he spent more time there than in the recreation room. In order to explore this possibility, I not only measured Jimmy's distances from the disturbed objects but also the distances of Lucille, his sister, to the objects which had moved. The activity of the two children in the home seemed similar with respect to their proximity to movable objects. There was no evidence of any attenuation pattern with respect to Lucille, nor did Mr. and Mrs. Herrmann show any. Similar studies were carried out for the Newark and Indianapolis cases. In all cases, the only persons whose positions with respect to the incidents showed the attenuation pattern were the ostensible RSPK agents. It seems that the decrease of incidents cannot be easily explained away in terms of some kind of artifact and that it may reflect something real in the RSPK process.

It was the Miami poltergeist which pointed to the lawful basis of RSPK occurrences. But this case also showed a feature which seemed completely meaningless. In fact, it seemed to contradict the attenuation pattern I mentioned before and again raised the possibility that this pattern was an artifact with no real meaning. This feature has to do with another kind of attenuation.

If there is such a thing as a psi field and if this field is strongest near the agent, we should expect that objects of the same weight which are close to him would move longer distances than objects farther away. There were not enough movements of large objects in the Miami case to show a reliable trend. If we consider the distances traveled by the smaller items, such as the beer mugs and ashtrays, which weighed approximately the same (a pound or less), we find that *the shorter movements were close to Julio, while the more distant objects moved farther.*

This made no sense at all. As in other situations when I have come up against a research problem I could not solve myself, I went to the experts. Another electrical engineer, Dr. William Joines, associate professor at Duke, had become interested in the work. I showed John Artley and Bill Joines a graph of the incidents giving the distance from Julio of each event, the length the object moved, and the direction it took. One of the striking features of this graph was that the directions of movement did not seem random. In the 23 cases where the direction in relation to Julio was known, this was counterclockwise in 18 and clockwise in five, a difference that has odds of more than 50-to-1 against chance.

One way to explain this is to suppose that the psi field is in circular motion around the agent. John and Bill observed that this is characteristic of vortex fields, such as whirlpools where the water rotates around an axis. Vortex fields are often found in nature, for example, they exist around stars and planets. Now if the movements of the objects are produced by a vortex field, this will not only influence their directions but also the distances they move. Since the angular velocity is higher farther away from the center of the field, an object located in that part of the field and affected by it for a certain period of time will move farther than objects closer to the center. (It may also move more rapidly—a prediction that can be tested when we have instruments to record and measure the flights.) Though the strength of the field may be greater toward the center so that more objects are affected here than farther away, the distances they travel are likely to be less.

In the four other cases I have analyzed—the Indianapolis, Newark, Olive Hill, and Seaford cases—the movements tended to be clockwise in relation to the agents, but only in the Newark case was this tendency statistically significant. In each of these cases, there was a gradual increase in the distances the objects moved up to 16 feet, when the effect disappeared.

Another poltergeist characteristic is the selection of special objects and areas for attention. This apparent focusing of the RSPK force is similar to a feature that has emerged in ESP tests. Some parapsychologists, including Drs. J. Gaither Pratt and Milan Ryzl have noticed that cards and objects which are used as ESP targets sometimes seem to have a special stimulating property [5] which makes them stronger ESP stimuli than others. Similarly, many of the poltergeist cases, including a large proportion of the early studies, involved one or more objects which were repeatedly disturbed by the poltergeist force. It was this observation which led to the experiments with target objects and target areas in the Miami case. Sometimes, it seems that this preference may be the result of a special psychological significance which the object may have for the poltergeist person. I shall give some examples of this in Chapter 13. At other times, it looks as if the object somehow becomes charged with a PK potential (or perhaps just becomes more sensitive to PK) for other reasons, for instance, as a result of having been disturbed or, possibly, as a result of having been touched by the poltergeist person. For instance, an Iron Beer bottle moved shortly after Julio had emptied it. So far, however, no one has come up with a theory to account for this phenomenon. All we can now say is that it seems to be a poltergeist characteristic which cannot easily be explained away. It does not appear to be an effect of the proximity of the poltergeist person. Once an object has become endowed with this special force or sensitivity, it may move even though the person is far away. For instance, the second time the male figurine moved in the Herrmann household, Jimmy was standing with his mother and sister in the hallway 15 feet from the figurine. This, incidentally, was also an example of an object relatively far away from the agent which then moved a considerable distance. The figurine broke against a piece of furniture 10 feet from its place.

Though we do not understand the nature of the focusing effect, it may help us explain another peculiarity of the poltergeist. Sometimes the poltergeist person is not at home when incidents take place. There may have been some examples of this in the Seaford case, but we could not be sure whether in fact Jimmy was away from the house, or perhaps entering or leaving at the time of the disturbances. In the Miami case, Mr. Jerome Eden, the TV reporter, said that one time when he was alone in the warehouse, the employees and owners having left for the day, a Pepsi bottle moved clear across the room, crashing 36 feet away. Also in the Olive Hill case there were reports of events taking place though Roger was absent. In all these cases, somebody else was at home when the object moved. It seemed as if the poltergeist person somehow imbued the objects with a special property or quality which made them sensitive even to the weak kind of PK any of us may be producing.

There is a great deal of speculation in the picture I have given of the energy responsible for poltergeist effects. And there is much else which I am not even prepared to guess about. But I think that one thing is becoming clear and this is that the poltergeist is a much less erratic creature than we have believed it to be. I hope there are enough indications of lawful processes to cause other venturesome scientists than those who have already collaborated in this work to take a close look at the poltergeist. It is clear, I think, that physicists and engineers will have something important to say about the poltergeist and the poltergeist, in turn, may add to their knowledge of the energies at play in the world. To make this work effective, hopefully we will obtain recording and detecting instruments needed to give a more complete picture of poltergeist effects.

It is natural to look to the physical sciences for help in unraveling the poltergeist enigma since the effects involve physical objects which are disturbed at a certain location in physical space and at a certain moment in time. This should not make us overlook the fact that at the center of the occurrences there is always some person, a living human organism. The poltergeist therefore also becomes the subject matter for the sciences which deal with people. In the next chapter I shall take a look at the poltergeist person from the point of view of the psychologist and the psychiatrist.

13

Poltergeist and Personality

After the alligator ashtray had broken, while Julio and Mrs. Rambisz were arguing, he seemed much less tense and angry. I asked him how he felt. "I feel happy; that thing [the breakage] makes me feel happy; I don't know why." This was the first occurrence that day, in fact the first after my return from Durham. During my earlier visit, on the morning of Friday the 20th, there had been another long period of inactivity, and I asked Julio how he felt. He said, "Now I am nervous because nothing happens." On the other hand, after a series of four incidents in the early afternoon of the 27th, Julio looked unusually cheerful and I asked him how he felt. He replied, "I feel good. I really miss the ghost—," he caught himself, "I mean—not the ghost, but I miss it when something doesn't happen."

Dr. Gardiner Murphy, the psychologist and former president of the American Psychological Association, says in his book, *Personality*,[1] that "the ultimate elements in personality structure are the needs or tensions." A tension is a concentration of energy in a particular tissue or group of tissues. These tensions are connected and spread from one region to another in the organism. "The result is a *tension system* whose lawful structure is expressed in terms of the relative strengths of tensions and the relative rigidity of barriers to their diffusion." It seems that for Julio the poltergeist breakages in a literal sense "broke the tension."

But all of us have needs and tensions, and yet we do not make ashtrays fly or produce unexplained knocks or lights. Is there something special about poltergeist people that will help explain their strange power? To help answer this question, Julio was invited to Durham for a program of psychological tests and other studies.

Dr. John Altrocchi, who had gone to Clayton with me and

153

had participated in the psychological studies of the Indianapolis and Newark disturbances, was now professor of medical psychology and associate professor of psychology at Duke. John's specialty is the MMPI test (Minnesota Multiphasic Personality Inventory). We gave this to Julio on February 10, 1967. It was clear that he was not a very happy and content person. John found evidence of "anger, rebellion, a feeling of not being part of the social environment, a feeling that he doesn't get what is coming to him and lack of strongly pleasant experiences in life."

Other psychological tests were given under John's supervision by Dr. Randall T. Harper, a psychology intern at Duke. Julio's IQ score was close to average, but cultural and language difficulties may have hampered his performance. Harper used three other standard psychological techniques. One was the Thematic Apperception Test (TAT) which consists of a series of pictures of people in ambiguous situations, about each of which Julio was asked to develop a story. He was also given the Rorschach inkblot test and told to state what he saw in the blots. The TAT and Rorschach are called projective tests; that is, people tend to project their emotions, beliefs, fantasies, and so forth, in the way they interpret and perceive the pictures. Finally, he took a word-association test consisting of a list of words, to each of which he responded with a different word. The time it takes a person to respond and the word he uses may tell something about him.

An associate of Murphy and an active research worker in parapsychology is Dr. Gertrude Schmeidler, professor of psychology at the City University of New York.[2] Dr. Schmeidler has developed a method for investigating haunted houses. She has also assisted in psychological studies of poltergeist personalities. She found that Julio's responses indicated "(a) early family tenderness, love, and training in high moral standards; (b) feelings of unworthiness, guilt, and rejection; (c) development of the personality traits of passivity and inaction; (d) development of inner feelings of detachment and unhappiness; (e) dissociated tendencies, especially in relation to expressing aggression. The lack of feelings of inner worth and the passivity would then naturally combine to a resentment of the need to work, especially because of lack of confidence in a happy, successful outcome of the work. The resentment would be exacerbated by a boss who was seen as phony and cheating, that is, a father figure who demands virtue but does not deserve it because of his own low moral standards. The outcome of the dissociated tendencies toward aggression, the moral resentment of the work situation, and the unhappiness in the work would then seem to be dissociated (poltergeist) aggression against the boss's possessions accompanied by outward compliance with the work demands."

In this report, the words, *"seen as* phony and cheating" must be emphasized. In the course of the many hours I spent in the business, Laubheim gave the impression of being a kindly, even warm-hearted person. He seemed to be liked by the employees, several of whom had worked for him for many years. Laubheim took a remarkably relaxed view of the losses caused by the destruction and general confusion in the warehouse and treated the phenomena with equanimity and even humor. He did not seem the kind of person who would be unethical in business dealings. I knew Lewis less well since he was present less often. He seemed to be a more distant and business-oriented person and was not liked by Julio.

Dr. Harper's observations were similar to Dr. Schmeidler's. He found that Julio had a vey rich fantasy life associated with changing emotions. Of these, "the most notable are the many examples of aggressive feelings and impulses which are disturbing and unacceptable to him. He prevents the direct expression of these feelings. Indeed, he not only controls the expression of aggressive impulses which at base could be sadistic and quite destructive, but he also feels it necessary to even control impulses of a more assertive, as distinct from aggressive, nature. This is not to say that Julio is not often aware of these feelings. Much of his fantasy must be filled with aggressive themes and its imagined expression and he is often aware of his anger. There is little self-understanding in relation to these feelings and there may very likely be a sense of personal detachment from them. Since they cannot be expressed or acted upon in any direct way, they are a source of difficulty to him. The feelings themselves remain internal and diffuse. The outward behavior would typically be socially very conventional." [3]

Several of the stories Julio gave to the TAT pictures showed grown children in relation to parents and parental figures. In these stories the younger person is unable to achieve independence or to communicate his need to do so. There are feelings of guilt, a wish for independence, and anger over the inability to achieve this. The response to parental control is "fantasied achievement or aggression or a more passive-aggressive stance in which he appears to capitulate but in some indirect manner manages to show some hostile resistance." Since these methods do not solve the problem, and do not lead to feelings of accomplishment or independence, this adds to the anger, results in attempts to withdraw from the negative feelings, and produces feelings of guilt.

Sometimes the poltergeist incidents begin at a time which is significant to the person. The first occurrence in the home of Ernest Rivers happened on his birthday; and, in Mrs. Beck's house, on her father's birthday.

There had been problems in Julio's home in the beginning of December, some 10 days before the incidents began in the warehouse. His stepmother apparently wanted Julio to move out, which he finally did at the end of the month. Some months before then, in October, he began having nightmares which became increasingly worse during November, December, and January. In these he would get killed and even sometimes see himself at the funeral. When Julio told me about this, he also revealed some of his attitudes to life and death. He told me he liked to go down to the sea at night or along the train tracks. It was as if "some force" made him do this. I asked him if he was not afraid of getting run over. "I am not afraid of dying—sometimes I hope I die. . . . I don't mean too much to . . . my family . . . because I don't have my mother and my grandfather." [4]

Julio's unhappiness not only resulted in anger but also in suicidal tendencies. As we shall see shortly, these nearly succeeded. But the anger also led to guilt and the guilt to a need for punishment. And this need was not satisfied by the poltergeist disturbances. Julio tried to deal with it in another way.

As I mentioned in Chapter 10, Julio was suspected of having broken into the warehouse on the night of January 30. An old portable typewriter, a movie camera, some pieces of costume jewelry, and some petty cash had been taken. Everything pointed to Julio. His car had been seen outside the business during the night, and two young men were carrying a box to it. Al Laubheim and Glen Lewis did not press the charges, but the police sergeant reported to the newspapers that Julio had confessed to the theft. The sergeant also claimed that Julio had told him he caused the incidents in the warehouse by trickery. This supposedly was done by a system of threads and by perching the items at the edges of the shelves so that vibrations from jets passing overhead caused

them to fall. I later learned from Susy Smith that the officer never examined the warehouse. However, Al Laubheim
arranged a meeting with him and Julio in his office the morning after the newspaper article appeared. Julio told the detective that he was lying and that he, Julio, had not confessed
to having caused the disturbances fraudulently. Laubheim
said that the sergeant did not deny the accusation and only
became red in the face.

If it was punishment Julio wanted, his plan did not succeed since the charges were dropped. A few days later he
was more successful. He was at a jeweler's looking for a ring
for his fiancée, and he walked off with a ring. The jeweler
called out, and a policeman who was passing by arrested
Julio. This resulted in six months in jail. Susy Smith and I
tried to help in his defense by offering the results of the psychological tests, but neither Julio nor his counsel responded.
When he was out of jail, we made arrangements, with the
help of Dr. John Artley and others, for financial support so
he could attend Durham Technical Institute. This would give
him an education in electronics, which interested him. It
would also give him an opportunity for psychotherapy by the
psychologists who had already examined him. And it would
enable us to continue our research with him. But Julio preferred to pursue his tortured life in Miami. He changed jobs
frequently, and sometimes reports would filter back about
moving objects. In June 1968 he married and nine months
later had a daughter.

Then, on the evening of March 3, 1969, there was a
holdup in the gas station where Julio was working. He refused to hand over the money and one of the robbers shot at
him but missed. Julio tried to take the gun away but a second
bullet hit him in the shoulder and a third in the chest, tearing
the aorta and nearly killing him.

After this encounter, wherein Julio nearly succeeded in
getting himself killed, apparently both his psychical and physical life settled down. In the meantime Susy Smith left Miami,
and it was more difficult for me to keep in touch with Julio.

The personalities of the other RSPK agents who have participated in psychological studies differ in many ways from
Julio's, but in all cases there is evidence of tension, mostly
anger, which cannot find ordinary ways of expression.

Poltergeist disturbances often erupt in the home of the central person and seem to express family tensions. In a TAT
story by one RSPK agent, the theme was hostility between

father and son. The Rorschach responses had images of rockets, bombers, and fighting animals. However, the aggression which gave rise to such images was not experienced by the person as coming from himself but as existing in outside situations. There was a barrier in his personality which diverted emotions directed against the parents so that he was unaware of his hostility. Perhaps this block was a factor in causing the tensions to be directed into his physical environment. Here they could show themselves for what they were by the breakages and turmoil created with the parents' belongings.

Another agent had lived through a great deal of violence between his parents. Apparently this resulted in a complete denial of even having angry feelings, let alone showing them. The poltergeist destructions seemed to be expressions of tensions which could find no other outlet.

The red thread running through most of the cases I have investigated, or am familiar with, is tension in family situations or extensions of them, as in the Miami warehouse. Sometimes the objects that break express this theme. In one home where the main conflict was between mother and child, two phonograph records broke. One of these had the title "My Mother"; the other was "At Home With Me." The latter was one of four records which belonged to the mother, out of a rack of 35. In another case, two of the objects most often involved were figurines of a male and of a female belonging to the parents. The breakage of these figurines perhaps expressed the agent's hostility toward his parents. In several of the cases, it also seemed that the direction of movements of flying objects reflected the tensions. The objects often moved toward rooms belonging to the person who was the focus of aggression.

In general, we find hostility in the agent which cannot be expressed in normal ways, the main target for the anger being people with whom he is associated on a daily basis.

But this cannot be the whole story. For each poltergeist personality there must be thousands with similar problems who lack this capacity. There must be something else which eludes the psychological tests.

Perhaps, I thought, the electroencephalograph (EEG) which measures brain waves would tell more. Dr. Walter D. Obrist, professor of psychiatry at Duke, is an EEG expert. He has given EEG examinations to two poltergeist boys, Julio and Ernest, the boy who was the center of the Newark disturbances (Chapter 4). Ernest's record was characterized "by an intermittent 10.0 to 10.5 cps. [cycles per second] occipital alpha rhythm, averaging 30 to 50 microvolts, and bilaterally symmetrical. This rhythm extends to the parietal and posterior temporal regions. The frontal and anterior temporal areas revealed low voltage fast waves mixed with irregular low-to-moderate amplitude theta activity (4–7 cps.)."

Obrist's general impression was that Ernest was within the normal limits for his age. However, there was one somewhat unusual feature: A burst of 14-cycles-per-second positive spikes occurred during a short portion of the record when the boy was drowsy. If this effect had been more pronounced, it would have indicated a form of epileptic discharge which is found in adolescents who have behavioral problems, including dissociative episodes. However, in Ernest's case the effect was too small to give anything but the barest suggestion.

When the next opportunity came for an EEG study of a poltergeist agent, I wondered whether this feature would again show up. Obrist's description of Julio's record follows.[5]

This is a low voltage tracing with intermittent alpha rhythm in the posterior region of approximately 10 cycles per second. Low voltage beta waves are also seen, but these are not highly rhythmic. Over the precentral and frontal areas, irregular low-to-moderate voltage theta waves appear that become accentuated with drowsiness. There is a good bilateral symmetry of all frequencies, and no evidence of seizure discharges during waking sections of the record.

A fairly long sample of light sleep recording was obtained, which progressed to the spindle stage, and again, there was no evidence of seizure patterns and the bilateral symmetry was good. Three and a half minutes of moderately vigorous hyperventilation resulted in a slight buildup of slow activity with no unusual or pathologic manifestations. Recovery from the overbreathing was rapid. At the end of the examination, the subject was asked to recall certain previous events by Mr. W. G. Roll. No abnormalities were seen at this time; in fact, the above mentioned anterior theta activity was noticeably reduced, indicating that level of alertness is a factor in its production. No focal EEG signs were observed either awake or asleep.

This is perfectly normal tracing for age 19, awake and asleep and during hyperventilation. Some mild anterior slowing (theta activity) was observed, which is not regarded as unusual for this age, and was shown to be related to level of arousal (greater when relaxed or drowsy). No focal or epileptic patterns were seen at any time.

There was no indication of the fourteen per second positive spikes briefly seen in Ernest's record.

The fact that the EEG record did not show anything unusual is itself interesting, all the more so because Julio apparently still possessed his PK powers. But more about this later. It was also interesting that when Julio imagined he was back in Miami, and that the events were happening, faster brain waves took over. Other than this, the EEG did not show any patterns which might give a clue to the phenomena.

Since poltergeist incidents often occur around puberty or adolescence when there are marked changes in the body's endocrine system, perhaps hormone secretion is connected with the events. I therefore arranged for Julio to have a thorough checkup by Dr. Harry T. McPherson, associate professor of medicine at the Division of Endocrinology at Duke.

Julio had a slight case of acne and a sore throat but was otherwise healthy. The only slightly abnormal aspect of the endocrine system was with respect to the adrenals. Julio said he had had an excessive appetite in the past year. He now weighed 167 pounds, which is excessive for his height. It also came out that Julio had had no less than three childhood diseases—chicken pox, measles, and mumps—during a recent three-month period. McPherson noted that the termination of this period coincided with the onset of the phenomena in the warehouse. But again, we have no idea how this could have any bearing on the incidents.

Since the psychological situation in the area where poltergeist events erupt appears to have some bearing on them, perhaps if we knew what the agent was doing at the time of an incident, this might give a clue about psychological or physiological factors connected to the occurrences. An analysis of six poltergeist cases shows that RSPK incidents are only likely to happen when the agent is awake. There are generally no phenomena when he is reported to be deep asleep. Only in a few cases was he lying in bed and in still fewer he was apparently asleep. Not only is he usually awake but he is generally active, for instance, busy with his job, doing schoolwork, eating, walking somewhere, or talking about the disturbances. Making an educated guess about the agent's brain waves on the basis of his activities at the time, I will suggest that they are probably characterized by high-frequency patterns (such as beta waves) which are associated with mental activity rather than the slower waves (alpha and theta) which predominate when people are relaxed.

Research at the Psychical Research Foundation and elsewhere suggests that ESP reception is best when the person is in a state of relaxed awareness as shown by a predominance of the alpha brain wave. However, the transmission of ESP messages may involve a different state, as suggested by tests where highly emotional situations seem to be easiest to grasp by ESP and by spontaneous cases of apparent ESP in real life situations where accidents, sickness, and other traumatic situations are conveyed most easily. The same may be true for PK and RSPK. High-frequency brain waves may be associated with the RSPK process.[6]

14

PK and Consciousness

It was Julio's first evening of PK tests at the Institute for Parapsychology in Durham. Dr. J. B. Rhine, head of the Foundation for Research on the Nature of Man, of which the Institute is part, had offered the use of the PK instruments there so that we could find out if Julio could control his PK enough to influence them.

The opportunity to test the PK of a poltergeist person appealed to several of the younger members of the FRNM staff. These were Robert Brier and his wife Henie, John Stump, and Charles Honorton. We began with the rotating dice machine. This consists of a plastic rectangular container, four by four by 24 inches, with two dice. An electric motor makes the container rotate, causing the dice to tumble from one end to the other, hitting a number of baffles on the way. After one turn, the container stops automatically for a moment so that the faces of the dice can be recorded. There is no manual interference with the machine during a series of trials other than turning the switch which starts it. PK tests with this machine are usually of the round-the-die type where the person first tries for the number one face, then for two, and so on. In this way, any imperfections in the dice or the machine cancel each other out and do not contribute to the overall score. For instance, if there is a bias favoring the six face, this will add to the number of hits which are registered when that face is target but it will subtract from the hits when the person tries for the other faces.

The dice are inserted through one of the ends of the container. This is fastened by four spring clamps. We were only at the second trial when the end of the container fell out and the two dice tumbled to the table. The machine is a sturdy one, and the FRNM experimenters had not had this difficulty before. The bottom was put back firmly and the test contin-

162

ued. Then, on the fifth trial, it fell out again and this time the dice came up with two fives, a double hit. The sixth trial gave one hit. At the first trial of the second round-the-die test, there was again a double hit and again the bottom came off. The same happened on the first trial of the third and final round-the-die test we did that evening, and one hit was registered.

The total score of nine which Julio obtained in these 36 trials (18 falls of the two dice) was three above chance and not significant by itself. But it was curious that he got five of these hits the four times the bottom dropped out. Here the odds against chance are more than 100-to-1.

The second of the three nights Julio was at the FRNM, on February 16, John Stump did a few trials with him to see if the falling bottom effect would be repeated. It came off once, though John had carefully checked the machine beforehand. He noticed that this did not happen when the dice hit the bottom of the cage, the time when it seemed most likely that it might come loose. The bottom dropped *after* the dice had come to rest and as the cage was moving up for another trial.

On the first evening at the FRNM, we also tried some of the devices built by W. Edward Cox (whom I mentioned in Chapters 3 and 8). But nothing of interest happened.

At 9:35 P.M., we were taking a break in one of the offices. Julio was standing in the doorway to the hall with a cup in his hand when we suddenly heard a crash. When we went out to look, we found a large decorative vase or bottle which had been on a table on the other side of the hallway in pieces on the floor. The base of the bottle and the glass stopper were intact but the neck had broken into about 50 pieces, the area of impact being five feet or so from the bottle position on the table. It had been about 16 feet from Julio and had moved toward him.

Chuck Honorton and John were standing opposite Julio just inside the doorway and had him in partial view both before and during the incident. Obviously, he could not have reached it. Was it possible that Julio had tied a string around the bottle earlier in the evening and then pulled it from his position in the doorway? His left arm and shoulder were not visible to Chuck and John so the string theory was attractive. Supposing he could have pulled a string, the questions remained how he could have fastened it to the bottle and what happened to the string afterward. The moment we heard the crash, our attention naturally went to Julio. We saw no string or other reaching device in his left hand nor anywhere else on his body.

The string theory faced another difficulty. When the bottle fell, Julio and I had only been at the FRNM about an hour. The first half of this we spent in general conversation with the FRNM group so that Julio could become acquainted with them and with the PK equipment. At 9 P.M. we began testing and worked continuously, using four PK machines, until we took the coffee break shortly after nine-thirty.

During the time we were at the FRNM, there was no occasion for Julio to absent himself from the rest of us. When we moved from one room and machine to another we went as a group.

It also semed impossible for Julio to have prepared the event earlier that day. Julio and I had been together all day except when he was examined by Dr. McPherson at Duke Hospital. In short, it did not seem possible that he could have fastened a string to the bottle or prepared this incident in some other way either while we were at the FRNM or before.

If this was a RSPK incident, it gave us an important clue: Julio's PK was still working. I had tried PK tests in two other poltergeist investigations but nothing startling had come out. I could not tell whether this was because the RSPK ability of the agents was ebbing or had disappeared altogether at the time. Now we had a chance to test an active poltergeist agent and hereby to answer the question whether or not he could consciously direct his PK powers.

The only PK device that gave an interesting score was the rotating machine. The second and third evenings we did 144 trials, or 72 releases of the two dice, 36 each night.

To make the experiments more challenging to Julio, they were set up as a competition between him and Bob Brier. And indeed, significant results were produced; but not in Julio's tests! Bob obtained 36 hits, 12 above chance, which gave him odds of more than 100-to-1. This is an unusually good score for so few PK trials, and more than Bob had ever managed before. Perhaps, therefore, Julio's PK came through after all. He may have had just enough control to apply it in the general context of the experiment but not at the specific task requested from him. If the falling bottom effect was also due to PK, this would be another example of such an effect.

Julio was also tested for ESP. He guessed a total of 17

packs, each containing 25 cards with the five standard ESP symbols: A star, a circle, a square, a cross, and three wavy lines. He showed no evidence of ESP in these tests.

Julio had chalked up a first with the bottle incident at the Institute for Parapsychology. As far as I know, there have been no other apparently genuine poltergeist incidents in a parapsychology laboratory.

The second night Julio was at the FRNM, we put another vase on the table in the hallway and four empty Coke bottles in what we hoped would be strategic places. The poltergeist was not tempted. Nor did anything else happen during the 10 days Julio was in Durham. He stayed in my house and often walked down the long hallway with its shelves of porcelain and other possible poltergeist targets. Everything remained peaceful.

After the bottle moved, I wondered if anything had happened that day which would help account for this incident. Julio had awakened quite disturbed that morning. He had had a nightmare—not just an unpleasant dream, but a nightmare in the old and literal sense of the word—since "mare" means "evil spirit." He dreamed that a spirit was trying to get into the house. Julio attacked and killed it, but the spirit revived, took a Japanese sword from one of the shelves in the hallway and went for Julio with it. Julio told me he often had such dreams in Miami but this was the first and, as it turned out, only time he had a nightmare in Durham.

This was also to be the day Julio was to have his medical examination. It was a very thorough and lengthy one which followed a protracted waiting period at the hospital. Julio did not like his visit to the doctor. He later told me, "It doesn't mean that I don't like people that take care of me, but . . . I don't like going to the doctors—checking my blood and things like that. I was very sad because of the time we were losing—things like that. I was very sad." I agreed with Julio that he had indeed seemed sad and angry, and Julio commented, "This the only day I be very angry" during his stay in Durham.

He added, ". . . I know the doctor was taking care and things like that, . . . I get mad at myself [for becoming angry] and the rest you know. When we went to the house— to the place, the thing fall down."

It seems that I had inadvertently re-created the tension and frustration which had stimulated the events in Miami.

I also tried to do this deliberately in two PK tests. One of these involved a machine built by Dr. John Artley (to whom I referred in Chapters 8 and 12). It was a PK machine of the "placement" type which we had modified for use in RSPK investigations. It had an electrical release mechanism for two or more glass balls, a sloping incline, and a glass target surface. This was divided into two parts, the purpose being to cause the balls to move into one or the other by PK.

The glass covered a sheet of paper with an outline of the warehouse in Miami. The glass balls rolling down the incline to the floor plan represented the moving ashtrays, glasses, and so forth. To simulate the situation in Miami further, we placed a picture of Glen Lewis, the owner whom Julio disliked, at whichever side of the surface was a target. But the test did not arouse Julio's PK.

On the possibility that the poltergeist events involved some kind of electrical effect, John devised another kind of apparatus. Using the same photograph, he put this over a piece of plastic insulating material which covered a sheet of aluminum. On top of the picture and connected with a wire to the aluminum, he placed a thin gold film. An oscilloscope was added to measure changes in electrical potential between the film and the aluminum.

John found that "a d.c. potential of about 0.2 volts developed between the aluminum and the gold film as Julio was looking at and handling the gold film. The scope had to be reset to remove the voltage. My natural inclination is to say that the scope drifted but it had been sitting in an operational condition for about two hours prior to the 'drift.' I cannot be certain about how or what happened. It did not repeat."

The best evidence we got that Julio had some control over his PK came from the tests with the rotating dice machine.

Even in Florida some of the events happened under circumstances which suggested that the process was at least on the borderline of consciousness. Once a target object fell at the moment Julio was placing a toy alligator on a shelf. As he did so, he said humorously, "I make magic," and a zombie glass in a target area behind him fell to the floor. I had examined the glass myself beforehand; I had Julio under direct observation, and no one else was near. This was the glass which moved over some obstacles which I had placed in front of it (203rd event).

Another time, a sailfish ashtray fell to the floor north of the shipping desk (215th event). We did not know where it came from. When this happened, I was looking at Julio who was humorously gesturing with a beer mug in the air, perhaps again suggesting that he was "making magic." Julio was the only member of the firm who was present. Only seven minutes after this I was watching Julio coming toward me with a broom in his hand when he said, "I hope something fall down." Just then a target beer mug fell. None of the other employees or owners were present, and again I had examined the target area before the event (216th event). This mug also had to move up off the shelf in order to clear the objects I had put in front of it.

Occasionally, a remarkable individual turns up who seems to be able to cause things to move at will by PK. The British medium, D. D. Home, Rudi Schneider, and Eusapia Palladino were examples. At the time of this writing, a woman in Leningrad, Russia, Mrs. Nina Kulagina, reputedly has this ability and has been studied under informal conditions by Gaither Pratt. Apparently as a result of great physical and mental effort, she makes boxes of matches, cigarettes, and other small objects move on a table in front of her.[1]

Some of the events in Miami and the PK results in Durham suggested that Julio might also develop control over his PK abilities. When Julio came to Durham, I learned that this had already to some extent been tried. At the suggestion of Mr. Diaz, his father-in-law, Julio attended several mediumistic sessions. At one of these, Julio said, they succeeded in causing a key suspended in a drinking glass to hit the sides of the glass. Another time he went into a trance.

One day in Durham we tried to re-create this kind of situation. Mrs. Adriana Ciompi, who had participated in similar tests before and had experience with trance mediums, assisted in the session. Julio easily entered a dissociated state but nothing of parapsychological interest emerged. He had several mental impressions, the most significant theme being his relationship to his mother, which had been a very positive one, and the sadness in the separation caused by her being in Cuba and he in this country.

Hypnosis sometimes seems to be a short cut to the unconscious. I mentioned Dr. Feather's hypnosis interview with Ernest (Chapter 4) and his failure to uncover any awareness in the boy of his role in the disturbances. The only person who was hypnotized when poltergeist events were actually going on was Mrs. Beck. I hypnotized her, and Dr. David Blumenthal did the questioning.

There was no doubt in our minds that Mrs. Beck was primarily responsible for the effects in the home. Yet she had no awareness of any involvement, even when hypnotized. What did come out was that interpersonal problems were connected with the incident. When she was asked if she had any idea of "what the trouble is," she replied, "Mother."

I shall return to question whether PK can be brought under conscious control in the next chapter.

15

The Poltergeist:
Parapsychopathology
or Human Potential?

The idea that PK is a natural capacity is, as I noted in Chapter 1, what we have all along been told by body English. Most of us, at one time or another, have probably engaged in the "instinctive attempt of a player to control the movement of a ball or puck after it has been thrown, batted, stroked, or bowled by contorting his body in the desired direction." [1] It may be this intuitive acceptance of PK which soon makes most poltergeist victims habituated to the phenomena. When these things have gone on for a while, there is generally little incredulity though the events are miraculous from other points of view.

It is perhaps not too strange that the central person should accept the phenomena without too much surprise; thus Julio's remark, "I miss it when something doesn't happen," or Roger's "The table will flip over." It is more curious that Roger's father, a down-to-earth factory worker, could say to Roger's grandmother, humorously and at the same time seriously, ". . . whatever was up there on Zimmerman Hill is now down here on Henderson Branch" and "You had two months of it, and now we are going to get two months of it." The reaction of a person who is contending with poltergeist phenomena is not so much one of disbelief or consternation as it is of a practical kind. In one of the cases mentioned in Chapter 3, a chair which several times "went revolving in mid air" was put away so it would not be of any further "annoyance" and would no longer "disturb us." Its movements were not described as inexplicable or amazing but as "accustomed." In the disturbances surrounding the building

169

of a bomb shelter, a self-propelling hammer was "becoming a nuisance" and taken away. When it returned by itself, it was simply left there.

Though few of us have experiences of this kind with our tools or furniture, it probably would not take us long to become accustomed to such events. Perhaps this is not only because most of us have a streak of superstition, but also because we may all have some measure of PK—at least of the weak kind that can be demonstrated in dice and similar experiments.

But what is the cause of the concentrated bursts of PK which we call poltergeist phenomena? We do not really know, but we have a few hints.

In a poltergeist study in which Dr. John Altrocchi participated, he concluded that the relationship between the members of the family was "significantly more pathological" than were the people as separate personalities. This may be true also for the other cases. In general, poltergeist incidents seem to be symptoms of pathological interpersonal relations more than of pathological individual personalities.

Most of us have problems in our relations with others. Yet our furniture and other belongings remain in their proper places. Perhaps the poltergeist person is an individual who is unusually sensitive to interpersonal stress or a person in whose life such stress has been unusually severe. In the case of Julio, his forced separation from his mother, his stepmother's rejection of him, and his father's compliance with her must have produced unusual strain. In the case of Virginia Campbell, studied by Dr. A. R. G. Owen (Chapter 7), there was also a recent history of family separations. This was true to an even more marked extent in the case of Heiner, the "Bremen Boy" studied by Dr. Hans Bender. Traumatic interpersonal and family relations also emerged in two other cases in which I have been involved. In one, the father of the poltergeist person had sought divorce from the mother by trying to prove that a minor physical defect in his child was inherited from the mother. In another, there was a shocking family tragedy: The mother had shot and killed the child's father in a family argument.

If the psychological needs or tensions of a person can extend beyond his body to be released in physical events in his environment, then the usual picture we have of man and his relation to the physical world is incomplete. Gardner Murphy, the psychologist I mentioned earlier (Chapter 13), is equally at home in parapsychology. In fact, he has been president of both the British and American Societies for Psychical Research.[2] In his presidential address to the first of these organizations, delivered in London, in June 1949, Murphy said that it is no longer possible to think of human personality as a solitary and independent entity. Rather we should look at it, "as a node or region of relative concentration in a field of vast and complex interpenetrating forces." In this field, "none of us is completely individualized any more than he is completely washed out in a cosmic sink of impersonality."[3] If we accept this expanded view of human personality, we may suppose that a person's tension system extends beyond the biological organism into his physical environment. In other words, we can think of the psi field as consisting of psychic energy. This field surrounds its source, in our case the poltergeist agent, and interacts with physical objects in his environment, much as sunlight interacts with water molecules as it penetrates the ocean. In the course of this process, psychic energy is transformed, for instance, to kinetic or light energy.

Poltergeist incidents may be symptoms of a kind of parapsychopathology, to use a word coined by Rhine. They may suggest a malfunctioning not of the familiar organism, but of a wider, "extended" organism.

Since poltergeist incidents take place outside the familiar physical organism and since the people around whom they occur generally are unaware of having caused them, it is not surprising that people often locate the cause of the incidents in some distant person who mysteriously causes the event, as the elusive prowler in the Clayton case, or a demon, as in the Olive Hill case. In a previous chapter I mentioned that psychologists use the tendency of people to project emotions and conflicts to external situations to help their patients become aware of their emotions. Nowadays we generally do not attribute our emotions, dreams, and so forth, to spirits, although there are still words in our language which reflect these earlier beliefs. For instance, we no longer suppose that a person who has a nightmare is visited at night by an evil spirit, but this is what the word literally implies.

We now know that the way to deal with nightmares is not to chase spirits, but for the dreamer to face his tensions and problems by bringing them into awareness. We also know that though few of us may suffer from nightmares, these and other dreams can be helpful because they can inform us about the nature of our anxieties and concerns.

The same may hold true for poltergeists. Probably few families suffer from the kinds of violent and prolonged disturbances described in this book. On the other hand, there are undoubtedly many more poltergeists than reach the newspapers or the police complaint rooms. Perhaps most of them go unnoticed even by the family. Especially if the events are short-lived, they are likely to be attributed to normal causes: A few plates moving off the dinner table by themselves or a glass flying out of the cupboard and hitting somebody are likely to be dismissed in terms of settling of the house, passing traffic, or similar explanations. If the events continue for a long time but not violently, the person around whom they occur may be accused merely of being clumsy or accident prone.

If the poltergeist target is not an inconsequential object, such as a plate or an ashtray, but something more important, such as a can with paint thinner near the furnace in the house or the engine of the family car, then the situation could become more serious.

As we have seen from the cases reported in this book, people who produce PK are usually unaware that they do so. If they become aware that they are involved, because the disturbances center around them, they cannot just stop things at will.

At the same time, the incidents are not random. As I pointed out in Chapter 1, the results of some PK tests suggest that the process is guided by ESP. There also seems to be some kind of guidance in many poltergeist effects which would not be expected if we were dealing with a completely impersonal force or field. This seemed to be the case, for instance, with respect to the objects in the Miami case which had to move up in the air to clear obstacles in front of them. The guidance behind poltergeist occurrences seems to be the mind of the agent. This mind, we must suppose, in some way extends beyond the brain and body. Professor H. H. Price, the Oxford philosopher and parapsychologist, suggests that once an idea has been created, it "is no longer wholly under the control of the consciousness which gave it birth" but may operate independently on the minds of other people or on physical objects. Hereby thoughts and images may result in ESP and PK occurrences without the person in whom the thoughts or images originated being aware that he is in any way responsible.[4]

If people generate PK effects unconsciously, then there is no need to suppose that this is restricted to individuals with the abnormally high PK levels discussed here. It would still be significant if people were found to possess no more PK than is usually demonstrated in laboratory experiments. In other words, if PK were only of the weak variety that might cause tumbling dice to come up with sixes rather than ones, then there are many times in daily life when situations hang in the balance and when a slight physical effect might tip the scales. For instance, if the steering mechanism of one's car is at the point of breaking down, perhaps PK may determine whether this happens at home in the driveway or at a curve on a highway. Similarly, PK might conceivably determine whether a mechanical defect in an airplane becomes effective on the ground or in the air.

If people are angry, it seems likely from what we know about poltergeist phenomena that the PK effects will express this anger. Apparently we must consider the possibility that many of us are polluting the environment with PK as a result of our tensions and aggressions. If we are, there is no reason to assume that we stop short with inanimate physical objects. It can safely be said that parapsychologists have demonstrated that some people exert a positive psychic influence on living systems, by accelerating the growth of seeds, the healing of wounds, and the like.[5] Possibly hostile and tense emotions bring about the opposite effects. In today's world we live in ever-increasing proximity to each other. It is easy to suppose that unconscious and aggressive PK would add to the other harmful effects of overcrowding.

Poltergeist studies suggest that PK force is strongest on objects which are closest to the body of the agent. What about his own body? If psychological tensions have harmful effects outside the brain of the agent, it seems possible that such effects might also influence the "object" which is closer and more continuously associated with this brain than anything else—the agent's own body. In other words, what we call poltergeist effects may be "extrasomatic" expressions of psychological stress in the same way as an ulcer is a psychosomatic expression of such stress.

In addition to overcrowding, another characteristic of present-day living is likely to accentuate the PK problem. We rely more and more on machines and instruments; in fact most of us depend on them daily for our lives. If some of us are liable to bombard our environment with destructive PK, perhaps we should not be put in charge of such instruments. Perhaps people should be tested for destructive PK before we allow them to become airline or spaceship pilots, or even airline hostesses or members of ground crews. Within such a context, it is fortunate that the effective range of PK appears to be limited. It also seems as if the duration of an RSPK siege depends on the agent in question and that the PK episode may be stronger for some than for others. These are all questions for further PK testing.

One relatively easy and obvious first step is to use automated machines (such as the Schmidt and Cox machines mentioned in Chapter 1) to monitor the PK of ordinary people, with special emphasis on situations in which they do not know that they are being tested. Such tests would tell us how much PK different individuals exert. The work should include psychological tests to probe the role of repressed anger, and so on. It should also include investigations of the attenuation phenomenon in order to determine the effective range of PK and of the other patterns found in RSPK cases, such as its tendency to center on certain objects and areas.

A rare but important poltergeist phenomenon is the occurrence which takes place when the agent is absent. As I have mentioned, on a few occasions, the poltergeist agent was not present at all when there were movements of objects. Jerome Eden, the TV reporter, said that a bottle in the Miami warehouse crashed 36 feet from the place where it stood after Julio and all the other employees had left for the day and when Eden was alone in the warehouse. If an object can be "charged" with PK by the poltergeist agent so that another person may later set off this charge using only a "normal" amount of PK, this would further increase the physical range of PK. Again, experiments could point the way. It would be a fairly easy matter to determine whether a person may produce effects on a PK machine which show up after he has left.

If it were discovered that PK does at times act as a disruptive physical force in the world, the next question is whether or not it can be controlled or directed into positive channels. Psychology, which has been so important for our understanding of the poltergeist, again points the way. Psychoanalysis and other forms of psychotherapy have shown that when people become aware of their hidden emotions, these may lose their destructive force. When a person is able to face his feelings and to express them constructively, he is likely to find relief from temper tantrums, ulcers, high blood pressure, or whatever expression his emotions have taken. Together with a lessening of negative behavior traits or psychosomatic complaints, there is likely to be an increase of spontaneity and creativity. The person will not only become a happier individual, but he is also likely to become more energetic and effective in what he is dong.

When we talk about ESP and PK occurrences, the conception of the human organism as an encapsulated entity, cut off from its physical and social environment, breaks down. Therefore, the method for curing an attack of poltergeist phenomena, whether of the violent kinds discussed in this book or the milder forms that most of us may suffer from— or cause others to suffer from—perhaps requires a different kind of psychotherapy than is generally practiced.

What may be needed is a method for treating the psi field. Psychotherapy teaches us ways of bringing our individual tensions and frustrations into consciousness and giving them constructive expression. But most systems of psychotherapy do not recognize that the human organism extends into the space beyond the skin, and therefore they lack techniques for bringing this part of the self into awareness.

Sigmund Freud, the Austrian founder of psychoanalysis, accepted the reality at least of telepathy, but he did not incorporate it into his picture of human personality or into his method of therapy.[6] This deficiency was made up by his student, the Swiss analyst, C. G. Jung, and now many psychotherapists are aware of the importance of ESP in normal (and patient-therapist) interactions between people. Pioneers in the United States of a psychotherapy which incorporates ESP, include Drs. Jan Ehrenwald, Jule Eisenbud, and Berthold E. Schwartz. In Europe, Dr. Emilio Servadio, the Italian analyst, is its main advocate.[7]

Perhaps we shall see the development of a "parapsychotherapy" to deal with the problems of parapsychopathology. Such a therapy may include the work of these men, together with other procedures for bringing the psi field into awareness. Two possible methods are currently creating much interest, namely meditation and biofeedback.

Dr. Karlis Osis, director of research at the American Society for Psychical Research, did an experiment with Dr. Edwin Bokert, also a member of the ASPR staff, using a group of meditators as subjects.[8] They found that the people who did best in ESP, in other words those who were most aware of their environment in the ESP sense, were also most conscious of the psi field. These people had a "feeling of merging with the others; a sense of closeness and unity with the members of the group; and a feeling of oneness as if the boundaries between 'what is me and what is not me' were dissolving."

In most forms of meditation, the person seems to achieve a deep state of relaxation, yet remains fully awake.[9] Usually, the mind is concentrating on a single task, such as repeating a word or visualizing an object. The purpose is to reduce distracting thoughts so that the meditator becomes aware of a unity between himself and the rest of the world. A similar procedure is used by some ESP subjects. In a survey of successful ESP percipients, Rhea White, also of the ASPR, found that they would enter a state of relaxation as a preparation for the test.[10] At the same time, they remained alert and used some focusing device to center their attention, such as a mental image. After a period of waiting, this image was released and the ESP impression would enter consciousness.

Parapsychologists are beginning to explore meditation as a means of controlling PK. In some systems of meditation, it is believed that meditation is not only a way of experiencing the basic unity between self and world, but that meditation also generates a positive PK influence on one's surroundings. This is particularly true for Zen, the Japanese way of practicing Buddhist meditation. The effect of this influence is believed to be a beneficial one for the world as a whole and not only for the meditator. Sometimes, however, he tries to use it for some specific purpose as in the following story which a Zen Roshi told a group of meditators (the title of Roshi is equivalent to that of Bishop). He and a Zen monk had to be in Los Angeles for an important meeting. They were picked up at the airport but then, when they were on the freeway, the driver discovered that he had forgotten to fill the gas tank and that it must be empty. There was no possibility of getting off the road to a gas station for many miles. The two Zen people believed they had another energy source and applied themselves with all their might to chanting meditation. They proceeded several miles along the highway in this way. Finally, there was a turnoff with a gas station where they could take advantage of this more conventional power supply.

There is no way to tell whether it was Zen or a residue of gas that got them to the station. But the story illustrates the belief that Zen meditation creates a real physical force.

It is a long jump from poltergeists to Zen meditators, but there are some interesting similarities. Procedures used in Zen are reminiscent of the poltergeist situation. The Zen meditator tries to be completely awake and alert, and therefore meditates with open eyes. The poltergeist agent usually has *his* eyes open and is mentally alert and active when objects fly.

The poltergeist person is not only awake, he is also often angry; and he is tense and frustrated because he cannot fully express his aggression. Correspondingly, Zen meditation is a very intense form of meditation. It is quite different from the relaxed, submissive type of meditation associated with other systems. Zen involves a great deal of effort, both physical and mental. The meditator sits with his legs crossed, preferably in the full or half lotus position. This can become quite painful after some hours or days of meditation, even for people accustomed to this position. The back should be perfectly straight, with nothing to lean against.

The mental exertion is even greater. Most Zen meditators either concentrate on a special word which they constantly repeat to themselves, or on a *koan*. The latter is an intentionally frustrating and thought-stopping question or paradox; for instance, "What is the sound of one hand clapping?" By filling the mind with either a word or a koan, the ongoing processes of information integration, whereby the mind organizes and assimilates experiences, hopefully cease, allowing the meditator to see only the basic unity of existence.

Zen concentration is attempted with as much energy and determination as possible, but without any overt physical expression. A similar theme of tense inaction runs through many of the poltergeist cases. The poltergeist person is sometimes aware of his anger, his frustration, and so on, but does nothing about them. The main difference seems to be that the poltergeist person builds up tension and energy involuntarily, while the Zen meditator does so deliberately.

Research into the question of whether mediation and similar processes enhance psi has become more promising with the discovery that meditation is associated with certain brain waves which also are associated with ESP. If some meditation techniques are a favoring condition for PK, this would lead us to ask whether brain waves are also associated with PK. The door might then be opened to control of PK by biofeedback, which is now an active area of ESP research.

In experiments with a gifted ESP subject at the Psychical Research Foundation we found a relationship between ESP success and the alpha brain wave.[11] This is a rather slow wave, between eight and 13 cycles per second, which is likely to appear when a person closes his eyes and is relaxed and at the same time attentive.

In alpha biofeedback the brain wave recorder (electroencephalograph) is connected to a buzzer or some other signal which comes on when the brain shows alpha.[12] The person tested is asked to try to keep the buzzer on for as long as possible—and thereby the alpha wave. Many people seem to be able to do so.

It is still uncertain whether ESP can be controlled by biofeedback. If it can, this would suggest that PK too can be approached via this route. The psychological state of the poltergeist agent would lead me to expect that the brain waves associated with PK are other than alpha—or supplementary to it. I would look for brain waves or other physiological conditions which reflect the tension apparently connected with PK.

By being able to control poltergeist and PK effects, we may not only be able to deal with a disruptive force in nature, but also to gain insight into a potentially constructive and unifying principle.

As with other anomalies studied by science, the main importance of the "parapsychopathology of the anomaly of the poltergeist," [13] as J. B. Rhine puts it, may be that it throws light on a normal state of affairs, in this case a psychical relationship between man and his social and physical environment.

The exploration of this unifying force will necessarily be a joint venture. We have already seen the crucial role which psychologists, psychiatrists, and physical scientists have played in exploring the poltergeist. If research is to advance, it must continue to be interdisciplinary. A significant advance requires not only the goodwill of other scientists in collaborating with parapsychologists, but also far greater resources in terms of funds and personnel.

It often comes as a shock to people to learn that there are fewer than thirty full-time parapsychologists in the world. If the resources and manpower in parapsychology could even modestly approach those of the other sciences, important advances could be made in our understanding of ESP and PK. Though our present knowledge certainly is incomplete, it is becoming increasingly apparent that psi phenomena are not "odd" events in nature, but rather, components of a basic fabric which connects people with each other and with their physical environment.

This fabric has provisionally been called the psi field. But naming it so does not place it outside the physical world, in some occult realm. The psi field may be no other than the complex interrelations of forces and fields which present-day physicists are already probing. The exciting prospect which parapsychology has introduced is that this outer physical world and the inner psychical world may be one and the same.

APPENDIX

On Meeting Poltergeists
and Ghosts

As a result of the growing interest in parapsychology among scientists and professional people, many high school and college teachers are encouraging their students to select parapsychological topics for term papers or special projects. At several universities, courses for credit are given for this type of work. If there is a haunted house in the area, or reports of other unexplained disturbances, the students sometimes select this as their project.

Since there are so few trained investigators in this field, the student of poltergeists and ghosts can make important contributions by exploring cases on his own. To find out about active cases in his area, he should keep an eye on news reports in the papers, radio, and television. He might also inform the editors of the local papers about his interest and possibly the police or sheriff's department. As a help to the beginner, some suggestions are offered in the following pages.

To carry out a serious study, familiarity with the scientific literature is a requirement. A list of articles and books will be found at the end of this book.

It would also help the would-be investigator to contact professional parapsychologists, preferably before his investigation. People interested in such studies may become voluntary field reporters for the Psychical Research Foundation by writing to the PRF, Duke Station, Durham, North Carolina 27706. When we hear of a case in a certain area but are unable to send an investigator, we alert a field reporter if there is one in that locality.

The disturbances can generally be divided into either of two groups: Haunting and poltergeist phenomena. This book has dealt nearly exclusively with the latter. It is not yet known whether the differences between the two groups are only superficial or whether they result from different psychical processes. In general, poltergeist incidents are connected with an individual, while hauntings seem to be connected with an area, usually a house. Physical disturbances predominate in poltergeist incidents, hallucinatory experiences in hauntings. These experiences, which may include seeing ghosts and hearing footsteps, are called hallucinatory because they are generally experienced by some persons and not by others. Hallucinations in a haunted house differ from those of a mentally disturbed person because they more often resemble experiences others have had independently, or correspond to some past event or person—they are then "veridical" hallucinations, that is, instances of ESP.

Haunting occurrences may also involve physical disturbances, but these instances of apparent RSPK are generally less frequent and violent than in poltergeist cases. However, hauntings tend to stretch over longer periods of time. Poltergeist disturbances are usually of fairly short duration, rarely lasting more than a couple of months, while a haunting may go on for years. As a rule, there seems to be no (living) person around whom haunting incidents revolve. This makes them of special interest to the survival question. I have made preliminary analyses of two haunting cases which suggest that the process may be different from that in poltergeist cases, and raise the survival hypothesis at least as one of the contending explanations.

Field investigations of either poltergeists or hauntings are endangered from two sides, time and publicity. If a case has broken into the news, it is often difficult to conduct a serious investigation. The investigator should try to prevent publicity, at least until a study has been made. If the case has already been publicized, reporters and editors should be asked to postpone further publicity until after the investigation. They will often agree to this both out of consideration for the family and also because it makes a case more newsworthy if a scientific study can be completed. If the family has had some taste of the effects of publicity, they often need no further persuasion to keep quiet.

Genuine poltergeists are nearly always short-lived. If intensive research is to be undertaken, the investigator must arrive at the scene as soon as possible. For training purposes, an imaginary ghost or poltergeist or one which is kept going by trickery may be as useful as the real thing.

Whether or not the case is genuine and whether or not the investigator plans a personal study, he should try to get a good appraisal of the case before he arrives by talking to the family and others who have been present during the events. Dr. Pratt and I have developed a questionnaire for this purpose.[1] It will be found at the end of this Appendix. Its main purpose is to determine whether or not a case seems to be genuine and deserves serious investigation, and if so, what form this should take.

I shall not here describe the procedures for conducting on-the-spot investigations of hauntings or poltergeists. The reader already will have some idea of the attempts by present-day parapsychologists to study poltergeist cases. He should round this out with a careful and critical reading of the articles in professional parapsychological publications. These studies are still primitive and sparse and there is room for improvement. In particular, it is important to develop the experimental approach to poltergeist studies by bringing in additional controls and refinements. There is a need for physical instrumentation, such as closed-circuit television monitoring of the active areas, particularly if this can be introduced without disturbing the psychological situation.

In my opinion it is best to begin a personal investigation in a low-key fashion. The investigator should try to blend in with the psychological and social situation in the home or area where the disturbances take place. Controls, tests, and instruments should be introduced gradually and inconspicuously. In the Miami case, nothing took place when the television crews had their cameras focused on the active areas. However, by gradually developing the decoy procedure into experiments, it was possible to conduct controlled tests. If the investigator has access to compact television equipment or other detection devices, he should install them. The recording of flying objects by video tape or other means would be an important step ahead. When it becomes possible, for instance, to analyze the trajectories of moving objects, we might gain new insights into the RSPK process. A study of scientific articles in this area will give the student ideas about the needs and possibilities for instrumenting poltergeist and haunting studies.

Poltergeist and haunting occurrences are people happenings. However strange the events are, first and foremost they involve the people in whose homes or businesses they erupt. The poltergeist and haunting student soon finds himself intimately associated with several groups of people. It is well to come prepared for this. The primary group, the people in whose territory the phenomena occur, usually wish them to end as quickly and painlessly as possible. It is therefore likely that they have asked the help of a second group, namely people whose professions or skills seem appropriate. Depending upon the educational and social background of the family, they may seek help from members of the building profession, from police officers, the clergy, and so on. The members of this second group have their own attitudes. If a police officer, or clergyman, or another individual has consented to enter a case, it is probably because he believes that his skills may help the family, and he will proceed on this basis. If his approach is balanced by common sense, his contribution may be useful, whether or not he finds an explanation for the phenomena. In several of the cases mentioned in this book, police officers, reporters, and others were very helpful. However, if their attitude is rigid and closed, it may lead to further difficulties for the family. Examples include the Indianapolis disturbances where the police sergeant arrested Mrs. Gemmecke (Chapter 5) and the Olive Hill case where the religious leaders conducted an exorcism by burning Roger's clothes (Chapter 11).

If the occurrences have become known outside the primary group, and outside the group of investigators they may have called in, a third group, consisting of representatives of the news media, such as press, radio, and television reporters, is likely to enter the picture. Their main responsibility is to their media and they are often expected to provide dramatic and entertaining stories. These, in turn, are likely to draw in a fourth group, namely curiosity-seekers whose presence and behavior is usually extremely disruptive both for the life of the family and for the conduct of a serious investigation. Even the most violent poltergeist sometimes pales in comparison to the antics of its audience. Particularly at times such as weekends, when poltergeist fans bring "spirits" of their own, they can cause a great deal of damage, both psychological and physical.

If a parapsychologist or a serious student wishes to attempt an investigation of a poltergeist or haunting case, he cannot usually expect to settle down at once to a quiet and thorough study, but must first resolve the social problems presented by these four groups of people and by their different needs and activities.

Usually the parapsychologist is the last to appear on the

scene. He essentially has the same concern as the first group
—the family or others primarily involved—namely, to explain the phenomena. However, an investigation can generally best be carried out by examining the phenomena while
they occur. It is therefore not in the best interest of the parapsychologist if the incidents cease before his study has been
completed. His investigation is only likely to be successful if
the family realizes this and is willing to follow his suggestions,
even if these are not designed to put an immediate stop to the
incidents.

To obtain a record of earlier occurrences in the case,
which should be as complete and as accurate as possible, the
parapsychologist and student also need the cooperation of
the second group, the investigators and observers who have
probably been involved from a practical rather than from a
scientific point of view. Their collaboration may also be useful in gathering information about disturbances which take
place while the parapsychologist is on the scene.

When representatives of the news media have been alerted,
the parapsychologist or the student must reach an agreement
with them, so that there will be as little publicity as possible
during the investigation period. This is particularly important
since the fact that the parapsychological investigation is being
made is itself newsworthy and likely to draw in additional
reporters and curiosity-seekers if it becomes generally known.
If the student can deal satisfactorily with the representatives
of the news media, then the fourth group, the curiosity-
seekers, are not likely to present a serious disruption since
their interest is likely to cease once the publicity stops.

Questionnaire for Poltergeist and
Haunting Investigations

Poltergeist and haunting cases show different characteristics and have to be studied in different ways. The questionnaire which appears later in this Appendix will bring these
out. It should be answered by the people primarily involved.
When there have been outside witnesses, they too should be
interviewed. Especially in poltergeist cases, which are likely
to be short-lived, the questionnaire should be given as soon
as possible, either face-to-face with the people or by telephone.

The questionnaire is divided into five parts. The first,
"General Background," seeks an overview of the situation,

including the place of the disturbances (see Question 1) and the length of time they have been going on (2). Sometimes the onset of the events coincides with a birthday or other significant date. If this date is particularly important to some person in the house, this may indicate that he is involved in the events. If a personal investigation is contemplated, it is important to know if the case is still active (3) and how active it is (4).

The investigator will also need to know who the people are in whose home or business the disturbances take place. If there are children at the age of puberty or adolescence, this may indicate poltergeist disturbances (5). If the persons involved have had psychic experiences in the past, particularly if they are similar to the present occurrences, this may indicate that the persons are important for the phenomena, perhaps as ESP percipients of ghosts, or PK agents of poltergeist disturbances. Sometimes a description of supposed previous psychical experiences indicates that these are only the effects of an imaginative or diseased mind and that perhaps the present phenomena can be explained in the same way (6). If the persons have been excessively interested in psychic or occult matters in the past, it may be possible that the present incidents are only due to imagination or exaggeration of ordinary happenings (7).

Often attempts will have been made to explain the events in normal ways. The investigator needs to know which methods were used and what the results were (8).

In some cases, particularly of the haunting type, pets and other animals sometimes seem to be affected by the events. For instance, they may act as if they see or hear something which the occupants of the house are unable to perceive (9).

A case is particularly promising if visitors to the house have been present during the incidents and are willing to describe their experiences. This is especially helpful if they have some training or qualifications as investigators, as do police officers and reporters. In my experience, the latter are often much more cautious and objective than the newspaper reports sometimes suggest (10).

Usually the people who have witnessed the incidents have a theory about them. It may be important to know what this is, whether or not it has any basis in fact. For instance, someone who firmly believes there is a ghost in his house may imagine or misinterpret things to conform with his belief. The family's beliefs may also affect the investigation. The

Callihans' conviction that the disturbances in their home
were caused by a demon (Chapter 11) and the Howells' belief in a prowler (Chapter 6) are examples (11).

The second category, "Localization of Phenomena," is in-
tended to determine whether or not the occurrences are
clustered in time and space. If they are concentrated at certain times during the day or night, this will facilitate the investigation since the investigator can be particularly on his
toes during those times (12). Similarly, if the incidents are
centered in certain parts of a building, it may be possible to
have these under especially careful scrutiny (13).

Sometimes the fact that the events happen at certain times
can be attributed to the presence of a particular person—
perhaps because he is a PK agent or, in the case of hauntings,
the ESP percipient of the ghosts. The members in the household may not have noticed that the things are only likely to
happen when this person is present. It may therefore be necessary to mention each person in the family in turn and ask
if things ever happen when that person is absent (14).
Whether or not the phenomena depend on someone's presence, incidents may occur in empty rooms or areas. If something has happened in a place which the observer knew to
be empty, this may suggest that the case is genuine. Once
the investigator arrives on the scene, he may want to try
experiments using such active locations as target areas (15).

The third category, "Physical Disturbances," only concerns
cases where there are unexplained physical events, such as
movement of objects. It is not always easy to determine
whether or not sound and light effects are physical unless
tape recorders, film, and other means of instrumental regis-
tration are used. The rule of thumb is to classify knocks,
lights, and so on, as physical if everybody who is in a position to see or hear them actually does so. If the event is
noticed only by some of those present, it is not physical in
the ordinary sense of the word, and should be classified under "Nonphysical Phenomena." After a general description
of the incidents (16), it is important to know how frequent
the disturbances have been. This will both give a general picture of the case and also indicate whether a personal visit
might lead to observation of some happening. If the events
are very rare, it is, of course, less likely that the investigator
will observe anything himself, unless he plans on a prolonged
study, particularly since the investigation itself may put a
damper on the incidents (17).

In poltergeist incidents, the objects in motion often seem to behave in strange ways, sometimes moving around corners, sometimes accelerating or slowing down. Such features, particularly if unexpected by the observers, make it more likely that genuine incidents are taking place. On the other hand, an object falling directly to the floor from its shelf may more easily be explained by tremors caused by traffic, settling of the house, and the like (18). Also, objects that move in poltergeist homes sometimes produce unusually loud noises when they hit (19). In both haunting and poltergeist cases there may be thumps and bangs without visible physical causes (20).

If objects move while somebody is watching, this is particularly significant. It is usually easier to exclude normal physical causes when the beginning stage of movement is actually observed (21). The same is true for disturbances taking place in empty areas (22).

We have seen that in many poltergeist cases, certain objects or types of objects are singled out. Again, if this feature is found in a new case, it may suggest genuine phenomena. The investigator can then try to arrange tests using such objects as targets (23).

Particularly in haunting type occurrences, there are often other disturbances in addition to the physical ones. A fourth category, "Nonphysical Phenomena" is devoted to these. Again, the investigator should obtain a general description of the phenomena (24) and a statement of how frequent they are (25).

Often only one or two persons in the household are sensitive to the ghost or whatever is reported (26). Sometimes it seems possible that the person who sees a ghost is imagining things and that a second person who also sees it is responding by telepathy to these imaginations. This is particularly likely to be the explanation if the two people reportedly have had ESP interactions in the past (6, 27). If a second or third person who believed he saw a ghost knew that somebody else had seen a ghost in the house, it is usually possible to dismiss these second impressions as due simply to suggestion (28). It is characteristic of haunting cases that only one or a few people experience the ghost, footsteps, and so on, and this may suggest a genuine case rather than one produced by trickery (29).

Sometimes the experiences a person has in a haunted house appear to be connected with previous occupants or events.

It is important to obtain as many details as possible supporting this relationship (30). If the individual who believed he saw a ghost knew beforehand about the person whose ghost he saw, the experience can probably be dismissed in terms of imagination and suggestibility (31).

In case the student is thinking of making a personal investigation, he needs to know what the practical possibilities for this are. In the fifth and final group of questions, "Future Investigation," the first question will bring out whether or not the people welcome a serious investigation (32). If this is to be made, it is necessary to know whether the case has become widely known. If it has, attempts should be made to minimize further publicity, at least until the investigation has been completed. If the family is unwilling to agree to this, it will be difficult if not impossible to conduct a thorough study. In any case, it is likely that people who seek publicity for their ghost or poltergeist may be exaggerating the events or perhaps inventing them altogether (33).

Sometimes an active case dies down temporarily only to revive later on. If the phenomena have subsided, a personal investigation may not be worthwhile. In that case, the person should ask the family to get in touch with him if and when the events resume. In the turmoil of a resumption of disturbances, the family may forget this, so it is a good idea if the investigator from time to time checks with the family to determine whether or not the events have started up again (34).

Questionnaire

GENERAL BACKGROUND

1. Where have the disturbances taken place?
2. When did the disturbances begin?
3. How recently has anything happened?
4. How does the frequency and severity at this time compare with earlier periods?
5. Who are the members of the household or group involved? What are their ages?
6. Have any of the persons who witnessed the phenomena had telepathic dreams or other psychic experiences in the past? If so, state who they are and describe the experiences.
7. Were any of the persons who witnessed the phenomena interested in psychic matters before the present disturbances began? If so, indicate their areas of interest.

8. Have attempts been made to find an ordinary explanation of the events? For example, is there reason to think that someone is doing these things as a prank or that they could be due to settling of the house, rodents, or similar causes?

9. Are there pets or farm animals in the area? If so, how do they react to the disturbances?

10. Have any visitors to the house or area witnessed the disturbances? If so, are they willing to testify? (Give names and addresses of such persons.)

11. Do you or others who witnessed the phenomena have any idea or theory about their cause?

LOCALIZATION OF PHENOMENA

12. Are events more frequent at certain times during the 24 hours of the day than at others? If so, state which periods.

13. Are they more frequent in certain places (for example, in certain rooms of the house) than in others? If so, state where.

14. Do the occurrences happen more frequently in the presence or vicinity of certain persons than others? If so, state which people. Do events take place when they are not in the area?

15. Has anything been known to happen when no one was in the area?

PHYSICAL DISTURBANCES

Answer Questions 16–23 only if there are physical disturbances (such as unexplained movements of objects).

16. Describe these disturbances.

17. How frequent are the disturbances?

18. If there have been unexplained movements of objects, was there anything strange about the manner in which the objects moved or stopped (for example, objects that moved around corners, hit with unusually great force, and so forth)?

19. Are unusually loud noises caused by the moving of objects? If so, describe these noises.

20. Are there noises not connected with the disturbances of objects? If so, describe these noises.

21. Has anyone ever seen an object *start* to move when no one was near it? If so, describe these occurrences.

22. Have things happened when no one was in the area or room in which the disturbances took place? If so, describe the occurrences.

23. Are special objects or kinds of objects disturbed more often than others? If so, which?

NONPHYSICAL PHENOMENA

Answer Questions 24–31 only if there are unusual phenomena not caused by the movements of objects or by other physical disturbances (for instance, if there are "ghosts," "footsteps," sensations of heat and cold, unexplained sounds, sights, smells, and touches).

24. Describe these experiences.

25. How frequent are these experiences?

26. Who first noticed them and when?

27. What other persons, if any, have had these experiences and when did they have them?

28. Were the people who had these experiences aware that others had had such experiences in the area before they did?

29. Have there been instances where the ghost, footsteps, and so on were experienced by some persons in the room or area but not by others? If so, describe these cases.

30. Do the ghosts or images resemble actual persons and events from the past? If so, describe the evidence for this. Were these persons or events connected with the house?

31. Did the people who experienced the ghost or image know about the person whose ghost they saw *before* they saw it?

FUTURE INVESTIGATION

32. Would the family or group welcome a serious investigation of the disturbances by someone who could make first-hand observations?

33. Has there been any publicity about the events? If not, can you be reasonably sure of not letting any get started?

34. If things are relatively inactive at this time and the prospects for a visit uncertain, will you telephone us collect at once if the events become more active?

Notes and References

Numbers in heavy print indicate titles which appear in the suggested reading list. The following abbreviations are used: ASPR for American Society for Psychical Research; SPR for (English) Society for Psychical Research; and PA for Parapsychological Association.

Foreword

1. "Supernormal Phenomena in Classical Antiquity," E. R. Dodds. *Proceedings* of the SPR, Vol. 55, 1971, pp. 189–237.

Introduction

1. Many local and national news stories, including progress reports by the *New York Times,* followed the Seaford incidents. The first news story appeared on February 3, 1958, and subsequent articles appeared frequently through spring of that year.
2. Symposium on Incorporeal Personal Agency held at Duke, June 9–12, 1959. Several of the papers presented were published in the *Journal of Parapsychology,* Vol 24, issues 1, 2, 3, and 4. For Cox's paper on the poltergeist, see **21.**

Chapter 1

1. "The Pressure of Laser Light," Arthur Ashkin. *Scientific American,* February 1972, pp. 62–71.
2. *Extrasensory Perception,* J. B. Rhine (Reprinted by Bruce Humphries, New York, 1964).
3. These early poltergeist cases are described by Owen, **24,** pp. 94 and 235.
4. Crookes' work with D. D. Home will be found in *Researches in the Phenomena of Spiritism,* William Crookes (West London: the Psychic Bookshop, 1926).

5. The group of initial reports on Palladino will be found in "Report on a Series of Sittings with Eusapia Palladino" published in the *Proceedings* of the SPR, Vol. 23, 1909, pp. 306–569. See also **48**.

6. Some of the tests with Schneider are described in "The Physical Mediumship of Rudi Schneider," Anita Gregory. *Proceedings* of the Parapsychological Association, No. 5, 1968, pp. 19–21.

7. The history of experimentation in PK is summarized in **8**. For some of the full reports see **33–47**.

Chapter 3

1. The Cideville case will be found in "Poltergeist at Cideville," Andrew Lang. *Proceedings* of the SPR, Vol. 18, 1904, pp. 454–463.

2. Zorab's survey will be found in **32**. The other cases, together with some haunting cases, are referred to in tabular form in a paper by Cox, **21**.

3. The Swanland, Yorkshire, case will be found in "On Alleged Movements of Objects," F. W. H. Myers. *Proceedings* of the SPR, Vol. 7, 1891–1892, pp. 383–394.

4. The Oakland case will be found in "A Case of Poltergeist," J. H. Hyslop. *Proceedings* of the ASPR, Vol. 7, 1913, pp. 193–425.

5. The Derrygonnelly case will be found in **19**, pp. 390–394.

6. The Worksop case will be found in "Poltergeists," Frank Podmore. *Proceedings* of the SPR, Vol. 12, 1896–1897, pp. 45–58.

7. The Durweston case will be found in "Poltergeists," Frank Podmore. *Proceedings* of the SPR, Vol. 12, 1896–1897, pp. 90–95.

8. Lombroso's case will be found in *Haunted Houses*, Camille Flammarion (New York: D. Appleton & Co., 1924), pp. 274 ff.

9. The Sumatra case will be found in "A Poltergeist Case," W. G. Grottendieck. *Journal* of the SPR, Vol. 12, 1905–1906, pp. 260–266.

10. The Vienna case will be found in "Report of a 'Poltergeist' Case," A. Wärndorfer. *Journal* of the SPR, Vol. 13, 1907–1908, pp. 66–79.

11. The Douai case will be found in *Haunted Houses*, Camille Flammarion (New York: D. Appleton & Co., 1924), pp. 256 ff.

12. The Enniscorthy case will be found in **19**, pp. 380–390.
13. The Dale, Georgia, case will be found in **19**, pp. 404–406.
14. The Folkstone case will be found in "The Folkstone Poltergeist," W. F. Barrett and Thomas Hesketh. *Journal* of the SPR, Vol. 18, 1917–1918, pp. 155–182 and 196–198.
15. The Hopfgarten case will be found in "The Hopfgarten Poltergeist Case," A. von Schrenck-Notzing. *Journal* of the SPR, Vol. 20, 1921–1922, pp. 199–207.
16. The Poona case will be found in "An Indian Poltergeist," Harry Price and H. Kohn. *Journal* of the ASPR, Vol. 24, 1930, pp. 122–130, 180–186, and 221–232.
17. The case from northern France will be found in **32**, pp. 121–122.
18. The Washington, D.C., case will be found in "Report of a Poltergeist." *Parapsychology Bulletin,* No. 15, 1949, pp. 2–3.
19. The Indonesian case will be found in "The Surabaja Poltergeist," George Zorab. *Parapsychology Bulletin,* No. 34, 1954, pp. 1–3.
20. The Runcorn case will be found in **22**, pp. 68–85.
21. The Hartville case will be found in "Some Recent Poltergeist Cases," W. E. Cox. *Parapsychology Bulletin,* No. 43, 1957, p. 2.
22. These cases were both reported in personal correspondence.

Chapter 4
1. Douglas Eldridge, of the *Newark News,* wrote an article which appeared May 11, and ran succeeding stories throughout the month.

Chapter 5
1. " 'Flying Glass' Terrorizes Trio," *Indianapolis Star,* March 13, 1962.
2. For Bristol case, see **24**, pp. 97, 202–205, and 260–262.

Chapter 6
1. North Carolina's "strange lights" are treated in various publications, among them a booklet by the United States Geological Survey, published in 1922, entitled, "The Origin of the Brown Mountain Lights," and *Tar*

Heel Ghosts, John Harden (University of North Carolina Press, 1954).

Chapter 7

1. This presidential address was "The Psi Field," W. G. Roll. *Proceedings* of the PA, No. 1, 1957–1964, pp. 32–65.
2. "Spirit (Or Wife?) Jolts Icelander," Werner Wiskari. *New York Times,* May 17, 1964.
3. Examples of Price's, Tyrrell's, and Barrett's are: "Haunting and the 'Psychic Ether' Hypothesis," H. H. Price. *Proceedings* of the SPR, .Vol. 45, 1939, pp. 307–343; *Apparitions,* G. N. M. Tyrrell (London: Gerald Duckworth & Co., 1953); and W. F. Barrett, **19.**
4. Owen has recently published another book, see **14.**
5. Miss Stewart's letter to Owen is referred to in **24,** p. 162.
6. These cases are discussed by Bender in his presidential address to the PA, **20.**
7. This study will be found in "A Psychokinetic Effect Personally Observed," John Mischo, Ulrich Timm, and Geir Vilhjalmsson. *Proceedings* of the PA, No. 5, 1968, pp. 37–38.
8. This survey for attitudes on poltergeists is discussed in **20.**
9. The Rosenheim investigation is reported in "An Investigation of 'Poltergeist' Occurrences," Hans Bender. *Proceedings* of the PA, No. 5, 1968, pp. 31–33.
10. Karger's work is reported in "Physical Investigation of Psychokinetic Phenomena in Rosenheim, Germany, 1967," F. Karger and G. Zicha. *Proceedings* of the PA, No. 5, 1968, pp. 33–35.
11. The Nicklheim case is discussed in **20.**
12. Bender's idea of higher space is presented in **20.**
13. Imitative and total fraud are discussed in **21.**

Chapter 8

1. "Ghostly Events Rout Family of 5," John L. Dotson, Jr. *Detroit Free Press,* August 8, 1965.
2. This Institute forms the main part of the Foundation for Research on the Nature of Man.
3. Several articles appeared locally and elsewhere, the

first being "Saucer Eyes See Flying Cups," Joseph V. Phillip. *Virginian Pilot,* September 9, 1962.

Chapter 9
1. Many articles followed the Miami disturbances. The incidents were also treated in **16** and **17**.
2. *Prominent American Ghosts* is listed as **17** in reading list.

Chapter 11
1. "Callihans Again Plagued by Mysterious Movements," George Wolfford. *Ashland Daily Independent,* December 11, 1968.

Chapter 12
1. Summaries of all the papers presented were published in *Proceedings* of the PA, No. 5, 1968.
2. Summaries of all the papers presented were published in *Proceedings* of the PA, No. 1, 1957–1964.
3. Reports of these data analyses are found in (1) above.
4. *Fields and Configurations,* John Artley (New York: Holt, Rinehart, and Winston, 1965).
5. This "special stimulating property" of certain targets has been termed the "focusing effect," and has been treated in several parapsychological studies. Among reports on this are the following: "The Focusing of ESP upon Particular Targets," J. G. Pratt and Milan Ryzl. *Journal of Parapsychology,* Vol. 27, 1963, pp. 227–241.
"Token Object Matching Tests: A Third Series," W. G. Roll. *Journal* of the ASPR, Vol. 60, 1966, pp. 363–379.
"Confirmation of the Focussing Effect," J. G. Pratt and W. G. Roll. *Journal* of the ASPR, Vol. 62, 1968, pp. 226–245.
"The Focussing Effect as Patterned Behavior," J. G. Pratt and H. J. Keil. *Journal* of the ASPR, Vol. 63, 1949, pp. 314–337.
"A Wider Conceptual Framework for the Stepanek Focusing Effect," H. H. J. Keil. *Journal* of the ASPR, Vol. 65, 1971, pp. 75–82.

Chapter 13
1. *Personality,* Gardner Murphy (New York and London: Harper & Brothers, 1947).

2. Dr. Schmeidler's methods are presented in **23** and **30**.
3. The quoted passages are taken from private reports.
4. The quoted remarks by Julio are taken from a taped interview conducted in Durham, February 1967.
5. Dr. Obrist's remarks are taken from a private report.
6. EEG research at the Psychical Research Foundation will be found in: "EEG Patterns and ESP Results in Forced-Choice Experiments with Lalsingh Harribance," R. L. Morris and others. *Journal* of the ASPR, Vol. 66, 1972, pp. 253–268. Such research elsewhere will be found in: "An Exploratory Experiment: Continuous EEG Recording During Clairvoyant Card Test," R. J. Cadoret. *Journal of Parapsychology*, Vol. 28, 1964, p. 226; and "Relationship Between EEG Alpha Activity and ESP Card-Guessing Performance," Charles Honorton. *Journal* of the ASPR, Vol. 63, 1969, pp. 365–374.

Chapter 14

1. Work with D. D. Home can be found in **49**; Palladino in **48**; Schneider in "The Physical Mediumship of Rudi Schneider," Anita Gregory. *Proceedings* of the PA, No. 5, 1968, pp. 19–21; and Nina Kulagina in "Nina Kulagina's Mind Over Matter," Zdenek Rejdak. *Psychic* magazine, June 1971; and "Interview: Montague Ullman," *Psychic,* June 1971.

Chapter 15

1. This definition of body English will be found in Webster's Third New International Dictionary, unabridged.
2. Gardner Murphy was president of the (English) Society for Psychical Research, 1949, and of the American Society for Psychical Research, 1962–1971.
3. This presidential address by Murphy was published in *Proceedings* of the SPR, Vol. 49, 1949–1952, pp. 1–15.
4. The theory by Price is described in "Mind over Mind and Mind over Matter," H. H. Price. *Enquiry,* 2, 1949, pp. 20–27 (No. 1) and pp. 5–14 (No. 3).
5. The effect of PK on living systems is approached in "The Influence of an Unorthodox Method of Treatment on Wound Healing in Mice," Bernard Grad, Remy

Cadoret and G. I. Paul. *International Journal of Parapsychology,* Vol. III, No. 2, 1961, pp. 5–24.
6. Freud's comments will be found in *Studies of Parapsychology,* Sigmund Freud (New York: Collier Books, 1963).
7. The subject of psi processes in therapy has been treated in the following, among others:
New Dimensions of Deep Analysis, Jan Ehrenwald (George Allen & Unwin Ltd., 1954).
Psi and Psychoanalysis, Jule Eisenbud (New York and London: Grune & Stratton, 1970).
Collected Works, Vol. 1–17, C. G. Jung. Bollingen Series (New York: Pantheon Books, 1957–1965).
"Synchronicity: An Acausal Connecting Principle," C. G. Jung. *The Interpretation of Nature and the Psyche,* Bollingen Series (New York: Pantheon Books, 1955).
Psychology Today, Emilio Servadio (New York: Garrett/Helix, 1965).
Psychic Dynamics, Berthold Schwartz (New York Pageant Press, 1965).
8. Osis' work is reported in "ESP and Changed States of Consciousness Induced by Meditation," Karlis Osis and Edwin Bokert. *Journal* of the ASPR, Vol. 65, 1971, pp. 17–65.
9. Research on relaxation achieved through meditation is discussed in "The Physiology of Meditation," R. K. Wallace and Herbert Benson. *Scientific American,* February 1972, pp. 84–90.
10. White's work will be found in "A Comparison of Old and New Methods of Response to Targets in ESP Experiments," Rhea White. *Journal* of the ASPR, Vol. 58, 1964, pp. 21–56.
11. This work with a gifted subject at the Psychical Research Foundation is presented in: "EEG Patterns and ESP Results in Forced-Choice Experiments with Lalsingh Harribance," R. L. Morris and others. *Journal* of the ASPR, Vol. 66, 1972, pp. 253–268.
12. Biofeedback is discussed in "Feedback-Augmented EEG Alpha Shifts in Subjective State, and ESP Card-Guessing Performance," Charles Honorton, Richard Davidson, and Paul Bindler. *Journal* of the ASPR, Vol. 65, 1971, pp. 308–323.

13. This description by J. B. Rhine will be found in the Foreword to this book, p. xi.

Appendix

1. The questionnaire was first printed in THETA, Number 16, Winter, 1967.

Suggested Reading List

General Books on Parapsychology

1. Broad, C. D. *Lectures on Psychical Research.* New York: Humanities, 1962.
2. Heywood, Rosalind. *Beyond the Reach of Sense.* Intro. by J. B. Rhine. New York: Dutton, 1961.
3. Pratt, J. G. *Parapsychology: An Insider's View of ESP.* New York: Dutton, 1966.
4. Rao, K. R. *Experimental Parapsychology: A Review and Interpretation, With a Comprehensive Bibliography.* Springfield, Ill.: Thomas, 1966.
5. Rhine, J. B., and Brier, Robert (Eds.) *Parapsychology Today.* New York: Citadel, 1968.
6. Rhine, J. B., and Pratt, J. G. *Parapsychology: Frontier Science of the Mind.* Revised Edition. Springfield, Ill.: Thomas, 1962.
7. Rhine, L. E. *ESP in Life and Lab: Tracing Hidden Channels.* New York: Macmillan, 1967. Paperback: New York: Collier-Macmillan, 1969.
8. Rhine, L. E. *Mind Over Matter.* New York: Macmillan, 1970.
9. Smythies, J. R. (Ed.) *Science and ESP.* New York: Humanities Press, 1967.
10. Thouless, R. H. *Experimental Psychical Research,* Baltimore: Penguin Books, 1962.
11. Tyrrell, G. N. M. *The Personality of Man.* Baltimore: Penguin Books, 1963.

Popular Books on Poltergeists and Hauntings

12. Carrington, H. H., and Fodor, Nandor. *Haunted People.* New York: Dutton, 1951.
13. Hole, Christina. *Haunted England.* London: B. T. Batsford, Ltd., 1940.
14. Owen, George, and Sims, Victor. *Science and the Spook.* New York: Garrett Publications, 1971.
15. Sitwell, Sacheverell. *Poltergeist.* London: Faber and Faber, 1940.

16. Smith, Susy. *Ghosts Around the House.* New York and Cleveland: The World Publishing Company, 1970.
17. Smith, Susy. *Prominent American Ghosts.* New York and Cleveland: The World Publishing Company, 1967.
18. Thurston, H. H. C. *Ghosts and Poltergeists.* Chicago: Henry Regnery, 1954.

Scientific Publications on Poltergeists and Hauntings

19. Barrett, W. F. "Poltergeists Old and New." *Proceedings* of the SPR, Vol. 25, 1911, pp. 377–412.
20. Bender, Hans. "New Developments in Poltergeist Research." *Proceedings* of the PA, No. 6, 1969, pp. 81–102.
21. Cox, W. E. "Introductory Comparative Analysis of Some Poltergeist Cases." *Journal* ASPR, Vol. 55, 1961, pp. 47–72.
22. Dingwall, E. J., and Hall, T. H. *Four Modern Ghosts.* London: G. Duckworth & Co., 1958.
23. Moss, Thelma, and Schmeidler, Gertrude R. "Quantitative Investigation of a 'Haunted House' with Sensitives and a Control Group." *Journal* ASPR, Vol. 62, 1968, pp. 399–410.
24. Owen, A. R. G. *Can We Explain the Poltergeist?* New York: Garrett Publications, 1964.
25. Pratt, J. G., and Roll, W. G. "The Seaford Disturbances." *Journal of Parapsychology,* Vol. 22, 1958, pp. 79–124.
26. Roll, W. G. "Some Physical and Psychological Aspects of a Series of Poltergeist Phenomena." *Journal* ASPR, Vol. 62, 1968, pp. 263–308.
27. Roll, W. G. "The Newark Disturbances." *Journal* ASPR, Vol. 63, 1969, pp. 123–174.
28. Roll, W. G. "Poltergeist Phenomena and Interpersonal Relations." *Journal* ASPR, Vol. 64, 1970, pp. 66–99.
29. Roll, W. G., and Pratt, J. G. "The Miami Disturbances." *Journal* ASPR, Vol. 65, 1971, pp. 409–454.
30. Schmeidler, Gertrude R. "Quantitative Investigation of a 'Haunted House.' " *Journal* ASPR, Vol. 60, 1966, pp. 137–149.
31. Tart, Charles T. "Applications of Instrumentation in the Investigation of Haunting and Poltergeist Cases." *Journal* ASPR, Vol. 59, 1965, pp. 190–201.
32. Zorab, G. "A Further Comparative Analysis of Some

Poltergeist Phenomena: Cases from Continental Europe." *Journal* ASPR, Vol. 58, 1964, pp. 105–127.

Experimental Reports on Psychokinesis

33. Cox, W. E. "The Effect of PK on Electromechanical Systems: I. The First Electrical Clock Experiment." *Journal of Parapsychology*, Vol. 29, 1965, pp. 165–175.

34. Cox, W. E., Feather, Sara, and Carpenter, J. C. "The Effect of PK on Electromechanical Systems." *Journal of Parapsychology*, Vol. 30, 1966, pp. 184–194.

35. Dale, L. A. "The Psychokinetic Effect: The First ASPR Experiment." *Journal* ASPR, Vol. 40, 1946, pp. 123–151.

36. Humphrey, B. H. "Simultaneous High and Low Aim in PK Tests." *Journal of Parapsychology*, Vol. 11, 1947, pp. 160–174.

37. McConnell, R. A., and others. "Wishing with Dice." *Journal of Experimental Psychology*, Vol. 50, 1955, pp. 269–275.

38. McConnell, R. A., and Forwald, H. G. "Psychokinetic Placement: I. A Re-examination of the Forwald-Durham Experiment." *Journal of Parapsychology*, Vol. 31, 1967, pp. 51–69.

39. McConnell, R. A., and Forwald, H. G. "Psychokinetic Placement: II. A Factorial Study of Successful and Unsuccessful Series." *Journal of Parapsychology*, Vol. 31, 1967, pp. 198–213.

40. McConnell, R. A., and Forwald, H. G. "Psychokinetic Placement: III. Cube-Releasing Devices." *Journal of Parapsychology*, Vol. 32, 1968, pp. 9–38.

41. Pratt, J. G. "A Reinvestigation of the Quarter Distribution of the (PK) Page." *Journal of Parapsychology*, Vol. 8, 1944, pp. 61–63.

42. Rhine, J. B., and Humphrey, B. M. "The PK Effect: Special Evidence from Hit Patterns: I. Quarter Distributions of the Page." *Journal of Parapsychology*, Vol. 8, 1944, pp. 18–60.

43. Rhine, J. B., and Rhine, L. E. "The Psychokinetic Effect: I. The First Experiment." *Journal of Parapsychology*, Vol. 7, 1943, pp. 20–43.

44. Rhine, J. B., Humphrey, B. M., and Pratt, J. G. "The PK Effect: Special Evidence from Hit Patterns: III.

Quarter Distributions of the Half-Set." *Journal of Parapsychology*, Vol. 9, 1945, pp. 150–168.

45. Schmidt, Helmut. "A PK Test with Electronic Equipment." *Journal of Parapsychology*, Vol. 34, 1970, pp. 175–181.
46. Schmidt, Helmut. "PK Experiments with Animals as Subjects." *Journal of Parapsychology*, Vol. 34, 1970, pp. 255–261.
47. Thouless, R. H. "A Report on an Experiment on Psychokinesis with Dice, and a Discussion of Psychological Factors Favouring Success." *Proceedings* of the SPR, Vol. 49, 1949–1952, pp. 107–130.

Older Tests with Physical Mediums

48. Feilding, F. H. E, *Sittings with Eusapia Palladino and Other Studies*. Intro. by E. J. Dingwall. New Hyde Park, New York: University Books, 1963.
49. Zorab, G. A. M. "Test Sittings with D. D. Home at Amsterdam." *Journal of Parapsychology*, Vol. 34, 1970, pp. 47–63.

Index

agent, 9 f, 78, 118, 144 f, 148–50, 152, 154 f, 157–58, 159 f, 163–64, 169–71, 173 f, 177 f, 185 f; see also *psychological studies*
absence of, 28, 151, 174
adolescents and young persons as, 3, 20, 27, 30 f, 33, 35 f, 37 f, 39, 78, 85, 88–90, 91, 106, 119, 134, 141, 144 f, 160 f, 185
aggressive feelings of, 89, 95, 154–58, 173–75, 177; see also *tensions*
conscious, 20, 166 f, 172
dual, 148
ESP tests with, 90, 164
hypnotized, 49, 167 f
PK tests with, 17, 90, 162–67, 172
unconscious, 49, 171–73; see also *dissociation*
Adelphi College, 19
adolescents; see under *agents, adolescents and younger persons as*
alpha brain wave, 178; see also *electroencephalograph*
Altrocchi, John, v, 76–78, 153 f, 170
Altrocchi, Stella, 77
American Association for the Advancement of Science, xvi
American Psychological Association, 153
American Society for Psychical Research, 3, 171, 175 f
animals, 97, 185; see also *poltergeists, dogs affected by*
apparitions, xiv, 82, 97–100, 135, 137

apports, 30, 34 f, 37 f, 40, 88 f, 93 f
Artley, John, v, 98, 143, 146 f, 149 f, 157, 166 f
attacks, 24, 38–40, 53 f, 101; see also *punctures*
attenuation, 146–49, 174; see also *decline effect*

Barrett, Theodore H., v
Barrett, Sir William, 27 f, 84
bell ringing, 31
Bender, Hans, 88–95, 143, 148, 170
Bingen, Germany, case, 2
biofeedback, 175, 178
bites; see *punctures*
Blumenthal, David, v, 56 f, 59, 167
body English, 7, 169
Bokert, Edwin, 175
bottle poppings, 12, 17 f, 22, 62
brain waves; see *electroencephalograph*
breakage of objects, 15 f, 28, 34 f, 40 f, 43, 51, 61, 81 f, 89, 106–09, 113–15, 117 f, 122, 123–27, 129, 132, 135, 139, 153, 163
Bremen, Germany, case, 89 f, 170
Brier, Robert, 162, 164
Brier, Henie, 162
Bristol, England, case, 54
Brown, Donna, vi
Brown Mountain Lights, 65
Burdick, Donald S., v
Buta, John, 97 f

Cambridge University, 84 f
Can We Explain the Poltergeist?, 85
Chamberlain, Richard, 3

203